MW01278510

'SIMPLICIUS'
On Aristotle's "On the Soul 3.1-5"

'SIMPLICIUS'

On Aristotle's "On the Soul 3.1-5"

Translated by
H. J. Blumenthal

Cornell University Press

Ithaca, New York

Preface © 2000 by Richard Sorabji
Introduction, Translation and Notes © 2000 by
the Estate of H. J. Blumenthal

All rights reserved. Except for brief
quotations in a review, this book, or parts
thereof, must not be reproduced in any form
without permission in writing from the publisher.
For information address Cornell University Press,
Sage House, 512 East State Street, Ithaca, New York 14850.

First published 2000 by Cornell University Press

ISBN 0-8014-3687-7

Librarians: Library of Congress
Cataloging-in-Publication Data are available.

Acknowledgments

The present translations have been made possible by generous and imaginative funding from the following sources: the National Endowment for the
Humanities, Division of Research Programs, an independent federal agency
of the USA; the Leverhulme Trust; the British Academy; the Jowett Copy-
right Trustees; the Royal Society (UK); Centro Internazionale A. Beltrame
di Storia dello Spazio e del Tempo (Padua); Mario Mignucci; Liverpool
University; the Leventis Foundation; the Humanities Research Board of the
British Academy; the Esmée Fairbairn Charitable Trust; the Henry Brown
Trust; Mr and Mrs N. Egon; The Netherlands Foundation for Scientific
Research (NWO/GW). The editor wishes to thank Andrew Lockey who
prepared the first version of the Greek-English Index; Mary Ruskin who
prepared the first version of the Subject Index; William Charlton, Pamela
Huby, Donald Russell and Carlos Steel for commenting on the MS, and Han
Baltussen for preparing it for press.

Printed in Great Britain

Contents

Editor's Preface

Very sadly Henry Blumenthal died shortly after delivering the MS of this book. Few people in the world could match his knowledge of Neoplatonist psychological theory. He studied Plotinus with Sandbach in Cambridge in the early 1960s. His book *Plotinus' Psychology* was published by Nijhoff in 1971, but before that he was already recognised as an authority and was contributing to the then small number of conferences on Neoplatonism. Two of his articles are reprinted in the volume Richard Sorabji, ed., *Aristotle Transformed*, Duckworth 1990. His latest book, *Aristotle and Neoplatonism in Late Antiquity: Interpretations of the De anima*, Duckworth 1993, is precisely on the theme of the present commentary. Readers of his selected papers, *Soul and Intellect, Studies in Plotinus and Later Neoplatonism*, Variorum 1993, will be pleased by the photograph, a poignant reminder of his friendly character. He leaves behind, as well as the present volume, a MS commentary on Plotinus *Ennead* 4.3-5 *Problems of the Soul*.

His introduction to this book shows him at the height of his powers. Too cautious to plump easily for one interpretation, he was very good at thinking of alternatives, and in this case the alternative he somewhat favours is a very interesting one. It concerns the authorship of our commentary. He sides against Simplicius. But rather than backing Priscian as author, for whom a magisterial case was set out by Carlos Steel in one of our previous volumes, he suggests it may have been someone editing Simplicius' lectures, with his own additions, possibly Priscian himself.

In the chapters commented on, Aristotle moves beyond the five senses to the general functions of sense perception, the imagination and the so-called active intellect, whose identity was still a matter of heated controversy in the time of Thomas Aquinas.

'Simplicius' insists that the intellect under discussion is the human rational soul and not a transcendent intellect, as some other commentators had suggested (220,15-17; 25-35). He also disagrees with Plotinus' view that part of our soul has never descended from uninterruptedly contemplating the Platonic Forms, without our normally being aware of it (220,12-16; 6,12-14).

At the same time, 'Simplicius' disagrees with Proclus' compromise position. Proclus had also rejected Plotinus' idea of our having a soul transcending the world of change, but he had wanted to resist the opposite extreme, Galen's appeal to Plato's *Timaeus* 43B-44B, to show that our soul is wholly dependent on the state of the body. His compromise was to say that our soul is subject to change in its activities, but not in its substance (Proclus *in Tim.* 3,335,24-336,2; 338,6-13; 340,14-17). 'Simplicius' at 241,7-10, following the head of his school Damascius (*in Parm.* Ruelle 2. 252,11-253,26; 266,25-8), replies that our soul *is* changed in its substance.

Some of 'Simplicius' ' most interesting discussions concern the imagination (*phantasia*). At 211,33-212,27, he supports Aristotle's denial in *On the Soul* 3.3 that *phantasia* is the same as belief (*doxa*), a view which might seem to be implied by Plato *Sophist* 263E-264D. Unusually, he makes room for *phantasia* directed to universals, rather than to particulars, but only in the sense that what appears to the *phantasia* of grubs is food in general rather than this food from this source (209,17-25). 'Simplicius' further suggests that *phantasia* does not apprehend things as true or false (206,11-20), which requires a sort of awareness of one's own cognitions (211,1-8).

Just as for sense-perception earlier in the commentary, so also for imagination, 'Simplicius' postulates that projection (*probolê*) is involved. The imagination projects imprints (*tupoi*) into our physical spirit or *pneuma*. These imprints on the one hand correspond to the form or shape (*eidos*) of perceptible objects taken on during sense-perception, but on the other hand are in accordance with our concepts or reason-principles (*logoi*). The imaginative imprint of a mathematical object, for example, may be made like the form of a perceived figure, but it may be made more accurate, to accord with our mathematical concepts, so that the lines have no breadth (213,31-214,12).

'Simplicius' is aware that it is the Pythagoreans who most fully developed this sort of account and that Aristotle's view is different. Aristotle, he says, thinks of us as using not projection of concepts, but abstraction, and he thinks of mathematical entities not like the Pythagoreans as reason-principles and hence as substances, but as residing in the imagination's *tupoi*, abstracted from physical substance (233,7-25).

R.R.K.S.

Acknowledgements

The first two chapters of the commentary on book 3 have been read and discussed by the Liverpool-Manchester Ancient Philosophy seminar. I am grateful to its members, David Bates, Noreen Fox, Hans Gottschalk, George Kerferd, Owen Leblanc, Gordon Neal, Howard Robinson and Alison Samuels, for many useful suggestions and productive questions.

Carlos Steel provided me with numerous acute comments on the whole of the draft, and Willie Charlton on chapters 2 and 5. I have usually, but not always – perhaps unwisely – followed their advice, and the resulting improvement in the final version has been considerable. Further helpful suggestions were received from anonymous readers of chapters 1 and 3.

Richard Sorabji in his capacity as General Editor has been unfailingly helpful, and tolerant of ever-renewed delays. I should also like to thank Dr Anna Lenzuni, Director of the Manuscripts Department at the Biblioteca Medicea-Laurenziana, for arranging to supply me with photographs of Laurentianus 85,21, Hayduck's A, by far the most important source for this commentary.

H.J.B.

Introduction

Who wrote this commentary?

While it would be appropriate to begin with a brief biographical sketch of the author of the commentary translated, this cannot be done for the simple if uncomfortable reason that his identity is unknown, and perhaps unknowable. I say this in the full knowledge that some would identify him with Priscian,[1] probably a contemporary, while a few might still wish to maintain, as I myself formerly did,[2] the traditional identification with Simplicius of Cilicia.[3]

As it is, I now think there is no such simple answer to the apparently simple question, 'Who wrote Simplicius' *de Anima* commentary?'[4] Until some twenty-five years ago that question had been raised only once in more than fourteen centuries, by Francesco Piccolomini in the preface to his edition of the *de Caelo, de Generatione* and *de Anima* published, with some extracts from Simplicius, in 1608.[5] Piccolomini noted that while in the *Physics* and *de Caelo* commentaries Simplicius writes expansively, attacks Philoponus and often refers to Alexander, the commentator on the *de Anima* is laconic and preserves nothing from other commentators,[6] so, for these and other reasons which he left aside, he thought the commentary should be attributed to someone else. He then expresses a long-standing suspicion that that someone could be Priscian of Lydia, with whose paraphrase of Theophrastus he found both similarity of views and diction, which he duly exemplified. He also noted what appear to be self-references between the two works, but after further consideration, in which he noted that the philosophy of the *de Anima* commentary is no different from that of Simplicius, he concluded that the work may be either that of Simplicius in his old age – he does not quite say a senile Simplicius – or of Priscian.[7]

That it was indeed the work of a senile Simplicius was suggested by A. Torstrik in the introduction to his edition of the *de Anima*, where he wrote that there is something of an old man in the style of interpretation, adding what would now be regarded as the highly incorrect remark 'not to say of an old woman'.[8] Nevertheless the doubts about the commentary's authenticity raised by Piccolomini were forgotten for some 250 years,[9] until a by now well-known but rather less well read article by F. Bossier and C. Steel was published in 1972,[10] again questioning the attribution to Simplicius and making a case on a variety of grounds for transferring the ownership of the work to Simplicius' colleague Priscian of Lydia.[11] In 1978 their thesis was discussed by I. Hadot, who accepted that there were stylistic, but not doctrinal, differences between Simplicius and the author of the *de Anima* commentary, but preferred to leave open the question of whether Priscian was the author.[12] More recently the traditional attribution has been questioned, on different grounds, by J.O. Urmson, the translator of book 1 and the first 4 chapters of book 2 of the commentary in this series.[13] Urmson's criteria for separation are based on the knowledge of Simplicius' style and methods acquired in the course of translating book 4 of the *Physics* commentary.[14] Since his criteria are largely mechanical and involve what are, once stated, generally clearly relevant differences, they should meet widespread acceptance. Urmson does not, perhaps wisely, offer an opinion as to who his non-Simplician writer might be. Now Steel has produced a revised version, in English, of the article he wrote with Bossier: it appears in the second volume of the four covering this commentary.[15] As Steel explains, the revision is his own, but substantially reproduces the argument of the original article, while taking account of subsequent discussion and making use of new research tools not available in the early 1970s.[16]

Let us now look at the wide-ranging treatment by Bossier and Steel. Their case rests on both doctrinal and linguistic considerations, as well as one apparent self-reference which is the most important of their arguments for positively assigning the work to Priscian, rather than simply denying that it is by Simplicius.

Some of the considerations involved are of a fairly general nature. Such are the scale of the commentary, and the lack of the copious references and quotations which are so marked a feature of the other Simplicius commentaries on Aristotle, though one might note that they are not conspicuous in the *Encheiridion* commentary, whose authorship remains unquestioned. It is certainly true that the *de Anima* commentary is shorter in proportion to its subject than are those on the *Categories*, *de Caelo* and Physics: one might, however, point out that it is also closer to the two latter than they are to the *Categories* commentary. The *de Anima* commentary produces roughly 10 pages of commentary per Bekker page of Aristotle text, those on the *Physics* and *de Caelo* 16, that on the *Categories* 29. Thus in terms of the amount of comment on their texts the commentaries on the *Physics* and *de Caelo* are half as long again as the *de Anima* one, but the *Categories* commentary is nearly twice as long as they are: no one has tried to assign that to another author on grounds of disparate length.

That the method and style of the *de Anima* commentary is different from the others is certainly true, but there is more than one possible explanation of the differences. Before we consider such possibilities we should, however, look at the case made by Bossier and Steel and its restatement by Steel: space precludes a thorough examination of all the details of their case. A summary[17] of it is conveniently presented at the end of the 1972 article, giving what they saw as the main lines of argument and the conclusions to be drawn from them. That article has two main divisions, retained but reversed in the revision.

In the one they claim to demonstrate that the author of the *de Anima* commentary also wrote the *Metaphrasis in Theophrastum* which has been transmitted under the name of Priscian of Lydia.[18] This claim is based on two arguments. The first is that a reference in the *de Anima* commentary to the author's *Epitome of Theophrastus' Physics* is to a text in Priscian's *Metaphrasis*. The second, based on a detailed study of the texts, is that the method, style and language, as well as the thought of the two works, the *de Anima* commentary and the *Metaphrasis in Theophrastum*, is so close, including some almost identical turns of phrase, that the only possible explanation is single authorship.

In the other part of the paper[19] they try to identify the author of these two works, which the tradition has confidently attributed to different authors, pointing out that only internal criticism of the *de Anima* commentary can provide a way forward, in particular by comparing it with the other commentaries by Simplicius 'of which the attribution is certain' – a rather obvious comment is that on the basis of the manuscript tradition one could say the same of that on the *Physics*. Bossier and Steel find that three references to the *Physics* commentary cannot be found in that of Simplicius.[20] They maintain that the methods of the *de Anima* commentary and the others are different, the former lacking the rich historical documentation and discussion with earlier commentators as well as the lengthy but clearly organised exegesis characteristic of the latter,[21] while having a combination of phraseology and formulae alien to the other commentaries.[22] Their last point is that there are important doctrinal differences, such as the notion of the soul as determinative (*horistikê*, my trans.).[23] They conclude that the differences between the *de Anima* commentary and the others are so great that they cannot be by the same author. The attribution of the *de Anima* commentary must therefore be false, and since it is by the author of the *Metaphrasis*, it is probable that Priscian of Lydia was its author too.[24]

That there are differences between the *de Anima* commentary and Simplicius' other commentaries on Aristotle is clear enough. What we have to consider is whether these are such as to preclude authorship by the same commentator. Only if we find that they do should we embark on the search for an author other than Simplicius, bearing in mind that if we reject the traditional attribution we may not then be able to replace it with another. To begin with some generalities. The three long commentaries differ not only from that on the *de Anima* but also from the one on Epictetus' *Encheiridion*, and not only in subject matter. As far as I know no one has ever questioned the authenticity of the *Encheiridion* commentary, which would, of course, with the one exception of Piccolomini, have been true until very recently of the *de Anima* commentary as well. Then, though it is true, as Bossier and Steel have said, that the *de Anima* commentary is less prolix than the other three, its scale, as we have already noted, is closer to that of the *Physics* and *de Caelo* commentaries than it is to that on the *Categories*. Difference of scale is not, in itself, a reliable criterion of difference of authorship: one can cite examples from modern times where the identity of the commentator is in no doubt. As for the lack of the copious citation of early Greek philosophy, for which our debt to Simplicius is considerable, that could be due to his temporary absence – in consequence of Justinian's decree of 529, and the philosophers' exile in Persia described by Agathias[25] – from a city with a large library: it is in any case a feature shared with the *Encheiridion* commentary. The same explanation would apply to the sparseness in the *de Anima* commentary of discussions of any length with previous interpreters of the work in question. Difference of style is another matter, and though we must allow for differences arising from the type of composition, and from different periods of the same writer's career, there does come a stage at which the differences can no longer be seen as variations in a single person's output, and can only reasonably be explained by a difference of authorship. Just where this stage comes is, of course, very difficult to determine. No one could sensibly claim that the works of Thucydides and Lysias, or Demosthenes and Epicurus were produced by the same person. On the other hand one might be able to make a case for passages like the praise and defence of zoology in the *de Partibus Animalium* (644b22-645a36) being the work of someone other than the author of the *de Anima* or the early chapters of *Metaphysics* 12, to say nothing of the lost exoteric works which were probably, but by no means certainly, responsible for the praise repeatedly bestowed on Aristotle's style by so accomplished a writer as Cicero, and which has caused such puzzlement to modern scholars.[26]

Let us now turn to the other part of Bossier and Steel's case, that the authors of the *de Anima* commentary and the *Metaphrasis* are one and the same.[27] It depends initially on a comment in the *de Anima* commentary that 'I have defined this more clearly in the epitome of Theophrastus' *Physics*'.[28] Bossier and Steel take this to be a reference to the discussion of the function of the transparent as a medium in vision in *Metaphrasis* 8.1-14.15.[29] That is certainly possible, but by no means certain. In the first place, and most importantly, the *Metaphrasis* is not, as P.M. Huby has pointed out, an epitome.[30] Even if it were, we cannot be certain that the author of the *de Anima* commentary, being someone other than Priscian, did not also produce a summary of Theophrastus. Whether or not that someone was Simplicius is another matter, but in principle there is no reason why it should not have been. There is always the possibility that the group working in the 'Academy' at Athens were engaged in a co-operative project on the study of Theophrastus,[31] and those who are at all familiar with the practice of fifth- and sixth-century Neoplatonists need hardly be told that it is perfectly possible for contemporaries to produce parallel commentaries on the same works. One need think only of the profusion of *Categories* commentaries, an extreme case but not a unique one. The fact that Priscian wrote on Theophrastus' *Physics* does not mean that any reference to such a work must be to his. If it is not, and one can no more prove that it is not than that it is, the main objective argument for the attribution of the *de Anima* commentary to Priscian cannot be regarded as conclusive. That does not mean either that the work cannot be ascribed to Priscian on other grounds, or that the attribution to Simplicius is any less questionable. On the other hand the more one stresses the intellectual proximity of those whose names are linked with Damascius in the story of the exile to Persia,[32] thus increasing the likelihood that someone confused the names of Priscian and Simplicius at an early stage, the more likely does one make it that both men, or any set of two or more members of the same group, were engaged on related research projects and wrote on the same subject.

Apart from there being no known work on Theophrastus by Simplicius, which might make an available one by someone else a good candidate for being the target of a cross-reference, Bossier and Steel were impressed by similarities of diction and expression between *de Anima* commentary and *Metaphrasis*. In particular they drew attention to the similar way in which questions about the medium in perception are posed and answered in the two works.[33] In fact while such similarities are an argument for single authorship, they are not conclusive, since it is notorious that the corpus of Neoplatonic commentary is full of passages in different authors which resemble each other with varying but never negligible degrees of correspondence: at one end of the scale these amount to something like a correlation of one hundred percent. Some interesting examples may be found in I. Hadot's comparison of expositions of *Categories* 1.[34] Less obviously one could cite the affinities between Proclus' commentary on the *Cratylus* and Ammonius' on the *de Interpretatione*, identified and explored by A.D.R. Sheppard.[35] Proclus' commentary on the *Cratylus*, incidentally, differs sufficiently from his other Plato commentaries for that to be an excellent candidate for disattribution on the sort of grounds we have been considering.

One further point should be added. Though we know from Simplicius' that he and Philoponus were philosophically at odds, we do not have any named references to Simplicius in Philoponus' work. Nor are there any to Priscian, but we do have information from an unidentifiable third party that Philoponus engaged in controversy with Priscian:[36] that might be further evidence for the thought of Priscian and Simplicius being very close, whatever the correct ascription of any particular work might be.[37] Simplicius himself, incidentally, does not mention Priscian either. Indeed the incidence of named references to contemporaries is rather odd. We might mention as an example the fact that both Simplicius and Philoponus refer to Damascius by name in only one each of their works, Simplicius in the *Physics* commentary and Philoponus in that on the *Meteorologica*: since there are 18 such references in the former and 6 in the latter this is clearly more than a matter of chance, as the odd one or two might have been, but what the correct explanation might be is less clear. Let it not be suggested that it is an indication that these works too are by hands other than the rest of these commentators' oeuvre!

The greater part of Bossier and Steel's essays is taken up with detailed comparisons of the language and thought of the two works they are considering. Those who wish to examine their arguments in greater detail than I can do here can now do so in Steel's English update of their article.[38] For the moment let it be said that they amassed an impressive array of close parallels in thought and doctrine. From those they conclude, again, that the author of the two works must have been one and the same, and that this single author must have been Priscian.

That conclusion does, however, as they freely admit,[39] conflict with the unambiguous evidence of the tradition. They therefore embarked not only on a detailed comparison of texts in the *de Anima* commentary and the *Metaphrasis*, but also an examination of a number of philosophical issues, as well as questions of practice, style and usage which, they argue, separate the *de Anima* commentary from the other works of Simplicius. Some of these are matters to which we have already drawn attention while questioning their significance. Such are the lack of references to, and discussions with, earlier philosophers, as well as the generally dogmatic method of exposition as opposed to the more open-minded approach to be found in the other commentaries[40] and, perhaps the most difficult to assess, linguistic and stylistic differences.[41] More problematic still are doctrinal differences,[42] a question I have discussed elsewhere and which may therefore be left aside here, except to note that it is by no means immediately clear that there are such.[43] On the basis of these investigations Bossier and Steel conclude that, the traditional ascription notwithstanding, the *de Anima* commentary cannot be the work of the author of the other Simplicius commentaries. Since it is so close to Priscian, the work should be removed from the list of Simplicius' commentaries and reassigned to Priscian.

Should this conclusion be accepted? While Bossier and Steel have produced incontrovertible evidence of the intellectual proximity of the *de Anima* commentary and the *Metaphrasis*, I am still not convinced that the conclusions they have drawn are the only possible ones. What then may we conclude from this examination of the problem of the authorship of the Simplicius *de Anima* commentary? Though I have tended to resist this conclusion in the past,[44] partly but not only because the onus must lie heavily with the prosecution, I think it has to be admitted that the work differs from the rest of the surviving work of Simplicius in a manner and to an extent which makes the view that he himself was its author untenable.[45] It does not, however, follow from such similarities to that of Priscian as can be demonstrated that the commentary must therefore be attributed to him instead. There are other possibilities. Perhaps the one that is easiest to reconcile with the unwavering attribution to Simplicius in the tradition is that it is an *apo phônês* work,[46] composed by a pupil with no great gift for writing clear Greek and who, like others in the same relation to the original lecturer, allowed himself to insert ideas of his own – and some very interesting ones at that – in the same way that Philoponus did in publishing courses by Ammonius. In that case either the name Simplicius might be allowed to remain attached to it, but as 'Simplicius' with elucidation or, if Priscian were the pupil and recorder – we know nothing about his relation to the others in the list of exiles – it could be described as *Priskianou apo phônês tou Simplikiou* or ... *ek tôn sunousiôn tou Simplikiou*, 'Priscian, from the spoken words of Simplicius', or '... from the lectures of Simplicius'. Equally likely is that the work was composed by some other member of Damascius' 'school',[47] perhaps even by one of those who are otherwise known to us by no more than their names[48] and their participation in the abortive migration to the supposed Persian philosophers' paradise. That would make the divergences from the rest of the Simplicius corpus easier to tolerate than the retention of his authorship, and has the further advantage of allowing us to admit ignorance of what actually happened in the matter of ascriptions. A proper description of the author might then be simply 'school of Damascius', a frequent resort of art-historians when confronted with works that have traditionally been ascribed to a painter from whose hand they are highly unlikely to have come. Perhaps it should be used more often in dealing with those works traditionally ascribed to one commentator but showing clear signs that they were not his with which we are repeatedly confronted in this period of Greek philosophy. For convenience, and to fit the *status quaestionis*, I shall refer to our commentator henceforth as Ps.-Simplicius. It is a strange coincidence that two works of now uncertain authorship – the other being Ps.-Philoponus' commentary on book 3 – are numbered among the commentaries on the *de Anima*.[49]

The commentary

While its authorship remains in doubt, the philosophical orientation of our commentary is clear enough, and its general features can be described quite briefly. It is a typical product of fifth- and sixth-century Neoplatonic exposition of Plato and Aristotle in that it is not only an exegesis of a classical text but also, and sometimes predominantly, a vehicle for the expression of the author's own philosophical beliefs. I have argued the case for reading these commentaries in this way elsewhere,[50] and I think it can now be taken as generally agreed that this is how they must be approached.[51] The ideological basis for this use of commentary was the widespread, if not universal, belief among late Platonists that they were doing no more than expounding the philosophy of Plato, and that Aristotle too was a Platonist like themselves. Indeed the author of this *de Anima* commentary actually describes Aristotle as Plato's best interpreter.[52] Of course there was room for disagreement about what Plato himself meant, and also about the extent to which Aristotle followed him. But both the real Simplicius and our Ps.-Simplicius inclined to the view that agreement between them should be sought to the greatest possible extent. A good example is the discussion of the last lines of *de Anima* 3.5, where Ps.-Simplicius writes as if the *Phaedo* and the *de Anima* belonged together.[53] Indeed Simplicius in the *de Caelo* commentary claims that apparent attacks by Aristotle on Plato are really directed not against Plato himself, but against others who did not understand Plato properly.[54] Our commentator might be said to subscribe to the most extreme assimilationist tendency, perhaps a result of his allegiance to Iamblichus which is clearly expressed at the start of the commentary,[55] and whose extent has been carefully examined by others.[56]

One result of following Iamblichus was the adoption of his method of assigning a single *skopos* or purpose to each of Plato and Aristotle's works. This method sometimes produced bizarre results.[57] It was particularly inappropriate to Plato in so far as the dialogues – as is well-known – are rarely confined to a single topic, but it was always liable to lead to interpretations which it would not be entirely unfair to describe as prejudiced – in the strict sense of that word. In the case of the *de Anima* the commentator identifies the *skopos* right from the start,[58] and repeatedly thereafter, as being the rational human soul. That automatically excludes any interpretation of the 'active intellect' as being external to and superior to that part of the individual soul which was associated with the body of one particular person: such interpretations are the Plotinian view that we each have a transcendent component of the soul, or the one held by Alexander and Themistius that there was a superior intellect common to all individuals. The latter exclusion would have been comprehensible, if possibly unacceptable, to Aristotle, and perhaps the same could be said for the view proposed by Plotinus – not let it be said, as an interpretation of the *de Anima*, but that would have made no difference to the fifth- and sixth-century commentators, who regarded anything others said on a matter that Aristotle had discussed as commentary on the relevant treatise.[59] Further exclusions covered possibilities that Aristotle himself might well have found bewildering, and in contravention of his dictum that one must stop somewhere,[60] most notably the rejection of the notion that our intellect was to be identified with one of the members of a purely Neoplatonic triad of transcendent intellects, unparticipated, participated but not participating, and participating.[61] The introduction of these entities, if only so that they can be excluded, is as good an indicator as any of the extent to which this commentary is, whatever else it might be, a work of Neoplatonic philosophy.

That philosophy was the more easily compatible with the *de Anima* once it came to be read as a piece of Platonist philosophy. One major adjustment was, of course, necessary, for that – as we would see it – transformation, namely the metamorphosis of Aristotelian hylomorphism into Platonic dualism. The dualist view of the soul was, of course, crucial for a Platonist, and brought to the interpretation of Aristotle a curious reversal. While for Aristotle the main problem about the soul's relation to the body lay in the possible separation from body of its highest part, that caused no problems for a Platonist for whom the soul, and *a fortiori* its highest part, was anyhow separate. For the Platonist the most serious problem was at the bottom, namely how to translate into Platonic terms the indisputable – from an Aristotelian viewpoint – attachment of the soul as form and entelechy to the body as its matter. This caused a great deal of trouble: our commentator's solution was to split the entelechy, already relegated to the lowest phase of soul, into two, a part that informs the body, thus just, in Platonic terms, maintaining its separation, and another that uses the body so informed. Most of this business is conducted in the commentary on book 1,[62] but the question recurs during the exegesis of book 3,[63] and in any case Ps.-Simplicius' solution governs the rest of his exposition.

Previous commentaries on the *de Anima*

Of earlier commentaries only one survives, the paraphrastic commentary by Themistius, which belongs to the Peripatetic rather than the Platonic tradition, even if it shows some signs of Platonist influence.[64] It does not seem to have been of any great importance to our commentator, though it might have been to Priscian with his special interest in Theophrastus, perhaps mediated by Themistius' *Physics* commentary. Much more important was the lost one written by Alexander of Aphrodisias in the last generation of Greek philosophers before Neoplatonism became dominant. Some of its explanations may have coincided with views expressed in Alexander's own treatise *On the Soul*, which we do have, but such coincidence must never be assumed. In any case most of the references to Alexander were probably, and in many cases certainly, to his commentary.[65] Such references as we have are generally expressions of dissent.[66] Apart from these it may well be the case that Alexander's successors followed him in matters which were not controversial, that is in most questions to do with the soul and its operations between the level of its lowest body-informing phase and the active intellect: unfortunately the extent of such use is virtually inaccessible to us. Though doubtless most philosophy courses will have included some discussion of the *de Anima*, there is no evidence for any further formal commentaries before the late fourth or early fifth centuries,[67] when one was composed by the Athenian Plutarch, teacher of Syrianus and Proclus, who might be seen as the philosophical great-grandfather of the generation to which our commentator belongs. Plutarch's commentary certainly covered book 3:[68] a case can be made for its having been complete.[69] In any case, though it may have been more conservative, it will have provided at least a starting point for the heavily Neoplatonised type of exposition presented by Ps.-Simplicius. The Philoponus commentary may be seen as contemporary with ours: there are no clear signs of interaction.

Text, lemmata and translation[70]

The list of Textual Emendations includes both changes I have made, or suggested, to the text printed by M. Hayduck in *CAG* XI, and indicates places where the commentator's text deviates from Ross' edition. That is taken as a basis for comparison because it is now the standard edition in the English-speaking world, though some of Ross' textual choices are strange, and at variance with the practice of other modern editors.[71]

Unlike the lemmata in the real Simplicius commentaries, which are generally either complete, or give a catchword after *heôs tou* to identify the extent of the text on which he is commenting, this commentary frequently gives incomplete lemmata, citing only the first few words of what may be several lines of Aristotle that are to be discussed. Yet the commentary, as is not always the case with others, corresponds closely to the wording of the lemmata as we have them, which suggests that they were not subsequently inserted in some mechanical fashion from a text of Aristotle which did not always correspond to the one that the commentator used. Asulanus, either because he worked from a manuscript that was more generous in this respect, or because he did fill in missing text, provides much fuller lemmata than are to be found in A and so in Hayduck.

What may be of interest to students of Aristotle is that the text from which the lemmata come was, in terms of the Aristotelian tradition, probably rather conservative. Thus it often corroborates the reading of the less innovative editions of the *de Anima* and, for Anglophone scholars in particular, it frequently serves to draw attention to the somewhat arbitrary and idiosyncratic nature of some of the textual choices, and emendations, made by Ross.

The style of Ps.-Simplicius' commentary is generally neither elegant nor perspicuous – though there are a few examples of rhetorical writing. That presents obvious difficulties for a translator now, but it will also in the past have increased the chances of error in the transmission of the text and aggravated the task of editors, of whom there have been only two, the sixteenth-century Aldine editor Asulanus, who also translated the text in a separate publication,[72] and M. Hayduck, the *CAG* editor. Hayduck does not always seem to have been equal to the task and a new edition would be desirable. Nevertheless I have generally translated the text as he presents it: exceptions are noted in the list of emendations and explained in the notes. I would merely add that the lemmata, or such parts of them as the commentary provides – in contrast, as Steel notes,[73] with the full lemmata of the real Simplicius commentaries[74] are often at variance with the Aristotle tradition: I have usually translated the texts provided in the commentary, but supplemented them from the *de Anima* where appropriate.

The translation in this series is the first into a modern European language: there have been two Renaissance ones, that of Asulanus mentioned above and an earlier one by Faseolus.[75] On the whole I have kept rather closely to the Greek at the cost of some rebarbative English here and there. In the interests of doing so I have not striven for consistency in the rendering of Greek terms. Apart from the well-known case of *aisthêsis* and its cognates, which must be rendered in different ways in different contexts, the word *zôê* in particular presents frequent difficulties. Its normal meaning of 'life' is frequently inapplicable, and I have often translated it as 'faculty' since it then overlaps one of the meanings of *dunamis*.[76]

Notes

1. See below, 4ff.

2. With some reservations: cf. e.g. Blumenthal, 'The psychology of (?) Simplicius' commentary on the *De anima*', in H.J. Blumenthal and A.C. Lloyd (eds), *Soul and the Structure of Being in Late Neoplatonism. Syrianus, Proclus and Simplicius* (Liverpool 1982) 73-93.

3. cf. esp. I. Hadot, 'La vie et l'oeuvre de Simplicius d' après des sources grecques et arabes', in I. Hadot (ed.), *Simplicius. Sa Vie, son Oeuvre, sa Survie* (Actes du Colloque international sur les oeuvres et la pensée de Simplicius. Paris 28.9-1.10.1985. Peripatoi 15, Berlin and New York 1987) 23-7. An English translation of this article by V. Caston, incorporating some minor revisions, is printed in R. Sorabji (ed.), *Aristotle Transformed* (London 1990, hereafter *Aristotle Transformed*), where see 290-4; Simplicius, *Commentaire sur le* Manuel *d'Épictète*. Introduction etc. par I.H. (Philosophia Antiqua 66, Leiden, New York and Cologne 1996) 107-11. But see below, and n. 12.

4. The discussion that follows generally corresponds closely with the one that has just appeared in chapter 5 of my *Aristotle and Neoplatonism in late Antiquity. Interpretations of the* de Anima (London and Ithaca 1996) at pp. 65-71. I should like to thank Duckworth for allowing me to re-use it here.

5. Francisci Piccolominei Senensis *Commentarii in Libros Aristotelis De Coelo, ortu et interitu; adiuncta lucidissima expositione, in tres libros eiusdem de anima* (Mainz 1608). An earlier edition was published in Venice six years previously: I have not seen that edition and so do not know whether it contains the same discussion.

6. This is not quite true: he does several times mention, and discuss, views of Alexander and Plutarch.

7. op. cit. 1001-2.

8. '*et ipsum interpretandi genus quo in hac re utitur habet senile quiddam, ne dicam anile: tantopere a re proposita discedit et nescio quo evagatur*', *Aristotelis De Anima Libri III. Recensuit* A. Torstrik (Berlin 1862), vi.

9. Hayduck, the *CAG* editor of this commentary in 1882, whose 1897 preface to Philoponus' *de Anima* commentary shows that he – at least later – was well aware of similar problems, says nothing about this one.

10. Interestingly Bossier and Steel were not aware of Piccolomini's scepticism until their own work was well advanced, cf. (Steel 1997, [note 15 below]) 105.

11. 'Priscianus Lydus en de "in de Anima" van pseudo(?)-Simplicius', *Tijdschrift voor Filosofie* 34 (1972) 761-822. Their conclusions were quickly accepted by P. Moraux, *Der Aristotelismus bei den Griechen* I (Berlin and New York 1973) 172 n. 1. An updated version, in English, of Bossier and Steel's article has been prepared by Steel for the second volume of this translation of the *de Anima* commentary, see n. 15 below.

12. cf. *Le problème du Néoplatonisme alexandrin: Hiéroclès et Simplicius* (Paris 1978) 193-202.

13. Simplicius, *On Aristotle On the Soul 1.1-2-4*, translated by J.O. Urmson, notes by P. Lautner (London and Ithaca 1995) 2-4.

14. Simplicius, *On Aristotle Physics 4*, translated by J.O. Urmson (London and Ithaca 1992).

15. Priscian, *On Theophrastus on Sense Perception*, translated by P.M. Huby and Simplicius, *On Aristotle on the Soul*, translated by C. Steel, notes by P. Lautner (London and Ithaca 1997, hereafter Steel [1997]) 105-37.

16. ibid. n. 6.

17. In French, pp. 821-2.

18. Bossier and Steel 763-82; Steel (1997) 126-37.

19. Bossier and Steel 782-81; Steel (1997) 106-20.

20. Bossier and Steel 792-6; Steel (1997) 120-4.

21. Bossier and Steel 798-806; Steel (1997) 108-11.

22. Bossier and Steel 806-10; Steel (1997) 112-16.

23. Bossier and Steel 810-19; Steel (1997) 117-20.

24. Bossier and Steel 819-21; Steel (1997) 124-5. [The attribution to Priscian has been accepted e.g. by George Shaw, *Theurgy and the Soul. The Neoplatonism of Iamblichus* (Pennsylvania State Univ. Press 1995) 98 n. 2. (Ed.)]

25. II.30-1. On this cf. Alan Cameron, 'The last days of the Academy at Athens', *Proceedings of the Cambridge Philological Society* n.s. 15 (1969) 7-29; H.J. Blumenthal, '529 and its sequel: what happened to the Academy?', *Byzantion* 48 (1978) 369-85, repr. in *Soul and Intellect*, Aldershot and Brookfield VT 1993, Study XVIII. For the view that they never returned cf. M. Tardieu, 'Sâbiens coraniques et "Sâbiens" de Harrân', *Journal Asiatique* 274 (1986) 1-44; and 'Les calendriers en usage à Harrân d'après les sources arabes et le commentaire de Simplicius à la *Physique* d'Aristote' in *Simplicius. Sa vie, son oeuvre, sa survie* (see n. 3) 40-57.

26. cf. esp. the famous comment in *Academica* 2.38.119, *flumen orationis aureum fundens Aristoteles*, 'Aristotle pouring out the golden stream of his eloquence', and J.S. Reid's note ad loc., *The Academica of Cicero* (London 1885); W.K.C. Guthrie, *A History of Greek Philosophy* vol. VI. *Aristotle. An encounter* (Cambridge 1981) 56-59.

27. Bossier and Steel 763-91; Steel (1997) 126-37.

28. *kai saphesteron moi tauta en têi epitomêi tôn Theophrastou Phusikôn diôristai*, 'I have dealt with this more clearly in the *epitome* of Theophrastus' *Metaphysics*', 136,29.

29. Bossier and Steel 764-9; Steel (1997) 127ff.

30. cf. *Soul and the Structure of Being* (see n. 2) 95, in the discussion to Blumenthal's paper. See, however, Steel's comments on this matter in Steel (1997) 136-7.

31. A view first mooted by Alan Cameron, 'The last days of the Academy at Athens' (see n. 25) 24.

32. As Averil Cameron once pointed out (*Agathias*, Oxford 1970, 101), Agathias does not actually say that they all came from Athens.

33. Bossier and Steel 764-9; Steel (1997) 128-30.

34. cf. *Simplicius: commentaire sur les Catégories: traduction commentée sur la direction de Ilsetraut Hadot* (Leiden 1990,1) 127-35.

35. 'Proclus' philosophical method of exegesis: the use of Aristotle and the Stoics in the commentary on the *Cratylus*', in *Proclus. Lecteur et interprète des Anciens* (Paris 1987) 143-9.

36. cf. the remark in a MS from the Great Lavra monastery on Mt. Athos: *Iôannês ho Philoponos, hostis kai kata Priskianou êgônisato, pollakis de kai kata Aristotelous*, 'John Philoponus who argued against Priscian, and often Aristotle too', *Codex Coislianus* 387, fol. 153-4, quoted by P. Athanassiadi, 'Persecution and response in late paganism: the evidence of Damascius', *Journal of Hellenic Studies* 113 (1993) 27 n. 194. Steel, however, suspects that the name of Priscian here is a mistake for Proclus, cf. Steel (1997) n. 68.

37. One might further consider the fact that the ever pugnacious John also wrote against a work of their intellectual hero Iamblichus, *Peri agalmatôn, On Statues*, cf. Photius, *Bibliotheca*, cod. 215 = III 130-131H.

38. See n. 15 above.

39. Bossier and Steel 782-90; Steel (1997) 106-8.

40. cf. Bossier and Steel 798-806; Steel (1997) 108-11.

41. Bossier and Steel 806-10; Steel (1997) 112-16.

42. Bossier and Steel 810-19; Steel (1997) 116-25.

43. In the article cited in n. 2 above; cf. also I. Hadot (n. 12).

44. See e.g. the article cited in n. 2.

45. For some additional remarks concerning the authorship see further nn. 18, 160, 294, 355 to the translation. (Ed.)

46. One based on lectures by the person named, but composed by a member of the audience – with varying degrees of accuracy and coherence. On the meaning of this term and its changed usage over time cf. M. Richard, '*apo phônês*', *Byzantion* 20 (1950) 191-222.

47. Bossier and Steel, 821, note that some texts in Damascius can be connected with the *de Anima* commentary, cf. Steel (1997) 113-14. Steel has since (in 1994) told me, in conversation, that he thinks my suggestion is a possible solution: I think he would wish to put a strong stress on 'possible'.

48. Seven in all, of whom we have works by only three, Damascius, Priscian, Simplicius.

49. For two recent discussions of the more-often treated authorship of that commentary, which was questioned at the time (1897) by the *CAG* editor, M. Hayduck, on p. v of his preface, cf. W.W. Charlton, in the introduction to *Philoponus. On Aristotle on the Intellect* (London and Ithaca 1991) 4-12; P. Lautner, 'Philoponus, *In De anima III*: quest for an author', *Classical Quarterly*, n.s. 42 (1992) 510-22.

50. First in 'Some observations on the Greek commentaries on Aristotle's *de Anima*', in *Actes du XVIe Congrès International des Études Byzantines* (6-12.9.1971, Bucharest 1976) 591-8; more fully in 'Neoplatonic elements in the *de Anima* commentaries', *Phronesis* 21, 1976, 64-97; repr. with Addendum, in *Aristotle Transformed* (see n. 3) 305-24.

51. For discussion *in extenso* see now my *Aristotle and Neoplatonism in Late Antiquity* (see n. 4) passim.

52. At 245,12.

53. 246,17-248,17; cf. also, e.g., 211,32-212,27.

54. *in Cael.* 640,27-32. The commentator's task was to concentrate on the fact that in most matters Plato and Aristotle were of one mind, cf. Simplic. *in Cat.* 7,29-32.

55. 1,14-20.

56. cf. esp. C. Steel, *The Changing Self. A Study on the Soul in Later Neoplatonism: Iamblichus, Damascius and Priscianus* (Verhandelingen van de Koninklijke Academie voor Wetenschappen, Letteren en Schone Kunsten van België. Kl. der Lett. 40, 1978. Nr. 85, Brussels 1978), in particular pp. 142-5.

57. cf. e.g. Iamblichus' identification of the subject of the *Sophist* as the sublunary demiurge, *In Soph.* fr. 1 Dillon = G.C. Greene, *Scholia Platonica* (Haverford 1938) 40.

58. 1,22ff.

59. cf. esp. Ps.-Philoponus on *de Anima* 3.5, *in DA* 535,1ff.; see further 'Neoplatonic elements' (see n. 49) 72-8.

60. cf. esp. *Phys.* 8.5, 256a21-9.

61. cf. esp. 247,15-17; also, e.g. 218,29-31.

62. cf. 90,29-91,4.

63. cf. 227,13-17.

64. On Themistius as basically a Peripatetic cf. the revised version of my 'Themistius: the last Peripatetic commentator on Aristotle?', in G.W. Bowersock, W. Burkert, M.C.J. Putnam (eds), *Arktouros. Hellenic Studies presented to Bernard M.W. Knox on the occasion of his 65th birthday* (Berlin and New York, 1979) 391-400 in *Aristotle Transformed* (see n. 3) 113-23. For a different view cf. O. Ballériaux, 'Thémistius et le Néoplatonisme. Le *NOUS PATHĒTIKOS* et l'immortalité de l'âme', *Revue de Philosophie Ancienne* 12 (1994) 171-200.

65. On the evidence for the existence of this commentary cf. now Blumenthal, *Aristotle and Neoplatonism* (see n. 4) 184-5.

66. cf. Blumenthal, 'Alexander of Aphrodisias in the later Greek commentaries on Aristotle's *de Anima*', in J. Wiesner (ed.), *Aristoteles. Werk und Wirkung* II (Berlin and New York 1987) 96-102; repr. in *Soul and Intellect* (see n. 25) Study XIV.

67. It has sometimes been thought that Iamblichus wrote one, but I think it can be shown that he did not, cf. Blumenthal, 'Did Iamblichus write a commentary on the *De anima*?', *Hermes* 102 (1974) 540-56.

68. cf. Blumenthal, 'Plutarch's exposition of the *de Anima* and the psychology of Proclus', in *De Jamblique à Proclus* (Entretiens sur l'Antiquité Classique 21. Fondation Hardt, Vandoeuvres 1974), 124-36, repr. in *Soul and Intellect* (see n. 25) Study XII.

69. cf. D.P. Taormina, *Plutarco di Atene. L'uno, l'anima, le forme* (Symbolon 8, Catania 1989) 171-5.

70. The second and third paragraph in this section were (with one minor change) taken from Blumenthal's recent paper 'Some Notes on the text of Ps.-Simplicius *in de Anima*', in M. Joyal (ed.), *Studies in Plato and the Platonic Tradition: Essays Presented to John Whittaker* (Ashgate, Aldershot and Brookfield VT 1997) 213-28. The editor wishes to thank Dr M. Joyal, Ashgate Publishing Ltd. and Mrs A. Blumenthal for kind permission to reproduce the material here.

71. In some cases a fuller explanation may be found in the recent paper in Joyal 1997 (see previous note). (Ed.)

72. Venice 1572. The translation, also published at Venice appeared in 1553.

73. Steel (1997) 116.

74. These, if they do not provide the full text for discussion, often indicate the end of the section to be expounded, cf. e.g. *in Phys.* 236,13-14: 'We say that', down to 'we have said what from the non-existent means, namely from it *qua* not being', i.e. from 191a34 to 191b26.

75. Venice 1543.

76. In this respect this translation will not be consistent with that of books 1 and 2.

Textual Emendations

In this list <...> add words or letters which are not in the text, and [...] remove words or letters which are in the text.

CS = C. Steel, in comments on the draft of this translation, unless otherwise stated in the relevant note.

173,40	Perhaps *atelôn* for *holôn*
174,23	*dusmetalêptikon* for *dusmetalêpton*
174,23-4	Perhaps *stoikheiôn* should be read in place of *entelekheiôn*
175,26-7	(*panta gar ... aisthêta estin*), adding the parentheses, and substituting a comma for the stop after *estin*
175,32	Reading *hebdomôi* for *ogdoôi*
177,9	Reading *autois* for *autê*
177,12	Deleting *to anapalin*
177,36	Perhaps *haptomenê* for *haptomena* (sc. *zôa*)
180,9	Reading *dio* for *an* (CS)
181,17	*tên pronoian* <*tên*> *hêgoumenên*
181,22	Reading *autês* for *tês*
181,36	Perhaps <*peri ta*> *peri tên*
183,4	Retaining first *kinêsei* in *DA* 425a17
183,17	*hoion megethos kinêsei* as a new lemma
183,21	*kai* [*to*] ... [*kai*] *to*
183,37	Reading *suneisagei* for *suneisagein*
187,2	Reading *hautê* for *autê*
187,13	Perhaps *megethos* for *khrôma*
187,28	Perhaps *monou* for *monon*
188,25	Perhaps *pente* for *prôtai* (CS)
190,34	(lemma) Reading *to auto* for *tauton* (*DA* 425b27)
192,4	(lemma) Retaining *eipoi* against Ross' *eipeien* at *DA* 426a1
193,31	(lemma) Reading *ei dê sumphônia phônê tis* for *ei d' hê phônê sumphônia tis* (*DA* 426a27)
196,34-5	(lemma) Reading *krinomen tini kai aisthanometha hoti diapherei, anangkê dê aisthêsei* for *krinomen, tini kai aisthanometha hoti diapherei. anankê dê aisthêsei* (*DA* 426b14)
197,6	*met'aisthêseôs* [*hotan hôs atoma legêi*] *ê di'aisthêseôs*
199,8	Perhaps *kinêsis* [*hê autê*] *hê pathê*
199,12	Reading *tauta* for *tautês*
199,30	(lemma) *oukh hoion te* for *oukh hoion te*; (*DA* 407a5-6)
199,37	*ou, tôi energeisthai*

200,19	Reading *aülou* for *enülou*
201,13	(lemma) Retaining *dusi* against Ross (*DA* 427a13)
201,13	(lemma) Reading *kekhôrismenôs* (A) for *kekhôrismenois* (*DA* 427a13)
201,21	(lemma) Reading *hen, heni* against Ross' *heni, hen* (*DA* 427a14)
201,23	Reading *autê hê aisthêtikê psukhê* for *autêi têi aisthêtikê psukhê*
201,32	(lemma) Reading *krinein* for *phronein* (*DA* 427a18)
203,25	Reading *enantiotês* for *oikeiotês* (CS)
206,4	(lemma) Reading *hê autê noêsis kai hypolêpsis* against Ross *hê autê* [*noêsis*] *kai hupolêpsis* (*DA* 427b16-17)
206,21	(lemma) *esti poiêsasthai* for *esti ti poiêsasthai* (*DA* 427b18-19)
208,9	(lemma) *mia tis* retained for *<ara> mia tis* (*DA* 428a3)
208,19	Taking *dunamin de ê hexin* as a separate lemma
209,2	Reading *energeiai* (dative) for *energeias*
209,11	Reading *progegenêsthai* for *prosgegenêsthai*
209,15	*DA* 428a10-11 (not given in lemma): *hoion murmêki ê melittêi ê skôlêki* for Ross' *skôlêki d' ou*
209,15	*DA* 428a15 (not given in lemma): *tote ê alêthês ê pseudês* for *poteron alêthês ê pseudês*
209,22	Reading *hôrismenôs* for *hôrismenous*
211,16-18	Retaining lemma (*DA* 428a22-4), bracketed by Ross
211,30-1	(lemma) Reading *oute ... oute ... oute* for *oude ... oude ... oude* (*DA* 428a25)
212,7	Reading *diakekrimenôs* for *diakekrinomenôs*
212,10	Reading *hoion* for *hoson*
212,20	Repunctuating with comma instead of stop after *eiê*
212,29	(lemma) Retaining *kai dêlon hoti ... ekeinou, houper estin, homou kai hê aisthêsis* against *kai dioti ... ekeinou, eiper estin, hou kai hê aisthêsis dêlon* (*DA* 428b3-4)
215,7	Reading *prosekhei* for *prosekhê* or *<dia> tên ge prosekhê kai* [*dia*] *sômatikên pathên*
215,12	Reading *hoti* for *hote*
216,22	Reading *aisthêton* for *aisthêtikon*
216,38-9	*kai dia to ... prattei ta zôa* to be separate lemma (*DA* 429a4-6)
218,15	Reading *hote* for *hopote*
218,42	Reading *ton prôton* for *tên prôtên ton*
219,25	Reading *holôs, kai autos hôs hoion te tôi logôi tou exô* for *holôs kai autos, hôs hoion te tôi logôi, tou exô*
220,13	Reading *Plôtinôi* for *Platôni* (CS)
220,25	Deleting *hê*
221,17	Reading *hôristika* for *gnôristika* (CS)
222,20	Deleting *all'*
226,30	Reading *tês psukhikês <noun> noun* for *tês psukhês noun*

230,30-3   Retaining Hayduck's punctuation against *DA*
231,15   Reading *êi ê hê* for *êi hê*
232,8   Reading *autôn* for *autou*
235,34   (lemma) Retaining *dei* against *d<unam>ei* (*DA* 429b31, Ross
           following Cornford)
239,1   (lemma) Retaining *monon* (*DA* 430a6)
239,28   (lemma) Retaining *ekeinois* against *ekeinôi* (*DA* 430a8)
240,1   (lemma) Retaining *hôsper* (*DA* 430a10)
243,4   (lemma) Reading *pantê<i>* for *panta*
245,3   Reading *he autê d'estin* against *to auto d'estin* (*DA* 430a19)
245,5   (lemma) Retaining *all' hote* against *all'oukh hote* (*DA* 430a22)
245,23   Reading *deutera* for *deuteran*
247,36-7   Punctuating *sunäiresin, tês khôristheisês psukhikês ousias eis*
           ... for *sunäiresin tês khôristheisês psukhikês ousias, eis* ...

'Simplicius'
On Aristotle
On the Soul 3.1-5

Translation

The commentary of 'Simplicius' on Book 3 of Aristotle's on the Soul

<CHAPTER 1>

424b22 That there is no other sense besides the five [(I mean sight, hearing, smell, taste, touch) one would be convinced by what follows].

The primary purpose[1] in the third book is to discuss the soul which makes choices, that is the reasoning and intellective soul in mortal beings[2] since in the whole treatise he has embarked on the investigation of the soul in mortal beings, because from there we will perhaps be moved on, by some analogy, to higher souls, and especially so from the rational soul in these beings.[3] In the second book he taught mainly about the soul which is common to other living beings as well:[4] in the third he has set the main task as being about the rational soul.

He begins from sense-perception, at the same time making the argument continuous with the previous discussion, and also intending to make it easier to consider the rational soul's[5] difference from it by juxtaposition.[6] In addition he does this so that we can look at however much of a trace of the rational soul has arrived at the sense faculty, such as its indivisibility, its separability, in a way, and its ability to apprehend itself: it is also because the practical intellect[7] uses sense-perception too.

Right at the start he enquires if there is some other sense beside the five senses, so that from the inductive argument we can consider how reason differs from them and not claim that there is some other one, unknown to us, that has been left out, and also because it is proper to science to include, as far as possible, all kinds of objects of cognition. It is also useful for showing how each sense apprehends itself, for example whenever sight, seeing this colour, perceives at the same time that it is cognizing. For here reason is not cognitive in the first place, since the object of cognition is partial and discrete.[8] Nor is it the case that some other sense does this, since none of the remaining four does it and there is no other sense besides the five. So for this reason too it is necessary to talk about there being no sense apart from the five that has been left out, so that we do not suppose that the consciousness proper to each one belongs to that. He seems to attribute being in some way cognitive of itself exclusively or predominantly to the sense faculty of a living being equipped with reason.[9] Therefore he goes on with the subject[10] in the third book. It is proper particularly to intellect, and in the second place to reason, to have the capacity to cognize itself, and to the life that is separate from bodies (because body, on account of its being divided with

5   different parts of itself in different places, does not turn back to itself), so that it belongs to the kind of sense-perception that is like reason, if not quite, but is in a way free from any body.

On what basis then does he argue that there is no other sense besides the five? The belief in this does not come from induction: there are more unapparent types of living beings than ones we can clearly see.[11] Some are also mortal, the others are those that are superhu-

10   man.[12] Nor can it be argued from the elements, on the basis of each of them coming under its own sense, they being four, as well as the exhalation of which smell is said to be the sense, as sight is of fire, hearing of air and the other senses of the others, smell of water and touch of earth. For fire is cognized not only by sight but also by touch,[13] as being hot. So it is unclear whether it has some other quality which

15   we do not know about because we lack a sense which perceives it. How then does Aristotle make us believe that there are only five senses? From the perfection of the life in us and the fact that our sense-organs are not insufficient. Any sense would be insufficient either because the life is dim and is as if one had fainted, being too weak to act in respect of all of them, or because of the insufficiency of the instruments, which are the sense-organs.[14] If therefore the life is perfect

20   and none of the sense-organs is missing, it is reasonable and even necessary that such living beings have all the senses.

How then will we define perfect life, and in particular the life in mortal beings which is our subject? Since it initiates movement from within, and movement in respect of place is by nature, it is in the things that are moved in this way that we must seek the perfection

25   of the life that moves them. It does not come from some part only, as in the case of bivalves, but pervades the whole animal, and not in an indeterminate way as with worms and fleas, but in a determined way: they do not have this determination in some restricted way, like ants and bees,[15] but show the application of thought and contrivance, particularly those that are able to take notice of reason and to be organised by reason, and have the capacity to acquire habits and

30   understand the instructions given by reason. The sensitive life which is able to be combined with the faculty of reason which is superior to it is not the least perfect: that is a sign of high level.[16] If then this sensitive life is the most perfect, and is defined in terms of only the five kinds of sense, then there must necessarily be no other kind of sense. I am not saying that only the sensitive life in rational beings is perfect, because perfection exists also at the bottom:[17] this one is

35

the most perfect, and also that in irrational beings which listens to reason and shows contrivance, thought and determination in a way that is not restricted. What is restricted and indeterminate and immobile in respect of place is already imperfect, not as being moved contrary to its nature, but because it determines, according to its own nature, the things that live at the end of the continuum and in a dim sort of way. So by nature even a thing that is naturally imperfect determines[18] whole classes of things.[19] Enough has now been said about how in terms of the perfection of life no sense would be lacking in perfect beings.

It remains to consider whether the lack of an organ produces the deficiency. Since a sense-organ must necessarily be compounded from all the elements or simple,[20] we must enquire out of what kind of simple elements sense-organs can be made, to which senses simple elements should be attributed and to which the compound, and whether all possible sense-organs are present in perfect living beings, so that we can ascertain that no sense is lacking because of the absence of sense-organs.[21] Since then the first[22] organs are stimulated by sense-objects through some media (for they are not directly stimulated), he does well to find evidence for the nature of the sense-organs from the intervening media. For both receive the activities of the sense-objects and the media, being of similar nature and continuous with the organs, by transferring their activity to the sense-organs show that their substance is of the same nature. For example what receives a visible object must be transparent. Therefore this property belongs to both, to the medium and to the sense-organ. Further it is because of their mutual affinity that transfer from one to the other takes place without force and in a natural way. So it happens by virtue of contiguity and having the same nature. And so the medium is like the sense-organ.

What then are the media? Some are in us, as in the case of touch and taste; some are external, as in the case of the remaining senses. Of the ones in us the parts that are at the surface, which also become media, are thoroughly mixed because the nature of mortal living beings requires a hard and resisting outer cover, because that is resistant to affections but not completely unable to be stimulated: therefore it is not simple but mixed. Of the ones that are external the two simple ones, water and air, are able to transmit the activity of the sense-objects, or if they are mixed one of them is altogether predominant in the compound. The media are not made of earth because it is not subject to stimulation, not easily acted on and not easily able to participate[23] in the activities that come from the other elements,[24] nor are they made of fire because of its own active power, being an element that moves the others and rather gives something of its own properties to the others than being moved by the others

40
174,1

5

10

15

20

25

and participating in what is in them. How could the mixed in us, with
the earthy component predominating, receive the perceptible activities of objects of touch and taste immediately? One could say that it
is because it has life and is, as it were, made lighter by the life in us.
And how can Fire[25] be transparent and penetrable by sound?[26] An
30   answer would be that that fire is of an elemental nature, but that he[27]
now seems to reject the fire that burns and causes boiling as not being
a sense-organ in its own right, so that the Fire, being in the air, is
included in or common to all. Because nothing that is without warmth
is capable of perceiving: but what burns perceives nothing. Since then
two of the media are composed of simple elements, water and air
(there is an elemental nature in air too) or something that has them
35   in common, and the sense-organs are made of something similar, we
have both points: in perfect living beings not only is there the perfect
life, but also none of the organs is missing. So there would be no
missing sense either: if so there would be only the five senses. But
the great Iamblichus wishes us to have a large number of divine and
superior living beings which cannot be seen. And he says that we
40   should not make assertions about the number of the senses on the
basis of induction: he is right to say this. Of course Aristotle does not
175,1 rely on induction, but on the perfection of life, and the fact that we
lack no sense-organ.[28] But he[29] does say that the sense-perception of
the heavenly bodies[30] is superior in so far as it is not subject to
affections, is stimulated entirely from within and in no way requires
external objects to move it:[31] it is itself sufficient and dependent on
itself both in respect of its existence and in respect of its cognition of
objects of sense.[32]
5   Must we therefore posit more than the five senses precisely on
account of the sense-perception which belongs to the heavenly bodies?[33] Rather we should not count that together with the ones here,
taking it to be the cause of the ones here which are caused by it, and
being inclusive of all these in so far as they are unitary.[34] Further we
do not count the common sense in us as a sixth sense along with the
five. And yet it is inseparably situated together with them, because
of its capacity to include them in a common function.[35] So, *a fortiori*,
that which transcends them all, and includes them while being
10   separate and causative, is not to be counted together with them.
Moreover the sense-perception possessed by the heavenly bodies is
not different from the five simply. This is because difference lies in
definitions, because of the difference that attaches to the definitions,
and in the sense-objects. But the heavenly bodies' sense-perception
is not different in this way, but in its mode of operation, since its
sense-objects are no more numerous than those which we too are able
to apprehend. Indeed the whole demonstration of the point at issue
15   seems to me to be something like this: it relies on the perfection of

life in living beings which are not defective or possessed of charac-
teristics contrary to nature, and on the fact that no organs are
missing. This too he argued not by means of induction but from the
nature of the organs of perception, two of them being simple in the
case of the senses that cognize at a distance, with the mixed one
belonging to touch, since the body of mortal living beings is also mixed
– to put it in a general way.[36] It remains necessary to expound bit by
bit the words of the text that shows this.[37]

424b22 That there is no other sense apart from the five

This, to speak as geometers do, is the posing of the problem. The
marshalling of the argument starts from here.

424b24 If we now have sense-perception of everything of which
touch is the appropriate sense (for all the affections of the
tangible, *qua* tangible, can be perceived by us with the sense of
touch), ...[38]

Since the primary qualities that can cause affections are only four,
heat, cold, dryness and wetness, from which the others derive, as is
said in the *de Generatione*,[39] all of which touch can perceive since it
perceives all the primary qualities, and as all the things which are
tangible, in so far as they are tangible, are characterised by the
qualities that can cause affections, as is mentioned in the eighth book
of the *Physics*,[40] it is clear that it is rightly assumed that 'all the
affections of what is tangible, *qua* tangible', are cognized 'by touch'.
And if touch, though it is the lowest sense, leaves none of the tangibles
uncognized, so in general each of the remaining senses will not be
deficient in respect of any of its proper sense-objects. This follows from
the hypothetical premise, 'if <we have sense-perception> of everything of which touch is the appropriate sense.' Aristotle, however,
does not draw the conclusion, but there are other antecedent propositions, namely the words 'if a sense is missing it is necessary that
the sense-organ be missing too'. Then there is a third one, which he
constructs in the middle, that 'even if no sense-organ is missing in
us', and after a long interval he gives as the conclusion to all the
antecedent propositions in common the words, 'all the senses are
possessed by beings which are not incomplete'.[41] For if there is not a
sense-organ missing, as the third of the propositions posits, because
sense-objects are apprehended either directly or through the media
air and water, and we have what can touch both of the media, then
no sense is missing either since the text says, 'if some sense is missing
then some sense-organ is absent'. And in this way he also concludes
to the second of the antecedent propositions that has been set out,

10   that is to 'it is necessary that, if a sense is missing then we must lack
a sense-organ as well', that 'so all the senses are possessed by beings
which are not incomplete'. To the first, that 'if we have a sense
pertaining to everything of which the sense is touch', he gives the
same conclusion, 'so all the senses are possessed by beings which are
not incomplete', since thus we have all, for the reason that they do
15   not fail to be there for any of the appropriate sense-objects, because
we now have sense-perception by means of touch of everything for
which the sense is touch: the addition of the words 'and now' shows
that it had already been demonstrated before that there are only the
five senses. For we have touch which is perfect in so far as it does not
leave any tangible object uncognized, which he sets up by saying that
20   'all the affections of the tangible, *qua* tangible, can be perceived by us
with the sense of touch' if, as has been said, we are able to cognize by
touch all the simple qualities which cause affections, both of the first
simple things and also those that are compounded from them by
mixture. If then touch cognizes all tangible objects, it is necessary
that each of the other senses apprehends all the appropriate sense-
25   objects. So it is right that all the senses are said to be present in those
who have the five, in so far as there are no more and none of them
leaves its appropriate sense-objects uncognized.

424b26 it is necessary that, if any sense is missing, a sense-
organ is missing in us too.

30   This is, as has been said, the second hypothetical argument of the
series: what is meant by 'necessary' deserves comment. Why, if the
sense of vision alone is absent, and the organ of sight can be airy, is
this not present in a creature having hearing, so that it has the
sense-organ but vision, being absent, does not use it as an organ of
vision? It seems as if the absence of a sense-organ has two senses, the
35   first being that the basic body, whichever is useable for the missing
sense, is absent, as if air or water, unmixed, were not present in
themselves in some living beings. The other is that it is present but
not, shall we say, as able to see. For it would not have existed
pointlessly as able to see in a creature which has not the natural
177,1   capacity to see. Perhaps the argument is closer to the truth in the
case of perfect living beings. That is why he said 'in us', and not simply
'if a sense were to be missing then a sense-organ would be missing
too', but in us who have the five senses. If there were some other sense,
then the body would have some other kind of sense-organ,[42] or use the
existing ones[43] in some other way. But it is impossible for there to be
5   another sense-organ as an instrument, since there is no other perishable body apart from the four, and the heavenly body is not subordi-
nated to the divine soul as an organ:[44] for it is not subordinate to it

because the soul uses it, but because all of it belongs to the soul.
Moreover the bodies here do not have the capacity to be percipient in
some other way. For in a perfect form of life there would be some
power[45] using them.[46] Therefore it is necessary that those who do not
have this power, and this is not through a mutilation nor because of
imperfection, do not have the organ either. For all the powers are
present in the complete life, and their nature consequently provides
all the organs too, if the living being is not unnaturally defective,[47]
that is whenever[48] though the power is present the organ is missing.
Therefore it is not said that when the sense-organ is missing then the
perceiving faculty is missing too, but the other way round, that if the
sense-organ is not missing then the sense is not missing either, and
that this is so in us who have the five senses and are perfect, as being
able to move with the motion that is defined in respect of place.

424b27 And all the things which we perceive by touching them
themselves are perceptible by touch, which we do have [but
those which we perceive through mediums and not by touching
them themselves we perceive by means of simple things between, I mean such as air and water]

This is the third of the antecedent propositions, by means of which
he thinks he can show that we lack neither an organ nor a sense: for
it is necessary for sense-perception to take place either when we touch
the sense-objects or through the mediums. The division is without
mediation: it is impossible otherwise.[49] Since sense-perception is a
form of cognitive activity, and is of bodies, and these situated externally, and happens through a sense-organ which is a body characterised by this cognitive activity, it is necessary for the sense-organ
either to touch the sense-objects themselves, or to apprehend the
sense-objects by means of some other bodies situated in between (for
it does not do so through a void),[50] so that the actuality of the
sense-object is conveyed to the sense-organ. For Aristotle wants even
touch to take place through that which is a medium, but with the
medium not being external but in us, so that it too is alive in
accordance with the sensitive life: nevertheless he wants the sense-
organ which is primarily relevant to be different. So in respect of being
sensitive in the primary sense even touch is not immediate, in respect
of being perceptive in a general sense and in some way it is immediate. And perhaps what is called simultaneous perceptual awareness[51]
happens for us when we perceive some one of the parts in us being
cooled or heated by way of touch, the sense-organ primarily relevant
making contact with the affected part. All living beings have the
power of touch. But as for the sense-perception[52] which operates
through mediums, which perceives without touching the sense-

objects themselves, not all have it, and those living beings which do
do not perceive every characteristic of the sense-objects. For it is not
the case that when they are able to smell they can already hear, nor
that those which can perceive a sound can already perceive colour.
For how does he think that the things that are perceived through
mediums can be perceived by means of simple things in between when
178,1 these consist of air and water, and that each of the living beings which
have one of the two can perceive the objects which are perceptible
through both mediums? He says it is like this: 'but those which
perceive objects through a medium and not by touching them themselves do so by means of simple things between,⁵³ I mean such as air
5 and water'. That this happens through only two of the things that can
be in between, he will show when he has gone on a little.⁵⁴ The 'for
example' in the 'I mean such as air and water' is added so that, I think,
he can show that it is not just these two elements being in the middle
which transmit the activity of sensible things to the sense-organs, but
the things like these, such as heat, being like air, and also things
10 which are already compounds, but with air or water predominant in
them, like oil, wine and mist.

> **424b31** It is like this, that if more than one thing, different in
> kind from each other, is perceptible through one thing, it is
> necessary that a person having a sense-organ of this kind is able
> to perceive both of them,⁵⁵ [(for example if the sense-organ
> consists of air, air will be the medium for sound and colour) but
> if there is more than one medium for the same thing, for example
> both air and water for colour (for both are transparent), even a
> person having only one of the two will perceive what comes
> through both]

15 If more than one kind of sense-data from anything can act on the
sense-organ through one of the two mediums, he says that they are
'different in kind from each other', since they fall under different
senses. For the hot and the dry are not entirely different in kind, being
both objects of touch, but colour and sound are, because one is an
object of sight and the other of hearing. Nevertheless both are perceptible through air as they are through water. But even the class of
20 things that can be smelled works through both of the two mediums.
And he says 'that a person having a sense-organ of this kind', clearly
meaning one that is like water or air, or characterised by the predomi-
nance of one or the other, must be 'able to perceive both', since he is
discussing two things of a different kind and therefore saying 'both'.
So he has brought in two things by saying that air pertains to sound
and colour.
25   But why, as we said,⁵⁶ does the mole not see since it has air by

which it hears? And why does not the murex also hear, since it has that by which it smells, whether that be air or water? Because, I shall say, what is said[57] is neither held to be the case nor true simply, but applies to perfect living beings (hence, as has been said,[58] he carried on the discussion with reference to us, saying 'in us', and 'all the things which we perceive by touching them themselves') when the   30
power of sense-perception is present and perfect and, of course, none of the organs necessary for touch is missing (since no animal would exist without this sense), nor in perfect living beings any of those necessary for the perception that works through the mediums, even if only one of the two mediums were present: for in that case all the senses that work through a medium would use it, as they do the water or air that is external.

He has not yet shown that only the simple organs in us serve the   35
senses that perceive through the mediums, but has only taken it from induction that the two mediums are air and water, and now proposes one sense-organ only, the one through which most of the sense-data from various sources are cognized (where he writes 'that if more than   179,1
one thing is perceptible through one thing' and so on), sometimes mediums of this kind are more than one so that the same things are cognized through each of two, for example colour through air and through water. This he determines to be closer to the truth, adding the reason when he says 'both are forms of the transparent', since they do not transmit colour by virtue of being air or water but because   5
they are transparent.[59] In the first supposition he posits that the person having that one which transmits a multiplicity of sense-data from various sources is able to perceive both the two that come from different sources as though, as has been said, he is conducting the discusssion about two things, while in the second he posits that the person who has either one of the mediums perceives the sensible object that comes through either of them. For the 'through both' in   10
the words 'the person who has only one of the two will perceive what comes through both' is to be understood as saying that it comes through each of the two on its own, and not that it comes through both at the same time, nor that it comes from something that proceeds from both. This is so because whichever of the two mediums is present would serve the perfect faculty which is able to act in such a way as to see.

425a3 Of the elements sense-organs are composed of these two   15
only [(the eyeball is made of water, the organ of hearing of air and that of smell of one or other of these)]

Taking, above, the mediums to be only two, air and water, he wants the sense-organs too to be composed of these two simple elements only, since the organ of touch is a compound (it is made of all four, with the earthy element predominating), and taste is subsumed under touch. Of the organs which perceive through some mediums, 20 'the eyeball is made of water, the organ of hearing of air and that of smell of one or other of these'.[60] And from the induction he also makes the case for there being only two simple sense-organs in us by means of first taking the point that the mediums are two and the same two, showing what follows from the argument, that the simple sense-organs are two only. For the number and nature of the external elements that transmit sense-objects is the same as the number and 25 nature of the things in us that receive the activities of those sense-objects.

425a5 The organ of smell is made of one or other of these.

Either because air in us corresponds to water in fish, or because a medium consisting of both elements is in all living beings.[61]

30   **425a5** But fire either belongs to none of them or is common to all of them.

What causes burning[62] belongs to none, but the elemental nature of it is common to all. If so, then the simple organs too are called simple by virtue of what predominates. In fact the whole living being in the case of each mortal species consists of all four elements, and so does every part of it. So then do the sense-organs.

180,1   **425a6** Earth belongs to none of them, or is a major ingredient of touch alone.

Simple earth belongs to none of them, and in the compound ones there is earth strongly predominating, as in the case of bones and hair. It is a major ingredient in the case of touch alone because it is also present in the others, but not obviously. It shows in the case of touch 5 because it predominates, in the same way as the others show in the other senses. This is a peculiarity of the sense-organs that work by touch.

425a7 Therefore we would be left with the conclusion that there is no sense-organ apart from air and water.

These words are clearly presented as the apodosis to other clauses 10 because of the conjunction,[63] yet not to all the previous words. They are not the apodosis to the remarks about touch, but to the words that start from 'but those which we perceive through mediums and not by touching them themselves'. The words would be clearer, if as Plutarch thinks we should, we were to take the hypothetical conjunction to apply in common to all the protases in the words up to that point,[64] so that what is said would go like this: if all the things which we touch by means of mediums, not touching the objects themselves, are only two, the simple intervening things, air and water, and if the simple sense-organs in us must be of that number and that kind, then 'we would be left with the conclusion that there is no sense-organ apart from air and water', meaning clearly a simple one.

425a8 And some living beings do actually have these.

He says 'these' meaning the two simple elements, either really simple or predominating in such a way that the mixture does not show. He says 'some living beings' because of what are called zoophytes in which there is not one of the senses that perceives through the mediums.[65] Therefore neither air nor water are simple sense-organs, since both are in all living things in accordance with the mixture.

425a9 So all senses are possessed by living beings that are neither imperfect nor defective.

This is what provides the apodosis to all the protases that have been taken so far. If we now have perception of everything for which the sense is touch, and if where any sense is missing then a sense-organ would be absent in us, and if all the things which we perceive by touching the actual objects are perceptible by touch which we happen to have, but all the things which we perceive by touching them not themselves but through mediums are perceptible by means of the simple things in between, I mean like air and water, and if the sense-organs which some living beings now have are only operative on simple bodies made of these two, then all the senses are possessed by living beings which are not imperfect or defective. The connecting particle 'so'[66] as it now stands is either completive or syllogistic, since the apodosis provides the conclusion simultaneously. By adding the words 'by <living beings> which are not imperfect' he showed that he has set up the whole argument with reference to perfect living beings. Those are perfect which have locomotion in an ordered way.[67] Imperfect are those which do not have locomotion, not in so far as they are deprived of the life that belongs to their species (for all members of the species are of such a kind), but because they are deficient in respect of the life that belongs to the class of living beings *qua* living beings: the perceptive faculty belongs to a living being simply as such. Those that do not have the whole perceptive faculty are imperfect, not as living beings of a certain kind, but as living beings simply.

10   Those are defective which are individuals bereft of a sense which
belongs to those of the same species, because they are either damaged
in gestation or subsequently deprived of some organ.

425a10 Even the mole apparently has eyes under its skin.

The point is that though it is able to move locally it does not see,
15   because in its case Nature cares more about its being than about its
well-being, in so far as it digs the earth with its face and is nourished
from it.[68] I suspect the explanation is not right, because it makes
providence, which[69] is the origin[70] both of being and of any good that
may belong to each kind of thing, consequential. Because all animals
exist we shall say that not only the perfect ones exist, but also the
lowest and the ones in between, with no gap interwoven, the progres-
20   sion not being without intermediates.[71] In the case of the mole one
must consider, I think, that there is not a complete lack of the power
and activity of sight, but rather of the manifest power: it participates
in it[72] through membranes, in the way that we have some consciousness of light through the eyelids. For the animal would not have had
the eyes under its skin pointlessly if they were not able actually to
25   function under the skin: but they do so dimly and in darkness on
account of their weakness, like those of animals that feed at night.

425a11 And so unless there is some other kind of body or a
property which does not belong to any of the bodies here no sense
would be missing.

The words before us show the same thing, that the five senses are the
only ones, and that none is missing in those living beings which have
30   these. So this is attached as a conclusion to what was said before,
since it aims at the same target: the particle 'and so' indicates a
conclusion. And he shows in another way what was proposed at the
start. What comes up to this point has dealt with the problem,
starting from the perfect sensitive faculty and the not deficient
distribution of organs. I think that these words refer to the same point
starting from sense-objects. For if in the *de Caelo*[73] the simple bodies
35   are shown to be five only, and all the senses are concerned with their
substance[74] only in respect of quality or quantity or some charac-
182,1   teristic accruing to them in the nine categories (substance can be
apprehended by reason or intellect but not by sense-perception),[75]
then it is clear that no sense would be missing. For the five are able
to cognize the five bodies in respect of all the characteristics accruing
to them. If, therefore, there is no other body apart from the five, as
has been shown to be the case, and there is no 'property which is not
5   a property of one of the bodies here' (by properties he means what

comes after substance and the forms that proceed around it, like shape, sizes, movements, colours, sounds and smells: these are forms attached to the others which are substantial forms, and acquire their existence in them, and are therefore called properties, and 'the bodies here' are not those below the moon, but those in the whole cosmos), if then it is impossible for there to be either another kind of body or a property of another kind of body, because all sense-objects are made of these, as a man having an accurate knowledge of their substance would confirm, a knowledge from which he would know the number and nature of the things that follow from substance, no sense would be missing.   10

425a13 Nor again can there be some special sense for the common sensibles which we perceive incidentally with each of the senses [for example movement, rest, shape, size and number: for we perceive all these things by movement][76]   15

We have already defined which things are the direct objects of sense-perception in themselves, and by which the sense-organ is affected, and which are objects incidentally, that is things which exist along with what is perceived but do not come under the same sense. So sight perceives the yellow in bile directly but the bitter incidentally because it is affected by the yellow but not by the bitter.[77] Rather we say we perceive it too as it exists with the yellow in the bile, and this is so whenever the sensation proper to it is present, and has happened before, so that now in seeing the yellow the soul brings up the bitter with it.[78] Direct has been defined in two ways, primarily, that is what comes under a certain sense because of itself, and secondarily, that is as following a cause,[79] it too acting on the sense-organ, but with something else which is altogether prior. Thus sight sees the size and shape of a thing, being affected in some way by the colour, and also by the size and shape, but in so far as these are coloured and act by means of their colour. The primary direct sense-objects are those which are proper to each sense. But the direct objects of the senses which are apprehended secondarily along with the primary qualities are called common because they are not related to any one sense, as are the proper ones, but are cognized by more than one or by all of them.[80]   20, 25, 30

And when he has shown that no sense is missing in us, by showing that there is no other apart from the five, he solves the objection, as it were,[81] that thinks one should attribute a special sense to the common sensibles, since each of the five cognizes them incidentally. Just as when sight perceives the bitter incidentally in the case of bile, it is another sense which cognizes it in itself, that is taste, it is necessary for a special sense to be in control of the common objects if   35

the other senses apprehend them incidentally. But that the common
objects are cognized incidentally by each of the five is what those who
make sense-perception primary would say. That is why he used these
183,1   words 'which we perceive incidentally with each of the senses', since
they would say that. Yet it is not true that we do so incidentally, as
he immediately goes on to show, having first indicated the common
qualities. 'For we perceive all these things by movement'. That is by
the sense-organ being affected in some way by the sense-object, for
5   example by being dilated or contracted, or without being affected
actually receiving the actuality of the sense-object from outside, as
air receives light, and the sensitive soul perceives by virtue of the
affection of the sense-organ, as was said. In accordance with this there
comes about the actuality[82] that comes in from outside and also the
soul's own cognitive attention[83] itself, because it is stimulated by what
10   is outside and directs its attention to the outside. Each sense is moved
and affected by the common sensibles, but not at all by the incidental
ones, so that the common sensibles are not incidental, and therefore
it is not reasonable to require another sense for them. In addition
there would necessarily be no separate special sense for them, in so
far as more than one sense cognizes them directly in accordance with
what they have in common with each other. For the special is opposed
15   to the common, and the common power is present in more than one
sense, but would not be distinguished from them so that it would be
a special sense.

[425a17 For example size by movement][84]

That a sense-object as size acts on the sense-organ is shown by the
pain from snow spread over a large expanse of ground affecting sight
in so far as it is white, while the sound from a large stone falling is
20   more offensive to hearing.

425a17 And so shape too, for shape is a kind of size,[85] [but what
is at rest is cognized by its not being moved, and number by the
negation of continuity, and also by the special sense-objects].

He says this because in respect to its substrate shape uses size as its
matter. Thus we also call a bench wood, since all shape comes under
quality. How is it perceived by movement? Not because all sense-
objects are moved, but because what perceives is moved by them.
25   When he says that size and shape are cognized by movement, he says
'but what is at rest is cognized by its not being moved', to make it clear
in what sense 'by movement' is meant, namely that it is not by the
objects themselves being moved. For what is at rest is cognized even
though it is not being moved, in so far as it itself is not being moved,

but it moves the sense. For it is not the case, I think, that he is saying
that what is at rest is cognized by the absence of movement, by not
moving something as darkness does not move vision.[86]   30

It has already been said that we perceive all things by movement,
and rest too. And how we do so is said now, namely that it is not by
rest being moved itself,[87] but by the sense-organ being in a certain
state and the sensitive faculty being called into activity. And number
is not said to be perceived 'by the negation of the continuous' as in the
case of a privation. That is because number is perceptible in its own
right, like the one, and moves sense-perception, but not in the way   35
that darkness is cognized by not moving the sense of sight which is
trying to see, or the way that the soundless is cognized by the sense
of hearing, but because the one is the opposite of the many, in the
same way as plurality at the same time brings with it[88] the one that
is continuous[89] in respect of each of the components of the plurality.[90]
For in the sphere of what is perceptible what is one is one in so far as
it is continuous, and the continuous is not manifested as one in the
collection of all its components. And yet number exists as one and is   184,1
cognized as one through the collection, being a thing with divisions,
and not as being continuous. That is shown by the negation of the
continuous, the fact that it is not just one (for that is always continuous in the case of perceptible things) but is so in the collection of a
number of such things, the collection being a denial of the continuity.   5
The words 'and by the special <sense-organs>' do not, I think, refer
to number, but are used with reference to what was said above, so
that you should add to 'we perceive all these things by movement',
the words 'and by the special sense-organs'. Since the common sensibles stimulate these, they come after the special objects of the senses
which are primary, as has been said.[91]

425a19 For each sense perceives one thing   10

It perceives primarily the special sensible which is specifically one,
as in the case of sight. For the colour or the light is a single sensible
object, and a sound in the case of hearing. In the case of touch the
single sensible object is what is distinguished in respect of a quality
which can cause affections, or in any other way, even if we have no
common term to cover these.

425a20 And so it is clear that it is impossible for there to be a   15
special sense for any one of these.

For if there were a special sense for the common sensibles it would
be distinguished by contrast with the rest, and none of them would
perform its[92] function in its own right. Now they act and are stimu-

lated by the common sensibles. So if there were a special sense for them, the other senses would be in a similar relation to them,

20   **425a22** [For it would be like] the way we now perceive the sweet by sight. [This we do because we have a sense which perceives both, so that we recognize them]

that is they would be incidental to them, since we have a sense for both sets of objects which are clearly different senses, sight being for colour and taste for the sweet.

425a23 whenever they fall together.

Instead of saying 'in respect of which', in respect of having two different senses, he says 'when these[93] come together' (that is what is
25   meant by 'they fall together') so that we perceive the same thing simultaneously as yellow and sweet: 'we recognize' that this yellow thing happens to be sweet.

425a24 Otherwise we should not perceive them in any way other than incidentally [(as in the case of Cleon's son we perceive not that he is Cleon's son, but that he is white, and that to this is incidental the fact that he is the son of Cleon)].

If it is not the case that we perceive them by virtue of the concurrence
30   of the different senses, then there is no simultaneous cognition of both kinds of sensible, except incidentally, as when we see yellow and discern that the same thing is sweet because there has been previous perception in the case of the coming together of both qualities in the
185,1   same object. For this is how we know that the man coming towards us is the son of Cleon, in so far as we see he is very white, not on this occasion because we hear that he is the son of Cleon, but because we have perceived it beforehand.

425a27 But for the common objects we already have a common sense, [not incidentally. So it is not a special sense. If there were we should never perceive them except as has been said]

5   For example, in seeing the yellow we are also looking at its size or its movement, and sight is already working critically in respect of size as well whenever it sees a thing's colour.[94] The word 'already' shows this. And by 'common' he means the perception of the common sensibles, not in so far as it is working by a process of assembly in bringing together more than one kind of sense-objects, but in so far as it is present to each of the many in respect of what they have in

common with each other. For they are not separated to the extent of 10
not having anything in common. That is why they cognize the proper
object of each sense, and what these things are. So the sense is also
called 'common' in another way, that is the sense that when different
sensible qualities come together judges that the same thing is both
yellow and sweet, with, in the case of honey, sight working on the
yellow and taste on the sweet at the same time, but neither on the
combination, but with the one we call common bringing the two 15
sensible things together and judging the plurality simultaneously
when the special sensibles coincide. The sense that apprehends the
common sensibles is called common in a different way, since each
sense has a common function as well as its special one, just as we say
that being two-footed belongs to humans in common because it
belongs to each of them. And we use 'in common' in the former sense
when we apply the term 'a five' to the fingers, because they are all
together in so far as they are grouped with one another. So he 20
concludes that there is no special sense for the common sensibles. 'If
there were we should never perceive' them 'except as has been said',
as we perceive the son of Cleon when we see something white, not in
this case referring it to a previous act of perception. For by not having
a special sense for the common sensibles we would never have
perceived them in themselves. So how in general can the senses
perceive incidentally? 25

[The senses perceive each others' special objects incidentally,]
425a31 not *qua* themselves, but in so far as they are one sense,
[whenever perception takes place at the same time in respect of
the same object, for example bile, perceiving that it is bitter and
yellow].

If there are faculties which are corporeal because they are inseparable
from bodies, nevertheless even in their case the common features of
incorporeal being appear, because their unity and separateness go
together. For it is the case that these senses are clearly distinguished
from each other, as is shown by the special activity of each, directed 30
towards something determinate, and they are also united without
division, as is, again, shown by the sense cognizing at one and the
same time different objects which are apprehensible by different
senses. For sight does not apprehend the sweet, nor taste the yellow,
but there is one sense nevertheless which is one and the same and
also perceives both simultaneously and recognizes the difference
between them and the concurrence in the same object of both sensible 35
qualities, what is called the common sense coming into existence in
respect of the undivided unity in relation to each other of all the
senses. For it is only with each sense that it cognizes what is special

to each. In so far as they are separate each cognizes what is special
186,1   to it, but in respect of their undivided unity, when all of them are not
only many but also one, they perceive each others' objects too, incidentally in so far as they are separate, and in themselves in so far as
they are one. That, I think, is how the words in the text are to be
justified. 'The senses perceive each others' special objects incidentally' as, for example, sight perceives the sweet and taste the white
5   (by saying 'of each other' he has shown that they perceive those of
others too) not, he says, in so far as they are themselves, that is when
each operates on its own as itself, when they also act in separation
(in that case they do not perceive incidentally), but 'in so far as they
are one sense and operate in unison, so that at one and the same time
each deals with its own object, and the plurality of them taken
together deal with one undivided object. They cognize each other's
10   special sensibles incidentally in becoming one, with the one sense[95]
cognizing all things in themselves, while they[96] do so incidentally in
so far as they are separate. They become one 'when perception takes
place at the same time in respect of the same object, for example bile,
perceiving that it is bitter and yellow'. For sight must perceive the
yellow and taste the bitter in the bile at the same time, so that with
the common sense perceiving both in their own right each of those
two senses perceives the objects of the other one incidentally. That
15   the common sense then perceives both in their own right he shows in
the sequel.

425b2 Indeed it is not the function of any other sense to say that
both are one: [therefore it is deceived, and if something is yellow
it thinks it is bile]

'Both' means the yellow and the bitter. So that to know that it is one
thing that undergoes both affections is not the function of any sense
other than the one which perceives each of the two qualities in itself.
20   'Therefore it is deceived, and if something is yellow it thinks it is bile',
clearly at a time when both are not active simultaneously, but only
sight: this happens because of the previous coming together of the
two, with the common sense bringing in what is left over in the
activity of one of them, sometimes correctly and sometimes wrongly.[97]

425b4 One might want to investigate what we have more than
one sense for, and not just one.

One must also understand 'for the common sensibles'.[98] The philoso-
25   pher Plutarch[99] did well to make the point that Aristotle is not now
simply investigating why we have not one sense only but more than
one (for that there are other causes, the differentiated multiplicity of

sense-objects,[100] and the divided suitability of a body in the world of becoming for the different senses)[101] but why we cognize the common sensibles with more than one sense, and not with one only. The answer he gives about the cause also shows what is being investigated. 30

425b5 It is so that we are less likely not to notice the associated[102] common sensibles

That movement and each of the others[103] is present in all sense-objects in so far as they are sense-objects we know from the fact that all the senses cognize them. From that point we perceive at the same time 35 both that each of the common sensibles is a second thing alongside the special sensible pertaining to each, and that it is different in such a way as to be associated with all of them in common.

425b6 For if there had been sight alone, [and this was of white, 187,1 they would be more likely to escape our notice and all seem to be the same because size and colour accompany each other simultaneously]

If there were sight alone it would be able to perceive size: 'and this[104] was of white'. He now says 'white' for 'colour' as he shows by adding 'because colour and size accompany each other simultaneously'. And therefore it[105] would perceive size less since it is not present along 5 with its other objects. It would seem to go with colour only (not then just white because it shows in a black object too, but with colour). For this reason they would seem to be the same not, clearly, in definition but in virtue of the thing in which they occur, because colour and size accompany each other. But why has he now said 'and it would be more likely to escape notice the more', and above[106] 'so that they should be less likely to escape notice'? For in some way it escapes notice now 10 too. It is because now we grasp the precise difference between the common sensibles and the special sensibles by means of reasoning and not by sense-perception. Sense-perception does not discriminate except that the common is a different kind from the special sensibles, in the same relation as colour[107] to white and black. The reason shows that it does not by means of the difference between the terms used.

<CHAPTER 2>

425b12 Since we perceive that we are seeing and hearing, it 15 must be the case that we perceive by sight that it is seeing, or by another sense. [But the same sense will perceive seeing and the colour that is its object,]

The whole purpose of the third book, as has already been said,[108] is
focused on the human soul. For that reason he is investigating
humans right from the start and conducts his argument with reference to us when he writes 'now we have sense-perception',[109] and, 'can
20   be perceived by us with the sense of touch', and 'if any sense is
missing, then the sense-organ is missing in us too and all the things
that we perceive by touching them are perceptible by touch which we
do have'. And it is to show that our sensitive faculty too is perfect that
he appears to have adduced the argument about the senses in perfect
25   living beings not being more than five, and that there is no special
sense of the common sensibles, so that a human being can be shown
not to be deficient in respect of sense-perception. But many other
living beings too share this common sense. On the other hand perceiving that we perceive seems to me to be a special characteristic of
humans only:[110] for it is of a rational soul that reflexivity is a function.
30   It is also shown in this way that our rationality penetrates as far as
sense-perception,[111] if it is the case that human sense-perception is
able to cognize itself. This is so because in a sense what is perceiving
cognizes itself, when it cognizes itself while it perceives. And for this
reason it turns to itself (*epistrephein*) and belongs to itself, and its
being separate from bodies already shows through more,[112] in so far
as every body having different parts of itself in different places would
35   never be able to turn its attention to itself.[113] For this sort of activity
is gathered together and becomes undivided, while every body is
divided.[114] Therefore our power of sense-perception is rational. Indeed
even the body itself is provided with organs[115] in a rational way and,
which is what Iamblichus says, our power of sense-perception is
homonymous with the irrational power of sense-perception, that is
our power which turns to itself is homonymous with that which
inclines as a whole to the body,[116] but it does not turn to itself like
188,1 intellect or reason. For it is not able to cognize its substance or its
power, nor on the whole is it stimulated by itself: it is cognitive only
of its activity, and at the time when it is active.[117] And it is active
when it is being moved in some way by the sense-object.[118] Taking it
as agreed that our perceiving that we see, and likewise that we hear,
comes from our simultaneous perception,[119] and so too in the case of
5   the other senses, he immediately shows that we do this not with some
other sense but with that very sense with which we are perceiving,
for example with sight that we see. For in this kind of simultaneous
perception the same sense will be 'of sight and of the colour that is its
object', that is of a particular colour which is at this time the object of
the sense of sight. From this he shows that it is neither reason which
10   cognizes this in its own right, nor any other sense. For reason is not
in its own right capable of cognizing individuals, nor is any other
sense capable of cognizing colour or light, because this is the special

object of sight; and what cognizes the sense that sees the particular colour as seeing it also necessarily cognizes the colour that is being seen.

This is one proof, taken from the peculiar nature of each sense which is directed towards its special sensible and has its being in that. The other is derived from the argument to the absurd.[120] For if it were another sense which cognizes that sight sees, it follows reasonably that that one too would be cognized when it is in operation, that it is in operation, if each of the five is so cognized,[121] this will apply to a greater extent to that one which not only apprehends sensible objects but also the senses themselves. So this one too will be cognized by another, and that by another, so that an infinite regress will happen and this type of perception alongside another is abolished because nothing is the first, or there will be some sense which is itself able to cognize itself. But if this is so, the same capacity must be attributed to sight and each of the five, if in general any sense that exists is naturally able to apprehend itself. If it does so in so far as it is rational, then the first ones are rational too,[122] and one could say in addition that the argument which posits other senses apart from the five is an artificial creation, both because of what has already been said, by which completeness was shown to be present in these ones, and because every sense is primarily something that perceives a sense-object and not a sense. For if a sense happens to be perceiving a sense and also a sense-object of which it is the sense, it will have a special sense-object, like each of the five. What then? Is this to be granted to the so-called common sense as a special privilege? Perhaps the common sense alone cognizes nothing at all, but operates alongside each of the five. And so, cognizing sight it will also cognize, along with sight, the colour, with which sight is concerned. And so cognizing itself is not an attribute of the common sense alone but of each one, even if it belongs in a purer way to the common sense, since in its case being separate shows through more.

425b17 But there is a problem. If seeing is to perceive by sight, and what is seen is colour or what has it, if someone is to see what sees, what sees in the first place will have colour too.

Now that he has shown that it is able to apprehend itself in the simultaneous perception that it is seeing when it sees, he has a problem about this position: since what is being seen is colour or something that has colour, how will sight itself not either be a colour or have a colour if it is itself being seen? For it is being seen if it is cognizable to itself. The 'first' is added in the phrase 'what sees in the first place will have colour' so that, they say,[123] it will show the coloured body, to be distinguished from the form that comes to be in

5 the sense without its matter. For the form of the colour that is
apprehended in sense-perception is not primary, but derives from the
sense-object. So the form that is in the sense-object is primary. I think,
however, that it is better to understand 'first' instead of 'in itself'
since, even if an object of taste is coloured, it is not tasted *qua*
coloured, but what is visible is what has colour in itself (and let light
10 be taken as colour). This is so since in solving the problem he will say
that sight too is in some way coloured. So it is not reasonable for what
will be admitted into the solution to be assumed in the problem.

425b20 So it is clear that perceiving by sight is not a single
thing. [For even when we do not see, we judge both darkness
and light by sight, but not in the same way. Further what sees
is in a way coloured. For each sense-organ is receptive of the
sense-object without its matter. Therefore there are sensations
and images in the sense-organs even when the sense-objects
have gone away].

He solves the problem raised about sight perceiving itself in two ways.
First, that it is not the case that if sight is primarily cognitive of
colours it does not for that reason not cognize some things in a
15 different way. Indeed in the very act of not seeing sight can make a
judgement as whenever, though it tries to see, a perceptible object
does not present itself, as whenever it is dark it judges that there is
darkness and that we do not see. If then in this case we judge by sight
that it is dark, by the fact that we do not see, *a fortiori* we shall judge
the very fact that we are seeing in the act of seeing. So that, 'perceiving by sight is not a single thing', is a good point. First because sight
20 does not only perceive colours that have light falling on them, but also
perceives light on its own (for we see air when it is lit), then because
sight perceives darkness in another way and, in addition to these
points, because it perceives itself, both not seeing anything and
seeing; it perceives itself acting, clearly, when it sees, and at the same
time it has simultaneous perceptual awareness of its own activity,
and in the case when it does not see it perceives itself being not
25 entirely inactive (otherwise it would not be simultaneously aware
because awareness is in addition to some activity), but is trying to
see, and in trying it is in act not in respect of the seeing but of the
trying, so that the awareness is not of seeing, but of the trying which
is, so to speak, failing: so the sense of sight makes the judgement that
it is not seeing.
He adduces another solution too, making a concession to the fact
that it is colours that sight cognizes. Indeed even if it does not always
30 do so, when it perceives coloured objects it picks up the form of the
perceptible object and sets itself in conformity with it, and just as

every form of cognition is characterised by the form of the object of cognition, the sense of sight too is in some way coloured itself, and somehow sees itself as coloured. He writes, 'is in a way coloured', because the sense of sight is not affected but actualises colours not by way of producing them but by way of making a judgement.[124] Therefore the sense receives its object not as something put into it from outside, but it stays in itself as it is while bringing into action the rational principles, bringing forward the one appropriate to the object of cognition,[125] and it brings it forward when the sense-organ has previously been affected by the sense-object. Therefore Aristotle applies the word receptive not to the sense but to the sense-organ, since the affection that happens in it comes about through the agency of the sense-object. Since it is affected not as are inanimate bodies, or the ones that live only the life of plants, but as a thing that lives a life of cognition,[126] it receives the affection in an active way: in respect of the life of the organ the activity happens in a passible way, while in respect of the faculty[127] which uses the organ the activity is a pure one, and is in accordance with the bringing into action the rational principles.[128] This has already been said at length.[129]

35

190,1

5

Now we must say something about how 'the sense-organ becomes receptive of the sense-object without its matter'.[130] It receives not the white thing but the activity of the white. The activity corresponds to the form of the sense-object. It is this activity with which the soul's power of discrimination is appropriately concerned when it is being stimulated[131] in respect of the sense-object's form: this is without matter and does not exist in the same way as that in the sense-object. That exists together with matter, the other does not in so far as it exists in the discriminating faculty in accordance with the cognitive activity. The sense-organ is receptive of the perceptible form, receiving it from both sides, from the sense-object which first stimulates the sense-organ, and from the faculty of perception which uses it, which comes into action in the first place in accordance with the judging activity of the immaterial form and brings the sense-organ too to fulfilment just as the organ itself, in accordance with the power of soul in it which makes it a living organ, is itself in the second place brought to fulfilment by the faculty which uses it, so that the organ receives from it the form without matter of the sense-object, that is its cognitive activity not yet being completed by the change that happens in the organ under the agency of the sense-object. For in all this the activity that is completed by this change is passible, whereas the one that comes in from the perception that is using it is impassible and immaterial. 'Therefore there are sensations and images in the sense-organs even when the sense-objects have gone away'.[132] For whenever there is clearer perception of something, some perceptual activity remains in the sense-organ even after the departure of the

10

15

20

25   sense-object and when it is no longer stimulating it. This activity
imitates the imagination[133] which throws up (*proballein*) impressions
of sense-objects even when they are not present. Therefore he combined imagination with the senses, since the perception that remains
after the departure of the sense-objects happens because of what it
has in common with imagination and is like imagination. He adduced
30   this point trying to show that the activity which is immaterial and
not completed by a movement of a body[134] goes forward as far as the
sense-organ. For if it stays even when the stimulus is no longer there,
it is clear that it was not the stimulus that brought it to fulfilment.

425b25 The activity of the sense-object and the sense is one and
the same, but their essence is not the same.[135]

35   When he has posited that the sense-organ is capable of receiving the
sense-object without its matter, and shown that it is not always in an
active state (he says, 'For even when we do not see' and, 'even when
the sense-objects have gone away'.[136] It is reasonable to say that the
sense-object and what perceives are sometimes in act and sometimes
in potency.[137] In things which are not always in act,[138] potency and act
191,1 are manifest in turn) he reasonably goes on to consider the question
when each state applies to both, the sense-object *qua* sense-object,
and what perceives likewise, and how each of the two, the sense-object
and the sensation, are the cause of the being in act. And that the
activity and completion of each is in accordance with reason and
simultaneous and not external, but in the perceiving subject. And this
5   section applies to other kinds of living being too, but this has been
raised in book 3 for the sake of showing the existence of sense-perception in accordance with reason in a rational being, and the purpose
of the third book is to talk about the rational soul.[139] Right at the start
of the section he says that the activity of the sense-object and the
sense is one and the same in its substrate, but it is not the same in
10   its essence. The special nature of each is different. The activity of the
sense happens whenever it is perceiving, that of the sense-object does
not happen whenever there is a colour or a sound, but when it is the
object of a sense so that it is in act as an object of sense. For the
sense-object in act falls together in every way with the sense in act,
since they are spoken of correlatively, just as what is double in act is
spoken of in respect of what is half in act, and so in a word this applies
15   to all relative things: and since every kind of cognition in act is such
in accordance with the limits of the object cognized, being completed
and characterised in accordance with it, without losing its own
characteristic of being a cognition, but staying itself and being more
than ever a complete form of cognition it becomes, all of it, the object
of cognition, the special nature of the cognizing subject being other

than the object of cognition, aiming at it and projecting itself towards   20
it and whenever it happens fastening on its object and laying hold of
it altogether, so that both are one, with both being two because of the
difference in their own nature (that of what cognizes is one thing and
that of the object of cognition another) but one because of their union.

425b27 I mean, for example, sound in act [and hearing in act.
For it is possible to have hearing and not to hear],

He is not talking about 'sound in act' as simply sound, but about the   25
whole thing[140] as perceived sound. This coincides with hearing in act.
For it is possible for there to be a sound and for it not to be heard. For
he says 'it is possible to have hearing and not to hear'.

425b29 and what has sound does not always make a sound.

Saying 'has sound' he means what is already making a sound, like   30
bronze being struck, but he says it 'makes a sound' when it is in act
as something being heard. Therefore he argues

425b29 When what can hear is active and what can make a
sound makes a sound, then hearing in act and making a sound
in act take place at the same time,

Granting the potentiality of sounding both to the bronze that is not   35
yet being struck and to that which is being struck but not being heard,
he applies the expression that it makes a sound and is active to its   192,1
being heard. By these means he has shown the sense in potency and
the potentially sensible object to be separate things and not to exist
at the same time, and when they are in act as sense and sense-object
they do exist at the same time.

426a1 of these one might call[141] the one hearing and the other
sounding.[142]

Hearing means the activity of hearing, sounding the activity that can   5
be heard in so far as it can be heard. So that we can follow more clearly
what comes next we should remark that if what is in activity is more
complete than what is potential, it is clear that a sense that is in
activity is more complete than one that is not in activity, and even
more clearly what is actually perceived than what is potentially
perceived. What is in activity is connected with life, and subsists in
respect of the cognitive life, and falls together with sense-perception,   10
being a form of cognitive life: it is certainly not the case that what has
no life is the cause of what has, or that what is imperfect is the cause

of what is perfect. Nor then is what is potentially perceptible the cause
of what is actually perceptible. Rather it is clear that what is perceptible is made perfectly so and brought into a state of activity by the
sensitive soul. That puts forward (*proballein*) a form of the perceptible
object too from itself, but it is stimulated in respect of the putting
15   forward (*probolē*) by the movement that takes place in the sense-
organ through the agency of the sense-object, because the sensitive
faculty is not entirely separate from the body, nor is it directly in
contact with the sense-object, but it puts forward (*proballein*) its own
rational form towards the soul-like affection, or the activity related
to an affection, that takes place in the sense-organ, fitting it to that
in due proportion and likewise in due proportion being stimulated by
20   it to the putting forward (*probolē*) of forms, for what is outside is at a
distance.[143]

426a2 If the movement and the acting and the being acted on
are in what is being acted on [then necessarily the sound and
the hearing in act must be in what is potentially hearing. For
the actuality of what acts and causes movement is in what is
acted on. Therefore it is not necessary for what moves to be
moved. So the activity of what can make a sound is sound or
sounding, and the hearing of what can hear is hearing].

He calls what is potentially perceptible capable of acting on something, and what potentially perceives he calls what is moved, undergoes affections and what is acted on. It is in what perceives that both
25   the sense-object in act and the sense in act are to be found. The acting
on something and the movement are not in what acts or what causes
movement, but in what is acted on and moved, as is set out in the
third book of the *Physics*.[144] That is why he says that what causes
movement is not in the full sense moved, since the movement that
originates from it is not in it. In this way, then, both sound, clearly
in so far as it is perceptible, and hearing in activity will be in the sense
30   when it is in a state of potentiality, clearly, that is, in what is potential
up to that point and comes into act when it receives a stimulus. What
is the acting on and the movement which the sense-object causes to
happen? Not, certainly, the cognition in act, nor the sense in act. For
the acting on is identical with the affection. Sense-perception in act
is not an affection or a movement, but rather forms and activities and
perfections: what is not alive does not produce things that are. But
35   since the sense-organ must be affected by some corporeal affection,
193,1   and be moved by the sense-object, in consequence of which the
sensitive soul is stimulated to the putting forward (*probolē*) of its own
reason-principles,[145] appropriate to the affection that takes place in
it, that is the reason-principles in accordance with which we have both

the sense-perception in activity and the sense-object in act, the potential sense-object is productive of the corporeal affection in the organ and the potential sense is affected in accordance with the organ 5 and its external stimulus, since the judging activity that follows on the movement and the undergoing of the affection and the bringing to completion of the object of cognition, and the form without matter of the object of cognition in the faculty, come from within, and the soul exercises its activity of itself, needing for this activity the undergoing of the affection by the organ through the agency of the sense-object. This is so since the movement that takes place in it 10 comes to it from the outside and is corporeal, while the sense-organ itself, in so far as it is alive in a way pertaining to sense-perception, is not affected in the way that things without soul are, but is affected in a way involving activity[146] and in this way calls up the pure activity of the sensitive soul, which is being continuously fitted to the soul-like movement[147] in a way appropriate to its nature.

426a7 Hearing has two meanings and sound has two meanings

He says this because in both cases there is being in potency and being 15 in act. But hearing, both the one in potency and the one in act, is in the sensitive faculty, but sound, that is the sound in act, is itself in the sensitive faculty as well. That is because it is in this *qua* perceived in act: *qua* potentially perceived it is outside.[148]

[The same account applies to the other senses and sense-objects …]

426a11 But in some cases they have a name, as for example sounding and hearing, [but in others one of them has no name. 20 For the activity of sight is called seeing, but that of colour has no name, and the activity of what tastes is called tasting, but that of the flavour has no name. Since the activity of the sense-object and what perceives it is one, but their essence is different, it is necessarily the case that hearing and sound, and flavour and taste, in this sense, are destroyed or preserved simultaneously, and so too the others. It is not necessarily the case for the things that are spoken of in respect of their potentiality. But the earlier physical philosophers did not put this well, thinking that there was no white or black without vision and no flavour without taste. In one way they were right, in another they were not. For a sense and a sense-object are spoken of in two ways, either in respect of their potentiality or their act: in the case of the latter what has been said is the case, in that

of the former it is not. But they spoke without distinctions about
things which are not spoken of without distinctions].

Hearing in act is an act of hearing,[149] while sounding is a sound
actually perceived. In the case of an object of sight or taste in act there
is no name, but both kinds of cognition in act have a name in the case
of these senses too, namely seeing and tasting. That point is well and
clearly made, that the sense-objects and sense faculties in act come
25   into being, remain in existence and come to an end at the same time
since, even if the sense-object and the sense faculty are different in
their peculiar nature, the activities of both are one in that in which
they happen. Those around Democritus[150] thought that the potentially perceived, like colour or a sound, came into existence in the
sense faculty and did not exist without the sense being in act. This
30   view is not correct: it is true only of sense-objects in act.

426a27 If indeed articulated sound is a kind of concord,[151] [and
hearing and articulated sound are in a way one, and the concord
is a proportion, then it is necessary that hearing is a kind of
proportion. And for this reason each one, the high and the low,
in excess destroys hearing. Likewise in flavours excess destroys
taste, as does the very bright or dark vision and a strong odour
smell, whether it be sweet or bitter, because the sense is some
kind of proportion].

I think Plutarch made a good point saying that the *eta* in the second
syllable is not an article, but part of a particle[152] so that there are not
three but two components of the phrase, 'if indeed ...', and so that the
35   'particular articulated sound' is the subject, with the 'concord' being
the predicate, and what he says starts from the predicate. The
194,1 argument proposed is made up of three premises, thus: hearing in act
is the articulated sound in act; the articulated sound in act is a
concord; every concord is a proportion; therefore hearing in act is a
proportion. The middle of the three premises comes first, starting
from the predicate. That the act of hearing in act is the articulated
5   sound in act, one and the same, because they are in the same subject,
but that these are not there as the same, being different in their
peculiar nature, can be seen from what has just been said. And the
asserting premise is true, namely that in a way the articulated sound
and the act of hearing are the same. And that he rightly predicates
concord of a particular sort of articulated sound, that is, the one in
act, we would see from the fact that the articulated sound in act is
10   lost when the tension of the high or the low is increased. Neither the
excessively low nor the excessively high sound can be heard, since the
excessively high destroys the hearing, as excessive brightness does

vision, and in the case of the other senses the whole constitution of
the living being is destroyed, clearly by objects of touch of greater
intensity and by the flavours that overwhelm them, and also some
smells, like the ones in the Charonian places.   15

So in respect of each of the senses he wants the sense-object in act
to consist in some sort of concord between the extremes, so that there
is no deficiency or excess of the stimulus, but it is somehow in the
middle. This is what concord is, like some sort of mixture between the
extremes, between the high and the low in hearing, brightness and
dimness in vision, and, in the case of each sense, between what causes
injury in each one and its corresponding privation. So it is appropriate 20
that he should predicate concord of the articulated sound in act, as in
the case of every object of perception in act. The most important of
the three premises posits that the concord is a proportion[153] in that it
is being produced according to some ratio from differing components,
leading to the bringing into being of one single thing. It is necessary
that some determining cause come first if it is going to produce any
one thing from more than one component, be it a natural effect or one   25
in the realm of artificial production. For unity in general resides in a
determinant and real unity in perfection. But the corporeal unity, in
so far as it is perfect and determined, like the concord of strings or
the well-fitting assembly of stones, bricks and wood for the construc-
tion of a house, is determined in accordance with a proportion in the
sphere of artificial production, just as the coming into being of flesh
from the four elements is in accordance with a natural one. The   30
perceptible concord in act, being the form of the sense-object without
the matter, and concentrated into something without parts, is no
longer in accordance with a proportion, but is a determinant, a
proportion and a completion. So hearing, and every sense, in act,
being the same as the sense-object in its subject, will be a proportion
(*logos*) and a determinant that discriminates.[154] For the thing determined would not coincide with the determinant, nor *a fortiori* would
what is not determined, but what does is a proportion coinciding with 35
a proportion and a definition with a definition. So every act of
sense-perception is a proportion, one that is active when it is in act,
but the power[155] that puts it into (*problêtikê*) activity is a substantial
reason-principle as the form without the matter, and inasmuch as it
is concentrated into something with no parts and more properly given
the honorific name of a reason-principle but not a form. This since
the perceiving substance is also a kind of soul, and the soul comes
after the forms and is a kind of deployed substance, being before   40
divisible entities, but not entirely undivided and a cause in a secondary sense.[156] And it is a kind of reason-principle, but not simply so.
Rather it is the discursively reasoning soul that is so in a simple
sense, the sensitive soul is some kind of reason-principle through its

195,1 lower position and its activity with the body. It is clear that every
sense is one reason-principle and many, its number being correlated
with the number of forms its object contains. 'And for this reason each
one in excess destroys', acting on the sense-organ and rendering it
inappropriate for the reception of the proportion. For each level of
soul is in its body in a way that is commensurate with a particular
5   sort of mixture of the elements being such as it is, both the one that
informs it so as to be an instrument appropriate for living and the
one that uses it as an instrument. The excess in the sense-object
destroys the commensurate mixture of the organ and thereby pre-
vents the sense from acting through it, 'because the sense is some
kind of proportion', not a relation and a kind of concord of the elements
10   in the mixture (for it has been shown that it is impossible for the soul
to be a concord)[157] but a substance being made such in accordance
with a reason which judges[158] sense-objects, and using an organ made
in such a way as to be appropriate to it.

> **426b3** So they are pleasant when they are brought to the
> proportion pure and unmixed [for example the high, the sweet
> or the salty, for then they are pleasant. But in general what is
> mixed, a concord, is more pleasant than the high or the low, and
> for touch that which can be heated or cooled].

15   When things which were previously unmixed are brought to a state
appropriate to a single proportion and made to correspond with some
mutual concord. Saying that in general perceptible concord depends
on a mixture, and that the high and the low are not unmixed in
hearing, nor in touch the hot and the cold – the extremes, obviously
– but it depends on the mixture of these, and so instead of 'hot' and
'cold' he said 'what can be heated' and 'what can be cooled', indicating
20   the pieces of matter which are at the extremes characterised by the
hot or the cold. And having said this he adds

> **426b7** The sense is the proportion.

That is the undivided[159] judging activity and the substance which
produces this kind of activity that goes together with the organ.

25   **426b7** things that are excessive cause it pain or destroy it.[160]

The sense-objects, clearly, which cause pain when they are a short
way outside the norm and destroy when they are seriously outside it

> **426b8** Each sense-organ perceives the sense-object which is its
> business, the sense being in the sense-organ *qua* sense-organ

He wants to go up to the sense called common,[161] being one sense   30
applicable to all sense-objects and thereby having its superior position. That we shall see more clearly from a comparison of the five,
each of them being considered on its own with respect to one kind of
object and not all objects. That is why he mentioned this at the start,
so that the difference between the common sense and them should be   196,1
easy to recognize, the difference not being that it cognizes some
special object over and above those of the five, but that it exists in
virtue of their all having something in common, and by virtue of its
being the common judging limit of all the others.[162] Therefore there
are not two senses perceiving colour, but one, vision. For common
sense is a sense of colour[163] by virtue of vision, just as it is a sense of   5
flavour by virtue of the sense of taste, but a sense of both at once, or
rather of all of them, depending on the fact that all arrive at one thing
as their term. The words 'being present in the sense-organ *qua*
sense-organ' give each of the five the characteristic of not being
separated, not from bodies simply, but from bodies as sense-organs
which are already alive and live this sort of life so that they serve the
sense like a tool.[164] So each is in the sense-organ in so far as it uses   10
it. This sense is the sense in the strict sense, since the one that gives
the sense-organ its form makes the sense-organ what it is by being
in body: it shares the body's affections and so falls short of pure
activity, while the sense that uses is said to be in it, in so far as it is
using the sense-organ as a tool.[165]

426b10 and it judges differences in the underlying sense-objects,   15
[so for example sight judges white and black, taste sweet and
bitter].

The judging is a pure activity, and an activity of the soul itself and
not of the body. That is why the sense-object comes in the end to be
an immaterial form.[166] And he has stressed even more the transcendent character of the sensitive soul and the fact that it is active on its
own without the body, by adding the point that it discriminates
differences in the underlying sense-objects. So that not only does   20
vision discriminate between white and black, but also their differences in respect of each other, which is an activity of something
indivisible, as he will say,[167] and in an indivisible point of time, and
which is free from affections. For it is impossible to be affected in
opposite ways at the same time, but nothing stands in the way of
opposite activities.[168] So it will be inseparable from the sense-organ,
in so far as it uses the organ which is already alive[169] for the stimulus
to its own activity, but when it has been stimulated it is active on its   25
own, *qua* incorporeal, if the discrimination between opposites at a
single time belongs to something indivisible, and if it applies itself to

them as indivisible (for sense-objects in act are forms without matter)
and is an activity which works indivisibly. For it is in the now.[170] But
a corporeal activity is divided. That is why the body's activity is
movement. And if not only vision but the other senses are like this,
then the common sense will be so even more in so far as it cognizes
30   the opposites of all the senses and does so from above, and it will have
its judging activity *per se*, being as it were the centre[171] of all of them
and the singular limit[172] which holds them together.

426b12 Since we judge white and sweet, and each type of
sense-object in relation to every other and perceive with some-
35   thing that they are different, we must do so by sense-perception,
since they are the objects of sense-perception.

Having mentioned that each of the five senses has a different perceptible object of its own, he shows[173] that there is one common sense for
197,1   all of the objects from the fact that there is something in us which
compares and judges each object, judging not only that it is a particular thing, but also that it differs from the others and from the objects
of the other senses, for example white from sweet. And there is no
faculty of the soul which cognizes the difference that characterizes a
particular white thing and the one that characterizes a particular
5   sweet thing other than the sensitive one. For it is sense-perception
that cognizes individual sense-objects, since opinion apprehends
them[174] together with sense-perception or through sense-perception,
if it goes up from them to the universal, or when it mentions the
individual things as well, it is operating together with imagination.[175]

426b15 it is clear that the flesh is not the ultimate sense-organ,
10   for it would then be necessary for what judges to do so while
touching the object.

His argument that the flesh is not the first[176] faculty of touch, but,
say, the *pneuma* about the heart,[177] or whatever else, is not about the
organ of touch.[178] For even if this organ does not immediately touch
that sense-object as does flesh, being body it would not receive the
different and opposing qualities of the sense-objects in respect of the
15   same part of itself. Flesh could not do this, nor could any other body.
Why has he made this point specifically about flesh? He clearly
mentions flesh in place of all body, calling the ultimate sense-organ
not the organ but the sensitive soul itself, where the sense-object
finally arrives, and which is also what judges. Since then what
cognizes the difference between any two or more things cognizes the
20   two, or all of them, at the same time and not with now one and then
another part of itself, but with one indivisible thing, it is clear that

what judges in the end is not body. For body judges as it touches, that is by making contact with each sense-object in its different parts, as things that touch judge only that part of what they touch in accordance with their hitting on each part. So it is as it would be 'if I were to perceive one thing and you another'.[179]

426b17 And it is not possible for things that are separate[180] to   25
judge [that sweet is different from white, but both must be apparent to some single thing – otherwise it would be as if I were to perceive one thing and you the other: it would be clear that they are different from each other but it is necessary for one thing to say that one is different. For sweet is different from white. So the same thing states this. And so, just as it states this, it thinks it and perceives it].

That is for different things. For both the sensible qualities must be apparent to one and the same thing if it is to be aware of the difference between them, because difference is a kind of relation, and the relation exists and is cognized together with the things between which the relation subsists. For it would not say that the sweet is other than the white if it did not know each of the two. For it is clear that   30
the subject who says this, being one and the same, before he says anything knows the quality in either a sensitive or an intellective[181] way.

426b23 And that it is not possible at a separate time either is shown by what follows

Since what says that the two are different in respect of each other is one and the same, so when it tells us about one of the two it tells us about the remaining one, whether it cognizes the one in some divisible time, recognizing the other in all of that time, if it is to know them as   35
different from each other in the whole of that time, or whether it does so in an instant, which is not time in the simple sense, but all of it is   198,1
an undivided time as being a limit of time.[182] Perhaps he is saying in a riddling way that the pure and perfect activities of the soul,[183] always in transition in respect of terms,[184] are also in time, the kind that is counted as the sum of instants, as of units, but not like physical time in continuity (I have said more about this in my comments on   5
the *Physics*).[185] For judging is not divisible, but is a complete activity: it all happens in an instant and at once.

426b26 The time when is not incidental [I mean, for example, I now say that they are different, not that they are different now

but it speaks thus, both now and that they are different now.
Therefore it does it at one time.]

Clearly 'in itself' is different from 'incidentally', both in the sphere of
10　entities and of causes, as has been said in the *Physics*.[186] And the 'now'
in 'the sea battle which is happening now and is being talked about
now' is predicated as such in both cases. But if it had happened before
and were being talked about now, the now is being predicated in itself
in so far as it is being talked about, but incidentally of the sea-battle
itself. It is not being used of its happening now, but of it as being
15　talked about now. But sense-perception is not cognitive of things in
the past or the future, but it is cognitive of what is present at any
given time, so when it announces the difference between sense-
objects, that is when it judges, it also judges that the difference exists
now. So 'now' is not said incidentally of the mutual difference between
the sense-objects, since it is being judged now, but of that difference
as such: the incidental is in the sphere of memory.

20　　　**426b28** And so <it judges> as something that is inseparable and
　　　in an inseparable time.

If the sensitive faculty were to judge the difference between any two
sense-objects, the same thing will grasp both, not in different parts
of itself, but it will grasp both with one indivisible part of itself. And
this inseparable thing will also grasp them at the same time at which
the difference exists. It exists in the now, since sense-perception is of
things that exist now. But why not simultaneously, but in a divisible
25　time? Indeed in this case too that the two objects are not the same is
cognized at the time when that difference exists. Save only that the
discrimination is an indivisible activity and not a divided one like
movement, so that it would be inseparable in the sense of being
undivided,[187] and so 'in an inseparable time' as in the now.

　　　426b29 But it is impossible for the same thing to be moved with
　　　opposite movements at the same time, in so far as it is indivis-
30　　　ible, and in an indivisible time. [For if it is sweet it moves
　　　sense-perception or thought in one way, but the bitter moves it
　　　in the opposite way, and white in another way].

Having shown that it is one thing that judges two or more, not in
respect of different parts, but as a thing that is undivided, and at one
and the same time, whenever it distinguishes their mutual difference,
he thus shows, consequentially on what has been shown already, that
35　perceptual discrimination is neither an affection nor a movement, but
an activity and a perfection, stimulated from within. For it is impos-

sible to undergo contrary affections or to change to opposites at the same time because contrariety, which conflicts, hinders and destroys, is to be found in affections and in changes. But to be active in opposite ways at the same time from a self-produced stimulus in respect of the different reason-principles in itself is not impossible, since this kind of opposition does not produce conflict when it happens to different things which admit of the opposing activities, e.g. when fire at the same time hardens mud and softens wax,[188] and the same sense at the same time discriminates between the white of the paper and the black of the writing. So perceptual discrimination is not one and the same movement,[189] or an affection or intake from outside. For there could be no perception of opposites at the same time, since to be changed in contrary directions, or to be disposed in opposite ways, is impossible. The tongue is moved in opposite ways by the sweet and the bitter. Therefore it would not be moved by opposites in respect of the same part at the same time. It[190] is affected by them in respect of different parts, and the sense of taste, because of its undivided nature is present as a whole in the different parts of the tongue, and is able to act in its own right in making judgements about the two.

427a2 Is what judges then numerically indivisible and insepa-rable but at the same time separate in its essence? [In a way what is divisible perceives divided things, but in a way it does so *qua* indivisible. For it is divisible in its essence but indivisible in place[191] and number].

Having established that the same thing while remaining indivisible could never be moved with contrary movements or undergo contrary affections, he accepts that point but nevertheless wonders whether perhaps the subject of these contraries is not indivisible in every way. Let it be undivided numerically and at one time, in so far as it receives contraries in the same time in respect of all of itself, but 'in its essence', that is in definition, it is divided and separate, since the receiving powers in it are different. So it will undergo contrary affections *qua* divisible. And if the judgement or the movement were to be an affection, what judges will not be prevented from judging contraries at the same time, since it would have been divisible in definition in respect of different reason-principles, being 'indivisible in place and number', in so far as it is one and the same subject undergoing both, or more, affections in all of itself, the word 'number' showing its unity, and the 'place' that it is not affected in respect of different parts but is divisible in its being, that is in its definition, since the substance of each is defined in terms of its form and its reason-principles.

30 **427a5** It is impossible:[192] the same thing can be potentially divisible and indivisible in respect of contraries, but in its being it cannot, but it is divisible in being made actual [and it is not possible to be white and black at the same time].

He says it is impossible for what is numerically one and the same, even if it is in its nature divisible, actually to undergo contrary affections at the same time. It is only potentially that the same thing

35 can move towards opposites at the same time, but it cannot receive them simultaneously in act, which is what he meant by 'in its being'. Therefore explaining how he now uses 'in its being in act' of the sense, he continues 'it cannot',[193] saying 'in being made actual'[194] so as to

200,1 indicate the affection and the movement. He shows this more clearly by means of the example, for white and black are passible qualities. And even more plainly he uses the very word for undergoing an affection in the conclusion.

427a8 And so it cannot be affected by forms of these, if sense-
5 perception and thinking are this kind of thing

Sensation and intellection do not receive the sense-objects themselves but their forms.[195] And sensation or intellection will not be affected by the forms of white and black at the same time, 'if they are this kind of thing', he says, like being affected and receiving something from outside, even in exercising their activity, as he put it. To undergo

10 contrary affections actually, so as either to change towards both or to be simultaneously disposed in accordance with them is impossible.

427a9 But like what some call a point, it is divisible in so far as it is both one and two. [In so far as it is indivisible what judges is one and judges at the same time, but in so far as it is divisible it uses the same point twice, at the same time].

By means of the example of the point both the impassibility and the
15 active nature of perceptual judgement are adequately demonstrated, as well as its indivisibility and its taking place in an indivisible instant. For the activities of indivisible entities are also indivisible whereas every affection and movement involves division because they consist in an alteration.[196] For that reason affections and other changes belong to the compound. Only circular movement, even if it is not a movement of something not in matter,[197] is a movement of something that has been informed. Therefore of something divisible,
20 since it is of a body. Everything that is in itself undivided has an undivided activity so that its activity corresponds to its being.[198] A point is undivided even though it has a position, being the limit of a

line and included in the line that is limited, say a cubit's length or whatever, and adds something peculiar in its own right, namely being the limit and the beginning, sometimes being the limit or end of one line and the beginning of another, and often the beginning and end of two or more lines, as the centre of the circle is the beginning or end 25 of all the lines drawn from it to the circumference.

The sensitive soul is compared to a point in so far as it is an immaterial and indivisible substance: it is one that uses a sense-organ which is divided and exercises its activity together with it while the organ is undergoing an affection and being moved by sense-objects,[199] when different affections impinge on different parts of the body which is subject to them, and it is on its own in the judging 30 activity, which is not altogether separate from bodies, since in the end it comes to the soul through the affection of the organ, the judging activity being neither an affection nor a movement nor a reception of material from outside, but an undivided activity proceeding from inside, not making sense-objects but cognizing them in accordance with the reason-principles of them which it has previously acquired, 35 sometimes singly and sometimes in groups, when it also cognizes the difference between them. For it is clear that the reason-principles of sense-objects are in it, if in exercising its activity from itself it is disposed according to the forms, without matter, of sense-objects. 201,1 Since there is no means by which it can be affected and moved in contrary ways and receive opposites actually and at the same time, but it is possible for it to exercise an activity, anyone who makes the underlying thing in some way one and two, indivisible and divisible, contributes nothing to its being affected and actualised in opposite ways at the same time, but does to its activity. For the point, when it 5 is the beginning of one line and the end of another, is one and indivisible in so far as it is the same being actualised in both ways, and again it is two and divisible in accordance with the different definitions of the beginning and the end. In this way the sensitive soul too, which is cognizing two sensible qualities at the same time, is one and indivisible since 'what judges is one and judges at the same time, but in so far as it is divisible it uses the same point twice, at the 10 same time', in so far as it exercises its activity in accordance with different reason-principles in an instant and simultaneously: therefore it is not impossible for it to exercise opposite activities at the same time.

427a13 So in so far as it uses the limit as two things it judges two things and they are separate as being judged separately.[200]

It is what judges that is using, and the limit is the sensitive soul itself. 15 Indeed what judges is the soul, but when it is already exercising its

activity, being a limit and a determinant and an indivisible nature in its substance. And it uses the same sense as two when it is concerned with two forms of sense-objects, whenever it is judging at the same time between two things which are separated from each other by definition and by their peculiar quality, so that in this way discrimi-
20 nations between different things are made as if they were in separate things.

427a14 In so far as it is one it uses it as one thing, and at the same time[201]

In so far as what judges is one in its being and the sensitive soul which judges is one substance, the sensitive soul itself uses the limit as one and exercises its activity simultaneously in an indivisible instant.[202]
25 What has been said fits each of the five senses: each of them is able to apprehend a plurality of opposites at the same time. It fits the common sense to an even greater degree since it is able to cognize many more of the things which are the objects of all the senses and is hierarchically superior and further above the sense-organs. Here the 'common' does not consist in the bringing together of a plurality of objects but rather in the pre-existing combination. The sensitive
30 soul is a principle both as a form and even more so as what uses.

<CHAPTER 3>

427a17 Since the soul is generally defined by two charac-teristics, spatial motion and thinking, judging[203] and perceiving

Moving on to another critical faculty of the soul after sense-percep-
35 tion, he does so in good order to imagination which is next to sense-perception. First he lays it down that this faculty of the soul too, which
202,1 appears in the soul's power to move things in space as well, is cognitive and not appetitive.[204] Then that it is not the same as sense-perception, since that for its own activity always requires sense-objects to be present and to be stimulating the sense-organs, whereas the imagination is sometimes stimulated by itself even when
5 they are not present and brings forward (*proballein*) the objects of cognition, having this capacity in common, in a way, with the rational faculties. Which gives it an intellective characteristic, the cognitive faculty's arousal from itself to the exercise of its activity. That is why he calls imagination intellect, since sense-perception no longer has anything in common with intellect in this respect, but only in respect of what judges.[205] So he opposes the critical capacity to the power of
10 spatial motion, as he does to the power of appetition, and subsumes sense-perception and intellection in this, taking intellection to repre-

sent any cognition which is self-stimulated. In the actual words he gives the clause answering to the conjunction 'since' after a long interval, when he writes 'that sense-perception and intelligence are not the same is clear', adding the conjunction 'therefore'[206] because of the great distance at which the main clause stands.

427a19 Thinking and understanding seem to be like perceiving   15
something.[207] [(for in both the soul judges and cognizes something that exists), and the ancients say that thinking and
perceiving are the same thing – as Empedocles said, 'men's
wisdom grows according to what is present to them',[208] and
elsewhere 'whence they are always able to think different
thoughts'.[209] And Homer's words 'such is the mind of men'[210]
mean the same as these, for all these people suppose that
thinking is something corporeal like sense-perception ...]

As has been said intelligising is taken by him in place of every
cognitive faculty which puts forward (*proballein*) its own activity from
itself, but thinking[211] is mentioned in the place of rational cognition:
it too shows the distinctive character of the cognitive activities itself,
even if some drag not only intelligising but thinking too down to a   20
state of identity with sense-perception, paying attention exclusively
to the critical and cognitive element – which Aristotle himself brings
in – since this is a common feature of the cognitive faculties. One must
not decline to believe that some physical philosophers or sophists
thought this. Plato's *Theaetetus* identifies knowledge with sense-perception.[212] But Empedocles and Homer should not be put down as   25
adherents of this view, even if Aristotle, focusing on what was crudely
put, refutes texts that are capable of another interpretation.[213] One
could take it that 'what is present' is an object of the senses. But that
is neither how it was intended by Empedocles,[214] nor is the truth like
this: for 'thought' always proceeds towards its completion not by
means of sense-objects but by means of intelligible ones which are   30
present to it, and thinking in dreams produces 'different thoughts'
not because of the residues from sense-objects, as someone might
maintain, (that is not what thinking is), but this happens when
reason is freed in some respects from its relation with the body and
there is some recognition of goodness or truth in dreams superior to
that which occurs in a state of wakefulness. The same is the case with   35
Homer: he says that the mind is changed by sense-objects not without
qualification, but the mind, as he says himself, of men who live
earthly and feeble lives.[215]

203,1   **427a27** and that sensation and thought are both of like by like,
          as we defined it in our discussions at the start.[216]

Where we too explained how the ancient philosophers' account which
claims that like is known by like is true, and how Aristotle correctly
5   grasps what he has heard.[217]

427a29 They should also have said something at the same time
about error. [For it is particularly the condition of animals, and
the soul spends more time in this state. Therefore it is necessary
either, as some say, that all appearances are true, or that
touching the unlike is error, for that is the opposite of knowing
like by like].

It does not seem to me that he brings in the point about error to refute
those who say that like is known by like, but that he objects to their
not setting anything down about error, while he brings in what
10   follows on the hypothesis. In fact they did not say anything about
error, either because it does not exist for those who think that what
appears is true[218] or because, holding that there can be false opinion,
they will say that it consists in contact 'with the unlike', assigning
opposite things to opposites.[219]

427b5 Error and the knowledge of opposites seem to be the same

15   The commentators[220] say that the introduction of this point is irrele-
vant to the hypothesis. For they say that not only is like known by
like in scientific knowledge, but that the opposite is also the case.
Similarly in error both are unknown, since it is one thing that knows
both or fails to do so. But it is one in what underlies, but in what it
actually is it is other, as Aristotle himself is in the habit of saying,
making contact with each of the two contraries in accordance with
20   different reason-principles. In an investigation that brings knowledge
it makes contact with like by like in both cases,[221] but in error it does
so differently with each of the two. One must make one comment, that
he does not here mean the error opposed to correct sense-perception,
but that opposed to knowledge. For, as he will go on to say,[222]
sense-perception of the special sensibles is always true but, he says,
the soul spends more time in making errors. A second comment is
25   this: that the opposition[223] of which Aristotle speaks belongs not in
the soul but in the living being,[224] since the soul is in a state of
ignorance for the majority of the time in its life with the body, since
being right is most closely associated with the rational faculty in
which thought resides. Therefore it belongs to the rational faculty.
How can he say that the contrary is more closely associated with it?

So, as he points out himself, 'the soul spends more time in this state'. That is because the living being, a thing that has come into being and is destructible, spends much time unable to receive the rational activities of the soul, and much of it being impeded by the affections that impinge on it. In addition it drags the soul round to the needs of everyday life and forces it away from the leisure needed for the pursuit of truth. And – the most important point of all – the strong inclination[225] of the soul towards the body, and its embracing the world of becoming, moves it away from the turning to itself in which thinking and truth in accordance with reason consist.[226]

427b6 That perceiving and thinking are not the same is clear. [All animals share the former, but only a few the latter].

Thinking, whether it be used in a more general sense to apply to all rational thinking,[227] or specifically to that which deals with action, is nevertheless always used of thinking which is correct and true and conducted with reference to causes. Therefore few living beings participate in it, for not even all human beings do, but only a few of these. On the other hand not only men, but also all animals have sense-perception. In this way he distinguishes and separates from sense-perception correct thinking in accordance with reason, and indeed any kind of thinking in accordance with reason, adding

427b8 Nor is thinking, in which there is correct and incorrect, [correct being practical understanding, scientific knowledge and true opinion, incorrect the opposites of these – this is not the same as sense-perception either. For perception of the special sensibles is always true, and all animals have it].

He now calls the simple activity in accordance with reason thinking, which includes both thinking correctly and thinking incorrectly, as Aristotle himself explains clearly. From this kind of thinking he separates sense-perception not because it has no share in truth (for perception of the special sensibles is always or for the most part true), but firstly because it is circumscribed by its activity through the body, whereas thinking has great depth and is separate both in the forms of cognition which always tell the truth, scientific knowledge and intelligence, and also in those which sometimes do, like true opinion, and secondly because it has the characteristic of always being true in the field of the special sensibles through a restriction, since it apprehends a limited number of objects, and does not sometimes fail to tell the truth like opinion, because it makes contact after some fashion with something by sometimes contemplating many other things and then making inappropriate pronouncements about it. But also be-

30

204,1

5

10

15

20

cause it is the lowest cognitive faculty, as it shows by being present even in the least prestigious living beings,[228] whereas thinking is present only in rational ones.

427b13 It is possible to think discursively and be wrong, [and no living being can do this without having reason].

25   He calls the activity of reason which moves from one thing to another discursive thinking. It always tells the truth when it grasps causes as it moves, but without the causes it sometimes gives false information. So discursive thinking is the activity of the reason which moves from one thing to another. Since the moving is related to terms and is not, like physical transition, related to a continuum, the assent of the soul to each term, and the supposition that takes place in respect of all of them as if they were one term, is the assent to that one as

30   being true. So discursive reasoning and the supposition are not the same thing, but appear together. For the activity of the reason always consists in moving from one thing to another and in assent to the truth as it appears. Sense-perception is neither discursive reason nor supposition. Not the one because it is not rational, since it is present in other animals too, and not the other because it does not move from one thing to another (for it does not collect things from other things)[229]

35   or give the truth in such a way that it is aware of itself telling the truth. For it has true cognition of the special sensibles,[230] so for

205,1 example sight has cognition that a thing is white, but it is not capable of perceiving that it is cognizing correctly. The cognition of a thing and the apprehension that the cognition is true are not the same. For instance the supposition comes after the apprehension of the thing: it makes a judgement whether the apprehension is true, assenting to and embracing the object of cognition at that time. Sense-perception,

5   however, only cognizes what impinges on it, and if it impinges falsely, as in the case of images, it does not have the power to discriminate. And even if it is always true in the case of the special sensibles, it will not know that it is true. But the discursive reason, whether it makes contact with the objects of cognition correctly or falsely, is not satisfied with the contact and does not give its assent, unless it also makes an additional judgement, correctly or otherwise, that the understanding

10   is true, and sometimes it makes mistakes in this additional judgement. And if the discursive reason sometimes produces falsehood, it is not thereby inferior to sense-perception which is always true in respect of the special sensibles. Its being wrong sometimes is due to it seeing many things simultaneously, and being right or wrong is not a function only of the first contact with and apprehension of a thing, but of the additional judgement of that apprehension.

427b14 For imagination is different from sense-perception and   15
reason, [and this does not occur without sense-perception, nor
does supposition without imagination].

The conjunction 'for', being indicative of cause, is now used because
it has been said that only rational beings have discursive reason, as
if he had added: imagination is not the same as reason since imagination exists in irrational beings too, as it is not the same as sense-
perception. He adds this too, since his subject for discussion is
imagination. Having said that it is different both from sense-percep-   20
tion and reason, for the reasons he gives, he explains at the same time
why it seems to some to be no different from sense-perception, and to
others no different from discursive reason or supposition (he sometimes calls the rational activity discursive reason, and sometimes
supposition, because these exist together) and at the same time, for
these very reasons, he thinks it right to distinguish imagination from
each of the two, sense-perception and reason. Since the images do not   25
arise without sense-perception, but always when it has happened
previously, because the modes of imagination consist in some separation, partition, division and shapes, and these things are objects of
sense-perception, and the objects of sense-perception are cognizable
by us using sense-perception, that is those of us who cannot go up to
intellect and are not capable of cognizing the furthest caused objects
by means of their cause, it is reasonable that some are misled because   30
they do not distinguish what supervenes from that without which it
cannot do so: while others do distinguish this kind of image from
sense-perception and know what it is.

Likewise they distinguish it from supposition. In the case of the
souls which incline outwards as a whole and depart altogether from
the activity which they exercise by themselves, and are focused on
sense-objects alone, with their situation in the world of becoming
contributing to their turning away from the life of reason, the discur-   35
sive reason needs sense-perception in the first place, then experience
and memory, so that it can for a time have knowledge of the universal
in the things that are defined in terms of the same species and then
be able to go up to the form that determines them and, in general, to
the causes, knowledge of which is a matter of reason and intellect. So
here too for those who do not distinguish what remembers from what
brings together the universals, confusion of the two follows, and those   206,1
who object to this position have sufficient evidence of their otherness,
namely that one is an end, and the other a necessary cause.

427b16 That thinking[231] and belief are not the same is clear.
[For this affection[232] is in our control, whenever we want].

5   He calls rational knowledge belief, as has been said, and now calls
     imagination thinking. He also calls imagination an 'affection', and
     wants to put it in the faculty that remembers. How then, if belief does
     not happen without imagination, does he distinguish it from belief?
     Because 'this affection is within our control whenever we want'. Not
     because all imagining is within our control (for imaginings can be
     present in us without our wanting them), but because some are within
10   our control so that we can make them ready for use, but not so that
     we can dismiss them in the same way.[233] So he calls the activity of
     imagination an affection because it is subject to division and to
     impressions[234] and is inseparable from bodies,[235] but is within our
     control because we do not entirely fashion the impressions in accord-
     ance with things, nor do we bring forward (*proballein*) images with
15   our minds altogether on the truth. Just as sense-perception does not
     apprehend a thing as true, but only as a sense-object, similarly the
     imagination does not do so, but apprehends only the impressions,
     taking only so much in addition to sense-perception, so that it does
     not require the constant presence of the sense-objects which the
     impressions resemble, but brings up (*proballein*) the impressions
     from itself and does not entirely follow what was seen in the first place
20   but adds and subtracts, transforms and embellishes in every way.

     427b18 It is possible to put something[236] in front of our eyes, [as
     do those who organise things in mnemonic systems and produce
     images of them].

     That is to bring up (*prokheirizein*) the impressions and exercise
     activity in accordance with them like, he says, 'those who organise
     things in mnemonic systems', that is, recollect them, so that 'memory'
     can be used rather than 'recollection'. This is Alexander's explana-
25   tion.[237] It is better to say[238] it is as, when we want to remember, we
     often exercise an activity in relation to an impression. 'Producing
     images' shows that one does not produce a projection of the images
     which is altogether like the things themselves.

     427b20 But having an opinion is not within our control, for it is
     necessary that it be either false or true.

30   Belief is a wider term than opinion, but opinion is taken to stand for
     any kind of belief. Being true or false is common to every kind, since
     every kind of belief consists in assent. Assent consists not only in
     apprehension of what comes along, but in discrimination between
     what is true and false. Truth and falsity consist in agreement or
     disagreement with things, and things are not in our control.

427b21 Besides, when we opine that something is terrible or   207,1
frightening, we immediately have the feeling that goes with that
opinion, and likewise if something produces confidence.

He finds confirmation for the soul's assent in belief from the affections
that follow it. It is afraid or confident in accordance with what it
thinks, since the thought consists in belief.   5

427b23 But in respect of imagination we are in the same
condition as if we were looking at terrible or confidence-inspir-
ing things in a picture.

Imagination produces likenesses, and just as the things in a picture
are representations of other things, so it is with the things in the
imagination. So the soul is not put together with things as if they   10
were real, so that it might be confident or afraid. In fact it does feel
pleasure or pain, not as being in the midst of things themselves, but
as being in the midst of a memory of those things.

427b24 There are different types of belief itself, knowledge,
opinion, understanding and their opposites.

Since he undertook to differentiate imagination from belief, and took
opinion, which is in a central position, to stand for all kinds of belief   15
(there are common features of every kind of belief and not just of
opinion: conviction, and the fact that the truth about things is not in
our control but pertains to these things, and that emotions, confidence
and fear, are stimulated in the case of the objects of belief being
supposed to be true), he divides the kinds of belief so that as we
progress we can see that what has been said on the basis of the
different kinds applies to all belief. Wisdom is practical cognition,   20
with the cause, scientific knowledge is theoretical cognition, whereas
true opinion has something in common with both, but lacks the cause
on either side. We must now understand true opinion,[239] since it is
put together with wisdom and scientific knowledge, and where in the
case of opposites we have, as it were, lack of scientific knowledge and
unwisdom, so too we have false opinion.

427b26 The discussion about their differences must be dealt   25
with elsewhere

He distinguishes more clearly between the differences in belief which
he has mentioned here in the *Ethics*.[240]

427b27 About thinking: since it differs from sense-perception,
[and imagination and belief seem to belong to thinking, we must
speak about the second when we have defined what imagination
is].

We must understand both thinking and sense-perception as being in
the soul itself.[241] For the thinking that is superior to the kind that the
30   soul does is not imagination or belief.[242] Rather one must understand
what is being said as having been said 'about the thinking' of the soul.

208,1   **428a1** If then it is imagination in virtue of which we say we have
an image [and if we are not to speak about it in a metaphorical
sense].

Just as a sense-object is the object of cognition corresponding to
sense-perception and an object of knowledge to knowledge, so too the
image corresponds to imagination. And just as he defined each of the
5   senses on the basis of its own sense-objects, so now he gives an outline
of the imagination in virtue of which we have images, distinguishing
it from the one that is so called after this one metaphorically, when
we use imagination in connection with what appears[243] as well as with
sense-perception and opinion.

428a3 It is[244] some one faculty or disposition of those, in virtue
10   of which we judge and are either right or wrong. [Such are
sense-perception, opinion, knowing scientifically and intellect].

The faculties of the soul are various, for example nutritive, locomo-
tive, cognitive, appetitive: imagination is a kind of cognitive faculty,
making judgements, that is it apprehends and cognizes an image. It
is right or wrong, being right when it portrays an image similar to
the object of which the image is an image, and wrong when it portrays
15   an image dissimilar to the object, whether this happens to it involun-
tarily, through forgetfulness for instance, or when it adds or subtracts
something, or in any way elaborates the image in virtue of its own
impulse. This is how he shows that imagination is a judging faculty.
For being right is a feature of every cognitive faculty, as also is being
wrong of some. He says 'power or disposition',[245] calling the essential
20   character in virtue of which we say that every human being is rational
'power', and the projected condition disposition. And imagination is
both an essential power and a projected disposition[246] according to
which we make impressions of images either determinately or inde-
terminately, and either truly or falsely and in an ordered or a
disordered way. After he enumerates the cognitive powers, sense-perception, opinion, knowing scientifically and intellect, he proposes to

show imagination differing from these. So sense-perception is cogni- 25
tion through an organ which first receives the activity stimulated by
the sense-object, being cognition of the sense-objects themselves but
fitting contiguously the forms of the sense-objects which arrive in the
sense-organs; opinion is belief about things which can be otherwise
and conviction about things that are necessary without the cause,
scientific knowledge is the rational deployment, with the cause, of 30
things which are unchanging, and intellect the compact and undivided contemplation of determinants.[247]

428a5 That imagination is not sense-perception is clear from
this. [For sense-perception is either the faculty or the activity,
for example vision and seeing.]

First he distinguishes imagination from sense-perception with the
following argument. Sense-perception means both the perceptual
activity, for example, seeing and the faculty, when it is not operative, 35
for example vision.

428a7 But something may appear to us[248] when neither of these 209,1
is present, [for example things in dreams].

Not to the living being when neither actual[249] nor potential sense-perception is present: this is impossible.[250] But to imaginations when
neither is present. For something appears, that is an image comes to
be, like the dream images in sleep, neither perception as an activity
being the same as they are (for sense-perception does not operate in 5
sleep), nor the faculty, which is not then active, since the images are
actually present.[251] So that imagination is working, and sense-perception is not. Therefore they are not the same.

428a8 Further, sense-perception is always present, imagination
is not.

Perceptual activity can be present in animals as soon as they are born, 10
imaginative activity cannot. Sense-perception must have taken place
before,[252] and perhaps several times, so for this reason imagination
is posterior to it and is not always present, that is if it is stimulated
after sense-perception and by sense-perception. So this is a second
argument separating them. And this is a third:

428a9 If they were the same in actuality, it would be possible 15
for all wild animals to have imagination. [But it seems not, as
in the case of an ant, a bee, or a worm.[253] Then perceptions are

always true, whereas the majority of imaginings are false. And
then when we are exercising an activity accurately with respect
to a sense-object, we do not say that this appears to us as a man,
but rather when we do not perceive it clearly then[254] it is either
true or false. And, as we said before, visions appear to those who
have their eyes shut].

This third argument starts from perceptions and imaginings in act,
and distinguishes their powers and substances, using three arguments in succession starting from the activities. One is that an
20   impression of each sense-object does not occur in all animals, as in a
dog, as is generally agreed to be the case, in a horse recognizing his
groom, and in many others, but as in an ant or a bee or, more clearly,
a worm there is not an impression of each thing in a well-defined
way,[255] but a more general one of food, and even if it is of the food in
this grove, as in the case of bees, it is still not of that food in the
discrete individual object, this flower. It is in this way that one must
25   understand that imagination is not present in all, and not that it is
not present at all.[256] For it is in all, even if it is not present as a
determinate imagination. But the perception of the individual object
is always in act. So that the activity of the imagination would not be
the same as that of sense-perception. A second argument is drawn
from truth and falsehood, if perceptual activities are generally true,
unless distance or something external is an impediment,[257] whereas
30   most imaginative ones are false. But some happen to be true because
of its narrow scope, whereas others are false because they are stimulated by some indeterminate impulse. A third is from the clarity or
obscurity of the manner of cognizing sense-objects. Things that can
be imagined are more precise than sense-objects, for example a
straight line, a surface, shapes, but the activity of sense-perception
35   with regard to these sense-objects is clear, that of imagination is at a
remove and obscure. Therefore we use 'appearing' and 'being imag-
210,1   ined' by transfer of sense-perception which is not clear, when it
happens that the sensation is not entirely true and sometimes even
false. He says that visions appear to those who have their eyes shut
as in dreams, for he calls the images of things that are seen visions.

5   **428a16** Nor again will it be one of those that always provide true
information, [like scientific knowing or intellect. For imagination may be false too].

Imagination is neither scientific knowledge nor practical wisdom nor,
a fortiori, intellect. For always providing true information belongs to
intellect and the rational kinds of cognition, which are concerned with
causes. Every cause is a substance, and the cause in the fullest sense

is also the first substance. Imagination is a long way from a cause and from all substance.

428a18 So it remains to see if it is opinion. [For opinion may be   10
true or false. But opinion is followed by conviction (for it is not
possible for someone holding an opinion not to be convinced by
what he opines), and no wild animals have conviction, but many
have imagination].

The difference between imagination and opinion which is stated now
seems to me to be the same as the one that was mentioned before.258
There having an opinion was said not to be in our control because it
is necessarily false or true, and here it is said that conviction always
accompanies opinion. Conviction is assent to what has been cognized,
as being true: therefore it is not present in irrational creatures. For   15
judgement of a thing as being true follows the apprehension of it and
is rational. Intellect too knows that it is true, but in an undivided and
unitary way. But rational cognition which judges whether the apprehension is true, gives assent in this way: it is entirely dependent on
reasoning, whether it be necessary or convincing, or on the speaker
as being a trustworthy person, and it makes this judgement in
accordance with some reasoning process.259 It is like the double
cognition that takes place in the case of sense-objects, one that the   20
object seen is a man, the other that the cognition is true, the former
being perceptual and the latter pertaining to reason. The fact that it
is double appears clearly in the case of things being seen at a distance.
For I do not conclude that it is a man unless I reason that it is moving,
two-footed and upright. This escapes us in the case of things that are
close since the cognition of the fact that we are cognizing correctly
follows immediately on the cognition of what is seen. For the appre-   25
hension of anything is not the same as the understanding that it is
true, which is followed by assent, being a receiving of what is true.
For the soul loves truth and never accepts being disposed in accordance with what is false, but rather with the truth that has appeared,
entirely and immediately. So the double nature of cognition has been
distinguished in the case of all kinds of belief, but in the case of   30
scientific cognition of realities which is accurate the cognition that it
is true follows on immediately, as it does in the case of vision at close
quarters, but in the case of the cognition characterised as opinion the
difference is manifest in respect of its seeming and superficiality and
coming, as it were, from a distance, because it does not go into a thing
deeply and is not concerned with first causes. And he was right to say
that conviction follows opinion, since it is a constituent element of   35
opinion, but extends more widely, as 'animal' does in relation to 'man'.
Indeed conviction belongs to scientific knowledge, intellect and wis-

dom as well as to opinion itself. The nature of opinion resides in both,
211,1   in the more superficial understanding of things and in the assent to
it as being true. But conviction, which accompanies every rational
and intellective cognition, is not present in any wild beast since
irrational cognition cannot grasp something as being true, but is only
cognition of the thing which it is able to cognize, being true but not
5   judging the very fact that it is true. For the cognition which grasps
that it is cognizing the thing itself in general, or that is doing so truly
or falsely, turns towards itself, for it will itself cognize itself.[260] But
all irrational life is focused only on what is external, since it strives
only for things outside and cognizes those only. And the appetition
for these does not take place as for things that are good, but only as
for things that are pleasant, neither is the cognition of them as being
10   true, but only as being sense-objects. For in the simultaneous perception of something as being good or true it must necessarily bring with
it benefiting itself or proving itself true. What cognizes does not
consist in the judgement of the external object of cognition, nor what
takes pleasure in the accompanying perception of the pleasant. On
the contrary strong pleasure in things that are external, just like the
15   intense sensation of them, makes our soul depart from itself.

428a22 Further conviction follows every opinion, having been
persuaded follows conviction, and reason follows persuasion.[261]
Some wild animals have imagination, but not reason.[262]

The present argument also starts from the same idea. Yet it is not
20   exactly the same as the one that has been given. For that one began
from the end whereas this one begins from the movement towards
the end, because the end is conviction and the way to it is the process
of being persuaded. The strength of the other argument derives from
the definition of conviction, being assent to something as true, that
of this one from the notion of persuasion, which must precede convic-
25   tion, which supervenes on persuasion as its end. For persuasion is
assent produced by reason, just as already existing conviction is
assent. Indeed in persuasion there is a kind of investigation of the
apprehension of the things concerned and an acceptance of them as
true. He says some wild animals have imagination, calling imagination the kind that is limited and of some particular object.[263]

30   **428a24** So it is clear that imagination would be neither opinion
accompanied by sense-perception, nor produced by sense-perception, nor[264] a combination of opinion and sense-perception.

Plato in the *Sophist* and *Philebus* posits that imagination consists in
a mixture of opinion and sense-perception,[265] and with these words

Aristotle seems to be making an objection to this position. But in truth
he shows how one must understand mixture by his refutation of the 35
notions put forward.[266] For it is not the case that imagination has its
being in this kind of activity of both, with sense-perception coming 212,1
first and opinion following on (this notion he indicated with 'nor
produced by sense-perception'), nor with both happening simultaneously, nor with them coinciding but each one contributing its own
activity in its simple form, not mixed with the other (one must think 5
he means this when he says 'neither opinion accompanied by sense-
perception'), or with them coinciding and being combined with each
other and no longer distinct.[267] Rather there is one common activity
resulting from the two, not by merger with some destructive change
in each, as in the case of honeyed wine (for it is impossible to posit
this in the case of immaterial entities), but with them remaining as
they are and unmixed, but with all of each as it were[268] penetrating 10
the whole of the other. It is not, of course, just any kind of mixture of
sense-perception and opinion that is imagination. 'And for this reason
too' he says, meaning the things that have been mentioned, all the
things that are peculiar to each of sense-perception and opinion and
distinguish imagination from them. As, for example, that in dream
images there is neither potential nor actual sense-perception, and if
sense-perception is of things which are present, imagination happens 15
when sense-objects are not present, and if opinion is not within our
control and happens with assent to something as true and through
persuasion and reasoning, while imagination is within our control
and without belief or reason, imagination would not consist in the
activity of both of those, either coming together or one coming first
and the other following,[269] both for these reasons and because of the 20
argument which he now uses. So what mixture of them does Plato
mean? The one which consists in the middle components being simple
and themselves, but which is called a 'combination' and a 'mixture'
from the extremes because the middle terms have something in
common with both the extremes. This is how Aristotle says the
colours between come from white and black, and the *Timaeus*[270] says
that the soul comes from the substance that is undivided and the one 25
that is divided in bodies,[271] solely because of the participation of the
middle terms in the extremes by virtue of their simplicity. For
imagination too is in the middle between sense-perception and opinion.[272]

428a27 And it is clear[273] that opinion is not of something else
but of that which is, together with it, the object of sense-perception.[274] [I mean that the combination of the opinion of whiteness
and the perception of it will be imagination; for it does not come

from the opinion of goodness and the perception of whiteness. Appearing as an image will be to opine what it sees, not incidentally].

30 It is clear that what is being claimed is not that the imagination that derives from both is put together from perception of one thing and opinion about another: the opinion is about the same thing. And the 'about the same thing' is not incidental, for example about Socrates it does not come from the perception that he is white and the opinion that he is good (and so incidentally about the same thing, since
35 Socrates is the subject of the white and the good) but so that both are about the same thing in itself, that Socrates is white and good, if one act of imagination is to come from both.

213,1 **428b2** Things appear falsely, about which the soul has a true belief at the same time, [for example the sun appears a foot across, but is believed to be larger than the inhabited world. So a person has either rejected his own true opinion, which he had, with the object staying as it is, not failing to notice it or having been persuaded to change his mind or, if he still has it, the same opinion must necessarily be both true and false].

I think this too is clear, that not only must both be about the same thing in itself, but that they must not be in conflict with each other.
5 Conflict in cognitions is conflict in respect of truth and falsity. Whenever as in the case of the sun the perception is false but the opinion true, it will come about that the same imagination that arises by virtue of the combination of the two can be true and false at the same time, unless someone were to posit that the opinion too changes and becomes false. For it is clear that the perception about the sun is not
10 changed to the truth. But neither is the opinion changed to falsehood, if we have not changed our opinion and the sun is not different from what it was before. As is said in the *Categories*,[275] it happens in two ways that a person who has a true belief about something afterwards holds a false opinion, either because he himself has been persuaded to change his mind, or forgets, or because the thing itself has changed
15 unbeknown to him. So an image which is single will be about one single thing and be false because of the perception ('appear falsely' shows this) and true because of the belief. Therefore in the case of 'the sun appears a foot across' we shall understand the appearing as relating to the image that is produced through sense-perception, the same image becoming true by virtue of the belief about the sun that
20 it is larger than the earth.

428b10 But since when a thing is moved another thing can be moved by it.[276]

Having shown by what has been said before that imagination is distinct from the other cognitive powers, he next sets down what it is that it is, finding evidence for its nature in its activities. The sensitive faculty is moved immediately by sense-objects. It does not merely undergo an affection but is active in accordance with its status as a living thing, the pure[277] activity of sensation and judgement being stimulated on the occasion of this affection which involves activity. It is at rest in respect of the form of the sense-object and it is not externally or in respect of the affection but internally that it brings forward (*proballein*) this form in accordance with the appropriate reason-principles: it does so in harmony with the passive activity in the sense-organ. So the affection in the sense-organ produced by the sense-object is a movement, whereas the bringing forward (*probolê*) of the reason-principle, the pure judgement of the sensitive faculty, and the determination in accordance with the form of the sense-object, are not movement but an undivided activity. In succession to this the imaginative faculty, being immediately adjacent, is stimulated, using the same organ but not as a sensitive one that is somehow affected from outside, but as an organ of the imagination impressed and shaped by the imaginative faculty. It is not surprising if the same vehicle is set below different faculties; indeed it underlies even the rational faculty. Not only the *pneuma* but also the solid instrument is affected by our rational activities.[278]

In any case the *pneuma* is affected primarily as being sensitive and, when sense-perception is operative according to the activity in respect of the form, then the *pneuma* too becomes suitable for the reception of impressions which are objects of the imagination, and the imagination itself is stimulated to put forward (*probolê*) imaginative impressions in accordance with the appropriate reason-principles and in a way appropriate to the perceptual forms, sometimes needing the perceptual impressions for putting forward (*probolê*) similar ones, not just once or twice but more often. But when it has been stimulated it puts forward (*proballein*) the images from itself and impresses and shapes the figure from itself, either making it like the forms of the sense-objects or adding accuracy, as in <putting forward> a straight line with no breadth and figures which are completely accurate: but sometimes it is vague or elaborates the impressions in many ways. It shares the characteristic of needing sense-perception for its initial stimulus with our rational faculties (indeed these, because of the general turning of the soul towards the outside, initially need the impact, as it were, on the sense-organ produced by what is outside for the apprehension of their own objects of cognition), but the latter

move over towards the immaterial, unimpressed and undivided objects of cognition, whereas imagination is held back in the sphere of
the corporeal and that which causes impressions and is divided.
Indeed even if, as Iamblichus would have it, it takes impressions of
all our rational activities,[279] it still represents them in a way involving
20   shape and division in accordance with the sensible forms. Therefore
it is contiguous with sense-perception, but nevertheless above it
because after the initial stimulus and acting from itself it does not
need sense-objects which are always present, and because it adds
accuracy, which is perhaps a characteristic that not all imagination,
but rather that of rational creatures, will have. But all imagination
will have the characteristic of controlling and moving animals, some
25   as being the first cognitive faculty in them, but men whenever at any
time and for any cause reason is concealed. Let us now follow Aristotle's words.[280]

**428b10 But since when a thing is moved another thing can be
moved by it**

30   Like the stone moved by the lever moved by the hand. One must apply
the causal conjunction 'since', taking it in common, to the words that
follow too, as far as the point where he introduces the apodosis. Thus:
'since ...[281] imagination be a kind of movement and not to happen
without sense-perception but happens to things which are perceiving
and is of the objects of sense-perception' and 'since ... it is possible for
movement to happen through the agency of the activity of sense-per-
35   ception', and 'since ... this must be like sense-perception'. And then
he sets out the main clause with the words 'this motion would be ...'
and what comes thereafter.[282] But how, when it is a cognitive activity
and stimulated from within, is imagination a movement? He said
'seems'. It seems, in general, since what undergoes some sort of
affection and is moved has body: it is moved from outside as something that perceives, but as something that imagines it is impressed
40   by the faculty of imagination. Hence '... not to happen without
215,1   sense-perception but happens to things which are perceiving', at the
beginning,[283] clearly, is, as has been said, common to it, and to our
rational faculties. But 'and is of the objects of sense-perception' is
peculiar to imagination. For it does not move over towards the
immaterial, but remains with corporeal impressions and extensions
and shapes. That movement, or some other activity, happens through
5   the agency of the perceptual activity does not apply to imagination
alone, but is true and clear in the case of our rational forms of
cognition as well, but because of its contiguity[284] and through its
body-like affection imagination necessarily comes to be like sense-
perception. So he reasonably concludes that, being movement be-

cause of the bodily – as was said – configuration, it happens 'not without sense-perception'. For impressions and shapes are in every 10 way divided and corporeal, and things that are divided and corporeal are in the first place cognized by sense-perception, because[285] there can be no referral to universals without sense-perception.

428b15 Nor is it present in things which do not perceive.

It is not present in plants, nor in things which have no life at all, nor 15 in the things which are above sense-perception, which have their existence in accordance with intellect or intellective reason. This is so since the activities of imagination involve extension and shape, while those of pure reason, and *a fortiori* those of intellect, are above the division of extension and shape. Should one then not attribute imagination to the heavenly bodies? Yes, if one attributes even sense-perception to them, and in the same way as sense-perception, which is stimulated entirely internally and from itself, and is able to 20 bring into existence and cognize all sense-objects and, before external things, the determinate preconception of sensible objects which is situated in the divine vehicles themselves, in accordance with corporeal reason-principles.[286] These do not impart shape and are not different at different times, but they are contiguous with the ones that do impart shape, and they contain, from a position of superiority, the infinitude of things which are different at different times. 25

428b16 And what has it can do, and be affected by, many things by virtue of it, [and it can be true and false. This happens for the following reason: perception of the special sensibles is true, or very rarely false. Secondly there is perception of the presence of incidentals which are incidental to sense-objects. And here it is already possible to be wrong. We are not wrong about a thing being white, but whether the white thing is this one or something else is subject to error. Thirdly there is perception of the common sensibles which follow the things incidental to those which have the special qualities: about these there is the greatest possibility of being misled].

It can be affected in so far as it is moved by the senses, and do because it is stimulated by itself when it has already been moved and moves animals by means of memory. One must understand 'by virtue of it' not only in the sense that it determines, but also as meaning 'able to 30 cause movement', instead of <that movement is caused> 'through its agency', since it is the case that even the imaginative soul uses the living body as an instrument. 'And it can be true and false'. For imagination belongs to the cognitive powers in us, and the truth is the end of all cognition. But since, unlike intellect and scientific knowledge, it is not one of the ones that always tell the truth, he reasonably says that it is either true or false. Indeed sometimes it produces falsehood as if it did so willingly, as it were, for the produc-

35   tion of images that are unreal is, as has been said, within our power. Perhaps this would happen to the rational imagination which elabo- rates them in various ways because of the reason's ability to move to many things,[287] even opposites, while it would not happen to the

216,1 imagination of irrational animals because of its narrow scope. But he outlines the truth and falsehood that go with every kind of imagina- tion with respect to what follows on sense-perceptions, saying that the one that is moved by its own special objects is generally true, whenever the sense itself does not fall into error because of distance or because something else impinges on it. This is so because when the

5   sense tells the truth the image which has just been stirred up joins it in telling the truth, just as the image which is stirred up after a time, even when it is an image of special sensibles, is often false. That is why it was previously said that perceptions of the special sensibles are always true,[288] but most images are false, not when the percep- tions are still present but when they have already taken place and after a lapse of time. But with incidental sense-objects there are false

10   images even when the sense-objects are present, for example that the white man is the son of Cleon because sense-perceptions about these things too may be false. Perceptions and images of common sensibles are similar and are sometimes false even when their objects are present because, even if the senses do not perceive these things incidentally, they still do not perceive them primarily: it is the special

15   sensibles that they perceive primarily. Both common and special sensibles may be incidental to incidental sense-objects, which are the substances that underlie them. The words 'about these there is the greatest possibility of being misled' are to be understood as applying to both incidental and common sensibles.

[The movement that results from the activity of the sense will be different, that is the one from these three kinds of perception]. **428b27** The first is true so long as perception is present, [but the others would be false both when it is present and when it is absent, particularly when the sense-object is at a distance. If then nothing but imagination has the features mentioned (and that is what has been said), imagination would be a movement happening under the agency of sense-perception in act. And since vision is sense-perception pre-eminently, he has taken imagination's name from light, because one cannot see without light].[289]

Imagination is stimulated straightaway when the sensation is pre- 20
sent, even if it sometimes escapes our notice because of the impact of
the sensation which seizes our attention, particularly when the
sense-object[290] is at a distance, when it happens that not only the
imagination but also the sense may be wrong even about special
sensibles. On this basis he shows that what has been said applies to
nothing other than the imagination. What has been said is (1)[291] that
movement takes place through the agency of sense-perception in act 25
(movement belongs to bodies) and through the impressing and shap-
ing of the *pneuma* when the imagination is stimulated,[292] the movement being predicated of the imagination; (2) that imagination is
similar to sense-perception is because it is inseparable from bodies,
with the *pneuma* always being impressed by the activity of the
imagination; (3) that it is not present in things that do not have
sense-perception, and that it does not happen in them without sense-
perception, because the soul which operates wholly externally is 30
stimulated to project itself by sense-objects, while imagination remains with its sensible impressions. Then (4) that which has imagination acts on and is affected by many things by virtue of it (it has
impulses, which is to act, and blushes or goes pale, which come under
the heading of being affected). And (5) that it is true or false because
it is one of the cognitive powers, and of these not one of those that is
always true. And he does the etymology of the word *phantasia* in 35
terms of it having something in common with the senses through the
best of them, vision, whose activity takes place with light (*phôs*), from
which imagination received its name.

[429a4[293] And animals do many things by virtue of them because
they remain and are like sensations.]

For every action involves the objects of the senses, so that it uses 217,1
sense-objects in actions, and the memory of sense-objects in the
impulses to these actions: memory is an activity like the senses,
involving retention. In the other animals imagination is what initiates and controls actions because they have nothing superior. But in
human beings what initiates actions is the practical intellect, when 5
we operate in accordance with reason (but not without imagination:
reason too uses images, since actions are concerned with things that
can be perceived through the senses, and the impulse to them arises
with the memory of sensible objects). But because sometimes the
practical intellect is overlaid we too are moved by images which then
take the lead, most clearly when in dreams imagination without 10
reason darts here and there in an indeterminate way and sometimes
moves the living being, but also in emotions as in immoderate desires,
anger, pleasure, pain and fear, when the soul is not using reason, and

also in diseases like madness. Being of the age of a child is another cause of reason being overlaid.

15   **429a8** About imagination, what it is and why, let this much suffice.

He has defined it (the definition indicates what it is), particularly that it is a cognitive power which sometimes tells the truth and sometimes does not. Of the causes, which 'why it is' indicates, he has set out the **20**   efficient cause, sense-perception in act, and the final cause, that animals may act and be acted on in many ways in accordance with it.

<CHAPTER 4>

429a10 As for the part of the soul with which it knows and thinks, [whether it be separate or not spatially separate but logically so, we must investigate what differentiating feature it has and how thinking happens at any given time].

What the separate intellect of the soul is and what kind of thing it is, that it is first substance and is undivided, the best form of life and **25**   the supreme activity, and that the same intellect is object of intellection and intellection, and is eternity, completeness, rest and the determinant and cause of everything, has been dealt with more opportunely and more completely in what has been written on book lambda of the *Metaphysics*,²⁹⁴ following Iamblichus' investigations about it in accordance with Aristotle's purpose.²⁹⁵ Now we must rather discuss what kind of thing the intellect participated by our soul is.²⁹⁶ **30**   For there is a special intellect participated by each rational soul, which is determined by it: each soul goes down to what is determined and to reason rather than form. For every form is indivisible, since it is a determinant and a perfection, whereas the soul is not indivisible,²⁹⁷ as its diffused activity shows, proceeding as it does by division and collection at the same time. So, coming down to what is deter- **35**   mined and given form, it participates and is substantially in contact with the determinant and the form, and each soul is in contact with its own, if the individualised form is present in composite things too: in respect of this it is called the individual quality by the Stoics,²⁹⁸ which comes to or departs from things all at once, and remains the **218,1** same throughout the whole life of the composite, even when different parts of that composite change or are destroyed at different times. But if each of the composites is defined by its own form, that is the more true of the soul in so far as it is immediately adjacent to the forms.²⁹⁹ Clearly there will be a difference between this participated **5**   form and the first and unparticipated forms in so far as the former is

participated and does not altogether remain in itself and is not a
separate determinant but, belonging to some other thing, namely the
soul, it is precisely this, a determinant of the soul that goes down to
what is determined. So it differs from the soul itself in being a
superior substance, inasmuch as soul is determined by a determinant
and perfected by a perfection. And since the soul disposed in accordance with reason is a cognitive substance, what determines it will be
an indivisible cognitive substance. This is intellect, but participated   10
intellect, and all of it is the soul's intellect. Is this what Aristotle is
talking about now? No: this intellect is not a part of the soul, but is
its informing cause and a superior substance, in addition to it being
absurd for him to move immediately to it from imagination, passing
over rational substance when he always moves up to it from the
nutritive soul through intermediaries.[300] He defines this[301] clearly,   15
writing, 'I mean the intellect by which the soul thinks discursively
and makes suppositions'.[302] We must also take the definition of the
soul so that we can know it in a scientific manner, as in the case of
other things; for example knowing that man is a mortal and rational
living being we understand the form of man in the life that has its
substance in respect of reason and has finite limits in accordance with   20
time. So, having considered soul in its substance and its deployed life,
both practical and theoretical, sometimes turning to sensible objects
and sometimes to intelligible ones, we shall place its informing cause
in the indivisible and intellective substance and life, which is not
practical and does not consider things in a deployed way, but which
is a determining cause of soul and an activity which gives it action
and the power to engage in this kind of consideration. By informing   25
cause of the soul I mean the one according to which, it being inseparably present to the soul, the soul is itself already determined and
has gone down to what is determined, just as everything which is
determined is determined according to some determinant present to
it, which is shared with all things of the same species, and also
belongs to each one, on which basis things of the same species are
many. The subject set before us is not the intellect participated by the   30
soul's intellect nor, *a fortiori*, the unparticipated intellect, but rational
substance. This is the case because the treatise is about the soul, and
reason is a part of the human soul,[303] since the whole soul is one. It
has been said that it becomes one now when in the soul's declination
to the body reason is tied up with the secondary corporeal faculties.
And saying 'with which the soul knows', since the cognition of the   35
senses and imagination is also knowledge, so that he can show its
rational knowledge he added the words 'and thinks'. That is characteristic of a reason which has depth, with one aspect of it which does
not even use the second kind of faculties, but operates on its own and
is not affected by the objects of knowledge but actualises them, since

it does not have them from outside but advances (*proballein*) them
from itself, and also another which does exert itself in the direction
40   of what is outside and is involved with kinds of cognition that are
associated with body, and that is either imperfect or perfect but
perfected by the first and filled with forms. So that the soul's first
219,1 reason is double:[304] the one is separate and full, from itself, of the
appropriate objects of knowledge: this is the one by virtue of which
the soul's turning to itself (*epistrophê eis heautên*) and connection
with superior being takes place. The other is that in accordance with
which the soul as a whole steps outside its staying in itself and directs
itself to secondary being, or entirely stands apart from its causes,
5   because of the reason's greatly distancing itself from itself and higher
beings, possessing the forms only potentially and imperfectly, or is
completed even in the activity that is projected outwards in accordance with the reason that does not stay in itself, nor among the objects
of cognition which are substantially present in it, but nevertheless
does not entirely stand apart, but goes down to the kind of activity
that happens in accordance with projection outwards and in accordance with separation from substantial reason-principles, and receives
10   the objects of cognition proceeding from the substantial ones in its
dispositions pertaining to substance, as does the knower.

So there will be the material and potential and passible one, the
one that inclines outwards and is mixed up with secondary kinds of
cognition, imperfect and wholly external, and the other one which
does project but is complete and has perfection, but is nevertheless
concerned with being but not in accordance with substantial activity
itself, it too being passible because it is brought to perfection accord-
15   ing to secondary standards by the substantial and first objects, and
kinds, of cognition. So it is potential, but not in the category of what
is entirely imperfect, but it is potential in respect of what is already
perfect in respect of its disposition, but not acting, being of the second
rank. This is like the living instrument being said to have life
potentially, though it lives, because it lives a life which it has by
acquisition from elsewhere. In the same way what thinks by project-
20   ing, in so far as it is perfected by acquisition by the forms which are
static and the thoughts which go together with them, is said to think
potentially, even if it is already thinking.

The other is the first substantial reason, being itself the first object
of cognition in the soul and the first kind of cognition, and in so far
as is possible for the soul's reason it is in its substance activity,[305]
through its contact with intellect.[306] Just as the material and imperfect reason is like the sensitive faculty, because of its own general
25   inclination to it,[307] with it too, in so far as is possible for reason,
becoming focused on what is external, so the reason that stands
entirely apart from what is external and is united indivisibly with

itself, as far as possible, become like the intellect which is first, being
activity in its substance. That, I think, is how the reason of the soul
is double or triple, with the second sometimes imperfect and sometimes becoming perfect, and thereby being divided into two.

The division into two or three does not happen because the reasons   30
are altogether separate from each other, but because the two depend
on the one first one and proceed from it, and because the second and
third substances become substantial in dependence on the first. For
the first substance itself proceeds from itself and projects the second
and third forms of life in itself, these not being insubstantial activities
but just this, forms of life. Every form of life is a substance, even the
last, if what is determined in accordance with it is a living being, and   35
if the generative form[308] of life is capable of receiving opposites. But
the first does not proceed to the outside in such a way as not to remain
in itself. For its existence consists in remaining, and it provides
existence to the others by remaining somehow as it is. But whenever
it proceeds, it does not remain in the pure sense. So it is one reason
that purely remains in the first place and again relaxes the remaining
by its projection from itself to what is outside and its proceeding,   40
becoming imperfect or perfect in accordance with it, and again being   220,1
separate from the second level of projections and reverting to itself,
when it is what it is. For in its projection it somehow detaches itself
from itself and does not remain entirely in itself, nor is it purely what
it is, being somehow knocked out of its position even in respect of its
substance.[309]

This happens not because it is entirely destroyed, or because it does   5
not somehow remain when it goes outside, but it happens in a way
appropriate to its middle position as soul, as it is in the middle of what
is divided and undivided, and in this way it would be between what
always remains in itself and what sometimes detaches itself from
itself completely, between what does not come into existence and
what does, and between the immortal and the mortal, the activities
that go with the projection being sometimes available and then again
being collected together into the soul that remains in itself, while it   10
is sometimes knocked out of position in respect of its remaining pure
in itself and the summit of its existence which is realised in accordance with its turning to itself. So it does not remain always in the
same condition, as Plotinus[310] thinks, nor does it go out from inside
in such a way as to depart from itself altogether (for it would no longer
go out nor would it remain entirely) since its substance is realised in
its turning towards itself. Indeed all Aristotle's discussion here is   15
about the rational soul, and not about the intellect which is immediately participated by it.[311] It is possible, as we said, to move to it from
this one, without what happens to the soul happening to it, but it
exercises in a determinative way those activities which are what the

soul is and does when it is being determined by this intellect. This is
20   the soul that changes and remains, proceeding to the second order of
things and then again returning from its absence to pure and separate
substance. But the intellect which is participated by it, always remaining what it is and in the same condition, determines all the
states of the soul, like the physical and determinative form of things
that come into being, being undivided and remaining what it is,
determinative of things that are divided and change in every sort of
25   way. But intellect, they say,[312] is a[313] substance superior to soul, and
Aristotle is talking about intellect and not about rational substance.
And how, if the treatise is about the soul, is the best faculty of the
soul, the rational one, left aside? How, when he begins with the lowest
faculty, the nutritive one and goes up through the adjacent ones,
through the sensitive faculty and the imaginative one, does he not
30   deal with rational cognition, going up in good order, as appears when
he first gives the imperfect and potential one that depends on the
first, then the one that is perfect in habit, and so the one that is in
accordance with the static activity that goes with its substance, does
he go above all the rational soul and philosophise about the transcendent intellect of the soul which was not the subject of the discourse?
Surely it is clearly stated that what is now before us for consideration,
35   that with which it was said to think, is a part of the soul. Wisdom is
a rational kind of cognition, but does not belong to the intellect above
the soul. And again he makes the point, 'I mean the intellect which
thinks discursively and apprehends' (429a23). Apprehension[314] and
discursive thought are rational forms of cognition. But he also calls
the reason intellect: he extends the name 'intellect' even to the
imagination. So distinguishing opinion from imagination he writes,
40   'But that thinking and belief are not the same is clear: for the former
state is in our control', meaning by 'thinking' the product of the
221,1 imaginative faculty that is put before our eyes whenever we want,
like people who bring things up in remembering and make images.
He clearly calls it imagination when he says 'we are in the same
condition in respect of imagination as if we were looking at things
that cause fear or confidence in paintings'.[315] In these texts he calls
5   only imagination thinking, but calls the rational kind of cognition
belief, while using intellection of both in common in what comes next,
'but about thinking, since it differs from sense-perception, and imagination and belief seem to belong to thinking'.[316] By 'of this' he means
of thinking and not of perceiving, as he shows by referring to the
distinction between imagination and perception. But he calls reason
10   alone intellect, distinguishing it from imagination, and saying that
most animals operate by virtue of their imagination, 'some because
they do not have intellect, like wild animals, some because their
intellect is sometimes concealed by emotions, disease or sleep, as in

the case of humans'.[317] Indeed he seems to call intellect everything
cognitive that is stimulated to activity by itself, when he extends it
as far as imagination, and specifically the soul's reason, which is 15
defined contiguously in terms of intellect, not least when reason is
not involved with sensible objects *qua* sensible objects, but considers
either their forms which determine[318] these in terms of their substance, or the ones that are in reason's substance itself, or by means
of these reaches up towards the superior entities. Then it becomes
intellect in act in so far as it is cognizing the intelligibles, not sensible
objects *qua* sensible objects, which are the objects of sense-perception:
then it is only intellect in potentiality. So Plato, in all cases, was in 20
the habit of using the same name homonymously, for the forms and
the things that are informed by them.

Aristotle, on the other hand, whenever the thing that is informed
is divisible, avoids the same name because of the great distance
between the divisible entity and the indivisible form, but speaks of
the rational soul as being not only a thing determined but also a
determinant. For it is between the indivisible and the divisible and 25
so in some way is both, showing the duality of determinant and what
is determined, the one by being deployed, and the other in virtue of
its constant transition from term to term,[319] and also in virtue its
bringing together into one all the things that are deployed, in so far
as it is like the intellect that determines it. And for that reason in the
Eudemus, the dialogue he wrote about the soul, he shows the soul to 30
be a kind of form,[320] and in these words approves those who say the
soul is a recipient of forms, not all of it but the intellective one in so
far as it is cognitive of the true forms in a secondary way: for the true
forms go with the intellect that is superior to soul. Now that we have
set out these preliminary definitions let us take up Aristotle's words[321]
and see if the definitions are consistent with them.

429a10 About the part of the soul with which it knows and 35
thinks, whether it is separate or not separate in extension but
only logically, we must investigate what differentiating feature
it has and how thinking happens at any given time.

He defines the purpose of the words in question, saying that they are
about the rational soul in us. For this is a part of the soul taken as 222,1
one together with the sensitive soul and the appetitive and the
nutritive soul, and not for the moment in its capacity of causing
bodies' motion, but in so far as it is cognitive and deals with action.
Adding 'understanding' to 'knowing' he has not only conveyed what
kind of knowing he has indicated, but also shown its virtue in the field 5
of action. For the faculty that understands is not only rational but
practical. But one must take a form of cognition appropriate to the

rational soul, which either deploys the reason-principles it has itself
or reaches up to the things above, or considers the forms of the things
below it and, in general, substances, but not accidents or properties.
Sense-perception deals with these.

10   The words 'whether it is separate or not' are not to be understood
as referring to the body,[322] even if it was mentioned before, since it is
difficult even to contrive the notion that intellect holds together some
body, even if he now immediately adds the point that it is not mixed
with any body and does not have any organ, as does the sensitive soul,
but they refer to the parts of the soul already mentioned, the nutritive
and the imaginative.[323] Or rather, since, as has been said,[324] he will
tell us that what cognizes rationally is itself to be taken in three ways,
15   he undertakes to look at what understands in itself and to consider
whether it is separate in respect of its own extension or not, but only
logically. So that the enquiry would be whether there are three
intellects in us as substances separate from each other, or whether
the intellect is one and a single substance but different logically, being
sometimes turned to itself as a whole but sometimes inclining to what
20   is outside, with this one being either imperfect or perfect. So that even
if the substances are different, they[325] are not separated by their
substrate, but the three exist with the one at their centre, being
differentiated by the activity of the one intellect in accordance with
different reason-principles. Consistently with this <the sentence> 'we
must investigate what differentiating feature it has' does not refer us
to those our faculties already mentioned (it has already been men-
25   tioned that belief is different from these),[326] but rather to the differences in thinking itself, which he will do later.[327] Since our soul does
not always have perfect intellection, it is also necessary to consider
'how thinking happens at any given time'. Therefore he has necessarily taken the potential and imperfect intellect first. For all coming to
be starts from what is imperfect, and, by way of what is perfect in
30   habit ends with the perfection that exists in act.

429a13 If thinking is like perceiving, it would either be being
acted on in some way by the intelligible object or something else
of that kind

It is not about all thinking that he says that it is the same sort of thing
as perceiving. He does not mean the kind that is perfect in habit
whenever it can operate by its own stimulus,[328] with the intellect then
35   able to think itself, since sense-perception is neither able to cognize
itself nor is it ever stimulated by itself without the presence of
sense-objects. Nor, *a fortiori*, does he mean the intellect that consists
in causing[329] everything in the intellect that becomes everything, and
is analogous to a craft.[330] This intellect is clearly said to be exempt

from being acted on and separate, being in its substance actuality,[331] while the other is potential and material and is acted on by the intelligible object.[332] So he is not talking about every kind, as some 40 understand it and then condemn Aristotle of self-contradiction, and 223,1 then, so that he does not appear to be subject to that, they understand these things of the soul or the intellect that is participated by soul, saying that the intellect that is analogous to craft is said to be the unparticipated and transcendent one.[333] Indeed everything that cog- nizes and thinks that is brought up for consideration in this treatise has been clearly said to be a part of the soul,[334] and intellect is said 5 to be that with which the soul reasons and makes suppositions, and is about the one that is perfect in disposition, because at times it becomes like the knower and can sometimes operate and learn and find things out by its own stimulus. All these are characteristic of the human soul alone. But he puts not only the intellect that is acted on in the soul, but also the one that causes things. 'For it is necessary', 10 he says, 'that these differences should be present in the soul too'.[335] That is why he likens the intellect in the soul that causes things to a disposition and to light,[336] so that the intellect that stands above the soul[337] should be more readily located in terms of the one that illumines.

As has already been said, his whole treatise has the project of talking in these texts about the rational substance of the human being, which he calls intellect. Considering its thinking in three ways he begins from the lowest, as being most knowable to the audience 15 and as bringing forward this very point into the investigation, namely how thinking comes to be: every kind of coming to be[338] comes from what is imperfect. The lowest is the one called material because it is acted on in every way, as he will say,[339] and perfected from elsewhere, and because it is not yet the intelligibles, but is perfected by receiving them as sense-perception is by receiving the sensibles. That is why it 20 is likened to sense-perception. And for this reason he brings in reason hypothetically, using the hypothetical conjunction, 'if thinking is like sense-perception',[340] that is if that kind of thinking were to be consid- ered which happens to be like sense-perception, for example like that which detaches itself from rest in itself and turning towards itself, but inclines outwards, outside itself and its own forms, not com- 25 pletely, as though thinking itself, and the forms in it, did not remain somehow but, because of the inclination to the outside of itself and the forms in it, it is perfected and filled from things of another kind which remain, in so far as what proceeds is other. For our soul is one, I mean the rational soul, and at the same time it remains one and becomes multiple in its inclination to the body, and it neither remains purely as it is nor does it depart altogether, but it both remains, in a 30 way, and proceeds from itself and, by virtue of becoming other in respect of itself it becomes dim in respect of its sameness, and slackens the force of its return to itself because of its inclination to things of the second rank, without flowing away to the extent that it does not somehow turn back: every kind of rational assent involves a turning back, as has been said above.[341]

35   The intellect that is connected with the soul's flowing outwards does not think in its own right, nor under its own stimulus, nor with itself as its means, but just as sense-perception works under the stimulus of the sense-object, so it works under the stimulus of the intelligible object and the intellect that is co-ordinate with that, being stimulated and filled as another by something else because of the otherness of what flows out in respect of what remains where it is. And in this way thinking in respect of the intellect that flows out would be 'being acted on in some way' in so far as it is filled by

40   something other. 'In some way' is added to 'being acted on' so that we
224,1   do not understand being acted on as involving destruction. 'Or something else of that kind', as it is different from the being acted on that happens in sense-perception. For that is more properly applicable in that case because of the movement in the organ and because of the complete otherness of sense-objects as compared with the sense and their existence outside. But in the case of intellection the intelligible object is not altogether other nor is it on the outside but it is inside,

5   and there is no corporeal movement since it does not need the body as an organ, but what happens to it does so only in respect of its being filled as if by something other. In so far as it happens under its own agency, in a way, because the soul is a single substance, it is something else of this kind in so far as it simultaneously retains its similarity to the affection,[342] because of its being brought in from elsewhere, and at the same time is other than the affection because of its being completed by itself. For this reason the soul searches for

10   things as not having them and finds them by looking to itself as having them. Since our reference up to substances starts from activities which are of the clearer kind, it appropriately moves our investigation on from thinking to the substance[343] of what thinks in this way. It does not, as in the case of sense-perception grasping the objects of sense even before the sensitive activity, grasp the intelligible objects before it is active because the intelligible object is less accessible to

15   the thinking that takes place with the intellect that proceeds, since it is more substantial, as being more stable, as it is in general the first and highest part of the soul.

429a15 So it must be free from affections, but capable of receiving the form.

Since he said that receiving and having the objects of cognition from

elsewhere is to be acted on, he appropriately says that what is able
to receive but does not yet have is free from affections. For he sees
our rational faculty which proceeds and departs from itself, and this   20
one is still incomplete, like that of those who lack knowledge and in
no way have the strength to cognize the substance of things. Since
the soul cognizes even then, but cognizes the accidents and properties
of the substance, not individual objects in the way that sense-perception and imagination do, but common ones, being active in respect of
them in a rational way[344] and considering their mutual consequen-
tiality or contrariety, looking at the antecedent and the consequence,   25
as do all crafts which are concerned with things in matter: the
so-called mathematical sciences already do this. For these do not
investigate substances, but shapes and sizes, states, movements and
mutual similarities: they do not look at their substantial reason-principles (because they have no extension and are unified), but rather at
the extensions and divisions that come from them by separation and   30
as a result of otherness.

But if these too are derived from the forms, how will not the
intellect that proceeds outside cognize these as well by virtue of some
kind of participation in the forms, so that the intelligible forms are
not in the soul in vain, without operating on intellect at all? Indeed
they will be active then too, but not as intelligibles or as forms. For
the intelligibles are indivisible substances and determinants and
altogether form: in its imperfect inclination to the outside the intellect   35
participates in the intelligible forms not as substances or as indivisible objects of cognition, but in so far as they end by arriving at
division and affections and generally at the kind of being that is
consequent on substances. So, appropriately explaining his 'free from
affections' as meaning not yet having but 'capable of receiving', he
says not simply the object of cognition, but 'the form', which is an
indivisible and substantial determinant, and an intelligible. The   40
power with which we cognize definitions is intellect.[345]

429a16 It is potentially such as that is, but is not that.   225,1

It is not the case that, because the soul's intellect which has inclined
to the outside is imperfect, it is such as to be always imperfect, but it
can be perfected when, while it remains in its state of inclination to
the outside, it is perfected as the knower in habit, which is itself a
projection of substance. So it too exists in separation from substance,   5
and outside. In this way it is potential, both in so far as it receives
things from elsewhere and in so far as it is still imperfect and has not
yet received anything. For the intellect that proceeds from the one
that exists with the first substance is intellect in a secondary way. It
is not what is coordinate with that one but is subordinate, and

something of that kind, but not the thing itself. So it was right to say
10   that 'it is potentially such as that is, but is not that'.³⁴⁶

429a16 And the intellect must be related to intelligible objects
in the same way as what is sensitive³⁴⁷ is related to sensible
objects.

It is clearly the thing that thinks, which has been laid down as the
subject of the discussion, that is to be investigated. It has already
been said that 'if thinking is like sense-perception',³⁴⁸ and what
15   thinking comes from.³⁴⁹ To which he will reasonably add that which
has already become each of the objects in the way that the knower in
act is said to do.³⁵⁰ The intellect which has not yet become its objects
is in the same position in relation to the objects of intellect as 'what
is sensitive³⁵¹ to the objects of sense':³⁵² he calls what can perceive but
is not yet doing so 'what is sensitive'. As also in respect of its being
completed from elsewhere and becoming like in potency, and in
addition being not the things themselves, but something like the
20   archetypal forms that come in. For it is not the sense-objects that are
in what is sensitive,³⁵³ but their forms, being forms of properties.
Neither are the intelligible objects in this intellect, but something like
them. Except that things which have sense are superior to sense-
objects, being alive and included in what is indivisible,³⁵⁴ while things
that have intellect are subordinate to intelligible objects in so far as
the latter remain inside while the former proceed to the outside. And
25   because sense-objects are altogether different from things with sense,
whereas intelligible objects are at the same time different and the
same (for the intellect that flows out is not only different but also the
same as the one that stays in place). And also because sense-objects
stimulate the sensitive faculty through the sense-organ, acting on the
sense-organ (for the sensitive soul is disposed according to the form
by the projecting of its own reason-principles), while intelligible
30   objects complete the intellect itself directly: it too is completed from
there by its own activity.

429a18 It is necessary, since it thinks all things, that it should
be unmixed, as Anaxagoras says,³⁵⁵ so that it should be in
control, [that is so that it should cognize (for if it has anything
showing through, it hinders and puts an obstacle in the way of
what is of a different kind)].

It is clear that this too is said about the intellect which is the subject
35   of the present discussion, the one which proceeds and is still incomplete. This one is none of the intelligibles, but is available to them all,
unmixed,³⁵⁶ so that it can think them all by participation and not

through itself,[357] but by means of the completion that comes to it from outside. This is so since that intellect becomes each thing through itself like the knower, and is no longer unmixed, but is each thing, and, *a fortiori*, the intellect that is disposed according to the primary substance of the soul and is activity in its substance. But the intellect that thinks everything by participation is unmixed in respect of everything before it thinks. For it is the substrate of what it thinks, like matter, and what is purely material is completely devoid of form. That is why even in the case of bodies we do not allow that prime matter is one of the elements or, in general, anything that has been informed. For the elements have some sort of opposition to each other, by which whatever has substantial existence through one of them is impeded in receiving the others, since what is in them does or will put an obstacle in the way of all of them. So that this kind of mind should be in control and know each thing itself being purely what it is, let it be unmixed in respect of everything, just as Anaxagoras keeps the intellect unmixed, in respect of homoeomerous things,[358] so that it should control all of them, this one makes all things and thinks them in a transcendent way, while the soul's material mind does so in a subordinate way, so that it can participate in everything without impediment.[359]

226,1

5

10

429a21 So that of it there is not any nature other than this, that it is potential. [So the so-called intellect of the soul]

15

The words 'so that of it <there is> not' are not to be understood as referring to matter. For matter is without form, acquiring its existence only in respect of its being capable of receiving corporeal forms. But this intellect too has its substantial existence in terms of the rational soul and cognizes sensible objects, as has been said.[360] But one must not understand the words 'of it <there is> not' as though the sense has no nature. Indeed both the intellect and the sense have their own natures. But one must construe the lemma by transposing the word 'of it' in some such way as this, 'so that there is not any nature of it',[361] so that we should not be forced to take something else along with it as being like it. That 'there is not any nature of it' is true, if by nature we were to understand intelligible and intellective nature. For it neither actually thinks nor is thought. But it only exists potentially with respect to both before it thinks, while it is still incomplete. Even if it cognizes sensibles, it does not cognize intelligibles, which are substantial determinants. So it is not intellect, since intellect is the cognition of intelligibles, and intelligibles are the things which sense-perception cannot cognize. We are accustomed to divide entities into two, into intelligibles and sensibles. So it is appropriate that he says this kind of reason[362] of the soul is called

20

25

30

intellect,[363] because it does not yet exist on account of its not being in act, but it has its name nevertheless from the fact that it is potentially only intellect and is none of the intelligible forms, which he says exist as existing in the true sense and in act, before it thinks. For when it thinks it is completely determined in respect of one of the intelligibles and then it is like the thing that is being thought.

35   **429a23** [so the part of the soul which is called intellect] I mean by intellect that with which the soul reasons and apprehends [it[364] is actually none of the things that are before it thinks].

In the reason's transitions as it goes through things, transitions which the term *dianoia* (discursive reason) indicates from the word *dianuein*, to traverse in a cognitive way, and in its contemplation at 227,1 a remove, which 'apprehending' indicates, sometimes incompletion is an accompaniment, so that it thinks nothing, and sometimes completion in habit, when it has the capacity to think both other things and itself through itself.

    429a24 So it is not reasonable either for it to have been mixed with body. For it would assume some character, hot or cold, even 5 if there were some organ, as for the sensitive faculty. But now there is none.

Since he said that the intellect that has been talked about exists only in potency and is actually none of the things that are, and that it has no nature of its own except that it is potential, he has taken care not that we should not suspect that it has no substance or no life (for the nature that is able to think and understand and participate cognitively in intelligible forms is in every way life and substance). That is not what he has taken care about, but rather that it should not be 10 thought to be some kind of corporeal life and substance because being potential and incomplete, and also changes, exist predominantly in bodies, and so he shows that it transcends every life that is inseparable from bodies. The inseparable life is of two kinds, the one informing the living instrument – in respect of this one it is alive – and the other which uses as an instrument the body which is already alive,[365] like 15 the steersman in the ship,[366] in so far as it does use it, not being separate. Neither is able to fit the intelligibles when the life of the instrument is mixed with body and confused with the qualities in it. The body is below the forms of physical objects and, *a fortiori*, the intelligible ones, and passible qualities have departed from every kind of substance and fallen far away from the intelligibles. So the 20 life that is confused with these qualities and mixed up with the body would never have been fitted to the intelligibles. Having come to

belong entirely to the body, which is shown by the mixture, it also falls short of the form that gives the common determination to the things that come into being: I am not yet talking about transcendent entities. It also falls short of the turning to itself, so that it cannot think itself. And, even further, being filled up with qualities shows   25
its unsuitability for intellective activity and its lack of fit with intelligible forms. For the reason that is to grasp formal substances must be purified of accidents and particularly the lowest ones, like the passible qualities, and unmixed with body, so that it can think the indivisible and has the strength to turn to itself. But from where, since it has no organ, so that it can be entirely separate from bodies?   30
In fact he will demonstrate this clearly later when he has progressed a little, when the difference between the impassibility of intellect and the sensitive faculty becomes clear.

429a27 And those who speak of the soul as the place of forms do well [except that it is not the whole soul but that which is able to think, and is the forms not in act but in potency].

He praises those who say that the soul is the place of forms,367 and at the same time shows that his discussion is not about the intellect that   35
is participated by soul (that intellect is not soul, but a higher form of being) and also, at the same time, because he does not call accidents 'forms' (for the sensitive faculty receives these accidents) but rather the substances which exist in their own right or are entirely their   228,1
own, by virtue of which the things defined with respect to themselves have their substance. It is a place in so far as it receives things that it acquires, somehow from outside, so that the analogy with physical place is kept. If so, the faculty that is entirely intellectual will not be place, but rather the one that has been talked about and, in general, the one that flows to the outside, since the one that remains where it is is the forms corresponding to it, but does not receive them, and the   5
one that departs from itself is in potency and not in actuality, while the one that turns to itself as a whole and is at rest in accordance with its own substance is no longer potential but in act, or rather its act is it.

429a29 That the impassibility of the sensitive and thinking faculties is not the same is clear if one pays attention to the sense-organs and the sense. [For the sense cannot perceive when a sensory stimulus has been very strong, for instance a sound after very loud sounds, nor can it see or smell after very bright colours or strong smells. But when the intellect thinks something highly intelligible it is not less capable of thinking inferior intelligibles. For the sensitive faculty does not exist apart from body whereas the intellect is separate.]

10   With these words he wants to show what has been said before,[368] that there is no organ involved in the contemplation of intelligible forms.[369] He shows this by the comparison of intellect with sense-perception so that, knowing by means of sense-perception what affection is undergone by anything that cognizes through an organ, and seeing that the thinking faculty is free from this affection, we should place it above looking at things by means of an organ. He calls impassibility the

15   receiving that has not yet taken place in a thing that is capable of receiving. If then impassibility is not the same in what senses and what thinks, then neither is the capability of receiving, nor the receiving, the same in both.

What then is the dissimilarity? It is that the receiving of the sense-organ takes place with some alteration and change and a corporeal affection (for the organ must be affected in some way by the sense-objects if the sense is to operate), whereas that of the thinking

20   faculty is not subject to alteration and its participation is in accordance with its own activity. What shows this? It is that sense-perception, when it grasps some powerful special sense-object, such as vision apprehending a bright colour, is for the moment unable to apprehend less clear objects, but intellect is able to go from the contemplation of things which are highly intelligible (such are things that are more like forms, the determinants that are above, more powerful sorts of

25   perfection and purer substances) to think lesser intelligible objects, and is more capable of doing so than before it thought the greater ones. For thinking is made more powerful for the cognition of secondary objects by the contemplation of superior ones: hence cognition coming from principles and causes is the best cognition of the things of which they are the principles and causes.

So what is the cause of the difference? It is that the sensitive faculty

30   does not operate and receive forms without the body, with the organ being expanded or contracted and generally undergoing a corporeal affection in the receiving, and being most obviously disturbed in participating in strong sense-objects. So for example the sense-organ which has been expanded by what causes less expansion remains freer from affection and so does not stimulate the activity of the

35   sensitive faculty which goes with it. Intellect on the other hand, being separate from any body, needs no alteration or corporeal affection. Therefore it is not impeded in respect of looking at things below it, receiving the things that come from superior entities in accordance with its own pure special activity, and is said to be affected not because it is affected by body but because it operates in different ways.

429b5 Whenever it becomes each thing, as one who actually   229,1
knows is said to do

The intellect that somehow stands apart from itself and proceeds to
the outside sometimes revolves entirely around sense-objects and in
no way pays attention to forms or substances, which can be apprehended by reason or the higher intellect, but not by sense-perception   5
(and that is why they are called intelligible objects, since he calls the
reason too 'intellect'), is potential intellect, imperfect and material,
in so far as it is suitable for the receiving of intelligible forms and
thinking about them, but has not yet received them.

At other times it is already perfect and full of intelligible forms, as
far as is possible for the intellect that proceeds: it is not perfected by
sense-objects, but goes over these as being the last traces of the   10
forms,[370] and from there is stimulated, by its inclination to itself, to
the investigation of the forms themselves, and in this way it is in
contact with the static first substance of the soul. It is brought to
perfection by the forms that remain in this soul and by the cognition
that is united with it. It does not become what the soul's substantial
intellection becomes, nor does it become the forms that are at rest in
the soul's substance, but is perfected and filled in respect of the forms   15
that depend on it contiguously, and the cognition that is in contact
with the substantial one: this happens at the same time through the
agency of other things which remain at rest, in so far as it has
proceeded in a differentiated form, and simultaneously through its
own agency since being in a way one and the same it both remains
and proceeds. And the perfection in the intellect that proceeds is not
like the substantial perfection, but happens in respect of projection
and is second after the substantial one, and consists in disposition.   20
The disposition is in a relationship with substance but is not a
substance. In his contemplation of what are, as it were, parts of the
soul, the philosopher[371] goes up from subsequent entities to the first
ones by way of the adjacent ones, and starting from the material and
imperfect and potential intellect he goes on to the one that itself
proceeds but is perfected with the perfection that goes with projection.
This intellect is said to become all things as does, clearly, the one who   25
knows actually. He says this so that, even in the case of the intellect
which is perfect in this way, we do not make its activity identical with,
or always following, the disposition. But we should assume that the
intellect that proceeds is perfect as is the knower in act, that is the
one who has already acquired the perfect disposition but does not
always act in accordance with it. So let us say that the intellect that
has proceeded is perfect in this way, because through the proceeding
it is as if it were divided off from substance, and in this way has the   30
activity that belongs with the disposition divided from it[372] in such a

way that it does not always follow it, but only sometimes does so because the intellect too is itself only sometimes perfected. Therefore 'each thing' is correctly said of it because of the divided collection of forms in it, and the 'becoming' because of the perfection which comes 35 from elsewhere and is not permanent but happens sometimes.

429b7 This happens whenever he is able to act under his own stimulus. [In a way it exists potentially even then, yet not in the same way as before discovering or learning.]

Being able to act under one's own stimulus is characteristic of the intellect that proceeds but is perfect. For the material intellect is perfected by itself in so far as the soul's intellect that remains and the one that proceeds is one and the same, but it is unable to act and know 230,1 the intelligibles on its own so long as it is imperfect, but only when it has been perfected: this is the intellect that is the subject of investigation. Indeed not even the substantial intellect of the soul is able to act under its own stimulus, for its being consists not in being potential but in being already active. This intellect is potential because it is not 5 always acting: that is why it is said to be 'in a way in potency', both because it is not always active and because it is completed from outside, just as the already living body is said to have life potentially because of its having acquired participation in life not only from outside, but also as something given it at some time, but not 'in the same way as before learning or discovering', which was the condition of the imperfect intellect. For that one was potential in respect of the 10 perfection itself and differs from it by its fuller and clearer otherness from what perfects it.

429b9 And then it can think itself

Not incidentally, by having the intelligibles and being in a way the same as the forms that are thought, as primarily thinking the forms and not itself, as Alexander would have it,[373] but thinking itself too primarily. For what basis would Alexander or we have for writing 15 anything about it if it does not think itself and its intellection, its life and its substance, so that it can be intellect and not sense-perception, reaching out from itself to other things and having perception of itself along with its reaching out to them? Indeed it is not just intellect but also intelligible, as if it took a share in the other intelligible forms from the substantial ones that the soul has, thus becoming intellect 20 and intelligible by the agency of what is substantially intellective and is being thought. But, says Alexander, it undergoes no affection from itself.[374] Thinking seemed to consist of the intellect being affected by the object of intellection. Not simply, but in a way like sense-perception and what is somehow perfected from elsewhere, even if it does receive this perfection from elsewhere by its own activity.[375] So the material intellect is affected as is the one that has already been perfected in respect of its projection, in so far as it is perfected by the 25 substantial intelligible both as intellect and as becoming intelligible. But once it is perfected it thinks itself and the forms in it[376] without undergoing an affection, according to a perfect activity. For the being affected consisted in participation and being filled from elsewhere and not in some change.[377]

429b10 Since size and the essence of size and water and the 30 essence of water are different: this is the case with many other things, but not all: for in some cases the essence of flesh and flesh is the same: the soul judges them either by means of something else, or the same thing in a different condition.[378] [For flesh does not exist without matter, but like snub-nosedness is a this in a this].[379]

His purpose here is to explain the different kinds of thinking of the intellect that proceeds from substantial rest but is perfected in its 35 disposition by the substantial perfection that is in the soul so that it can produce different kinds of intellection: the one kind is of composite and divisible substances, the other of simple and indivisible ones, so that in this way he can distinguish the substantial contemplation of the soul, which remains at rest, as far as is possible for it, among 231,1 simple and indivisible entities, as does the intellect that is superior to the soul and does not move from forms to things that are informed, so that it can know the latter, but in the intellection of forms knows as from causes the things that are informed and their added proper- ties and, to put it simply, all things that are caused, the matter that 5 receives the last of these, and the things that somehow or other come into existence, in accordance with the intellection that deals with causes, in so far as things that are caused are causally anticipated in the forms. This <intellect> the soul (running up to its own substance as far as it can) imitates inasmuch as it is by its nature attached to it,[380] remaining among its own highest forms of reasoning and in no 10 way proceeding to the outside, but being in contact even with the forms in intellect: being among these it looks at the things that are caused according to the simplicity that causes things. Yet the soul that proceeds from itself, even though it already embarks on a contemplation that is perfect, does not remain in its formal simplicity, but because of the perfection which is given by its substance and its contact (not by union) with that perfection as itself somehow other, 15 it focuses on forms, even if it is further from them than[381] the soul that stays purely in itself, but because of its proceeding outside it does

not look at things from the causes alone but also, having proceeded,
it looks in a corresponding way at the things that are caused and have
proceeded.[382] It looks at sensible objects with sense-perception, at
composite substances and generally ones that are informed with
rational cognition, and one that is other than the cognition that
20   apprehends forms, and with the same one, but as it were deflected, it
thinks the things that are determined in this way too. For it thinks
the determinants with truth and without deflection. The determinants are perfection, and the thinking of them happens with perfection, since every kind of cognition accords with the object of cognition.
Things that are informed are perfect, as is the corresponding intellect
that focuses on them, but they are not perfection except by participation in perfection. The deflection shows the participation. Indeed a
25   doctor is like medicine deflected because he acts by means of medicine, but medicine that is a secondary manifestation and has proceeded, because it is what it is in the participation, being different
from what is participated though it exists by virtue of its relation with
it. A straight line which is bent, that is deflected, so as to make an
angle, has arisen from the straight line, but has departed from the
simple thing and has, as it were, submitted to division.
30   This is what Aristotle's says here[383] in his discussion about the
perfect intellect in its procession, reminding us above all of this very
point, that what is informed is other than the form.[384] Size and flesh
and water are things that are informed, but the essence of each of
them is the form of each of them. For the form is normally defined in
terms of the what it is to be something since it is according to that
that things that are informed have their existence. In their case the
35   form does not remain being itself and of itself, but is determinative
of something other and in these cases that thing is another, that is
the thing that is determined, and so is its essence which is the
determinant by which it is determined. In cases where the form is
without matter, remains on its own and is not the determinant of
another thing, in these cases the thing itself and its essence are the
same, like flesh and the essence of flesh. He has taken an example
40   which is not a true one[385] (he makes the point that flesh is in matter
and is like being snub-nosed), but he is trying to show that this is the
condition of an immaterial thing. But how can flesh, snub-nosedness
and, to put it simply, any compound of matter and form be said to be
232,1 'a this in a this', if the 'a this' is said of the form and the 'in a this'
either of the nature of the form in the matter or of any relation to
another as to something determined by it? For what is informed is
not the same as the form that is in another thing. For the latter is a
determinant, even if of something else, and the former is a thing
determined, even if it has no matter like heavenly body. Snub-nosed-
5   ness is not the same as the curvature in the nose, nor is the living

being the same as the life in the body, just as the doctor is not the same as the medicine in the human being. These things are cognized scientifically from the proximate causes which are their elements, for they are known from their[386] determinant form and the matter that receives it. So the 'a this in a this' shows not that a thing is compound, but the causes of the compound. The positioning of the form in the matter produces the compound.

10

429b14 It discriminates between hot and cold with the sensitive faculty, and also the things of which flesh is a sort of proportion. [But it judges the essence of flesh with something else, either something separate or something which relates to it as the bent line does to itself when it is pulled straight.]

Since he said that it judges size and the essence of size with something else, or the same thing in a different condition, he distinguishes which things it judges with something else and which with the same thing in a different condition: things that are sensible, such as qualities, 15 colours, shapes and sizes, and, as he said himself, 'the things of which flesh is a sort of proportion' (that is the things of which the determined substance is the proximate cause: for it is often the case that Aristotle too, like Plato in the *Gorgias* and the *Theaetetus* has taken the proportion in place of the proximate cause.[387] The determined substance is the proximate cause of all accidental properties because they exist in it and about it and from it: so flesh is taken to stand for any 20 determined substance) intellect – to resume – judges sensible things by means of sense-perception. For all objects of the senses are accidental and partial, and sense-perception apprehends them in a way corresponding to that. But intellect apprehends substances, so in the case of the things mentioned it judges them with something else, so with sense-perception which is something else as compared with intellect.[388] So the intellect which in all respects judges determined substance – since he thought fit to call reason too intellect,[389] as has 25 been said before – does not judge determinants with something else, but with itself being in a different condition, until such time as we look at forms with the intellect that proceeds and is perfected in us. This is so since the soul when it has run up to its own substance and stays with its own perfect activity, being united with the forms and entirely separated from the projection of secondary things, is other 30 than the life that proceeds. Therefore the words 'it judges the essence of flesh with something else, either something separate, or something which relates to it as the bent line does to itself when it is pulled straight', are rightly added here. For it judges forms with something else when that is separate, that is with its contemplation separated from things being projected to the outside and the activities that

35   proceed to dispositions and potentialities. Unless after all it does not
then judge with something else but with the same thing in a different
condition, because the soul as a whole is one, both the one that
remains and the one that proceeds. And it fits with the same thing
but in a different condition, when the intellect that proceeds both
cognizes determined substances and determines the forms in accordance with itself, being thus in a different condition, just as the straight
line is in respect of the bent one. Indeed the bent line, as we have
233,1 already set out, indicates the kind of cognition corresponding to
things that have been informed, and the one that has been straight-
ened out, as being straight and not bent, has been taken as a token
of the cognition of determinants and perfection, for the reasons that
we mentioned above.[390]

429b18 Again in things that exist by abstraction straight is like
5   snub-nosed, because both involve continuity. But the what it is
to be straight, if it is other than being straight and the straight,
it judges with something different. [Let it be a duality. So the
soul judges it by something different or by the same thing in a
different condition].

He usually thinks and says that the objects of mathematics exist in
abstraction, not, like the Pythagoreans looking for the rational principles which project the mathematical impressions which are in the
imagination,[391] being substantial in the bodily life of the soul, but
10   rather saying that the mathematical entities are in the imagination's
impressions themselves, to which in truth mathematicians devote
their whole activity. The Pythagoreans, attending to the living rational principles that project the impressions, made mathematical
objects substances.[392] Aristotle denies the substantiality of the impressions and says they arise from abstraction,[393] as the soul receives
15   them in accordance with an imitation in respect of sensible objects.
It is not because the soul does not project these too by its own activity
(that is shown by their turning one to truth and precision,[394] for the
perceived shape is not truly cubic, nor does the physical straight line
truly have no breadth: only the mathematical one does. For the
impressions come from inside, but the soul does not project them
20   without cognition of sensible objects, just as it does not do so for
superior or intelligible objects of knowledge). But, because of the very
great similarity of the things that are imagined to the sense-objects
they have the place of abstraction specifically among the things
imagined, as these are as nearly as possible the same as the sense-
objects, without the physical substance, since the impression in the
imagination is not like the form but like what is informed. For every
25   form is indivisible and undivided whereas magnitudes consist in

extension and numbers in division. So it is right that he said 'the straight is like the snub-nosed', because of the continuity and the extension, and because there is no form and what it is to be something, which is the being straight, apart from the straight. Aristotle said 'if it[395] is other' hypothetically, because it is not proposed to work these things out now, since he has worked them out and expounded them in the *Metaphysics*.[396] And now he reminds us saying 'let it be a duality', clearly meaning the straight. For the being straight is a unity because it is indivisibly one, whereas the straight is a duality not as being two things (for it too is one) but by being continuous and divisible and therefore dual. So the soul judges the objects of mathematics by means of something else, or by the same thing in a different condition, as is adequately explained in the case of the things that are determined. 30 35

429b21 Thus in general, as things are separate from their matter, so it is in the case of things to do with intellect.

Not with every kind of intellect. It does not apply to the soul's transcendent intellect,[397] nor to the one in the soul that is united with that one, being related to it.[398] For those are not apart from the cognition of forms. But it is about the one which is the subject of the discussion, the one that is perfected in its procession and cognizes things in a corresponding manner, so that because of its perfection it can focus on the forms as a determinant and, as a thing determined because of its inclination to the outside, on the things that are informed as proceeding from the forms. This kind of intellect thinks both things that are separate from any matter, like the substance of soul and the superior intellect, and also those that are separate in a way, like mathematical and physical forms, which do not require a substrate for their existence, and in this way are separate, but by being determinants of other things they are inseparable from them: in addition it thinks the things that are informed themselves, these being no longer separate from matter. He now seems to call the determined substance itself matter. As then things are in respect of being separate from matter or not, so do this intellect's contemplations (these are 'to do with intellect') *apprehend* either the things that are entirely separate, or those that are separate in a way, or those which are inseparable. But if its activities are such, it is clear that the intellect itself is neither only or altogether or in a way separate, nor only inseparable, but it is altogether separate because it is already joined to the soul's substance and the perfection that comes from it, and it is still separable in a way and again inseparable because of its reaching to the outside, both to the forms that determine other things and to the things that are determined in their own right. 234,1 5 10 15

20 **429b22** Someone might raise the question: if the intellect is simple and unmixed and free from affections and has nothing in common with anything, as Anaxagoras says,[399] how will it think, if thinking is being acted on in some way. It is in so far as two things have something in common that one is thought to act and the other to be acted on.

Having completed the investigation of the double intellect which proceeds, or which is two things, distinguished by being imperfect and

25 perfect, and in respect of its being double by potentiality and by its being involved as a whole with secondary forms of life or inclining up to itself and to substance, by which it is perfected, and being about to run up to the substantial intellect, he now sets out two problems about the intellects he has been talking about. The first pertains particularly to the imperfect intellect, but less to the one that is already

30 perfect, the second the other way round. Yet by both of them he conveys a certain commonality of the ones that have already been talked about with the one that is going to be talked about, the one being a more distant one and the other closer. Thus the last and material intellect is shown to have something in common with the one that acts, as being of a nature to be perfected, and the one that is perfect in disposition has more in common with the one that is perfect

35 of itself by being itself too intelligible and immaterial, since it thinks the intelligible in things without matter.

What then is the first problem, and from where does it start? From the intellect that is in act and above the soul. For that is free from affection in not being acted on by anything, and unmixed in respect of secondary things: these too are thought by virtue of the concept of them that pertains to cause, but not in a way that corresponds to them. Therefore it does not have anything in common in respect of a

40 coordinate commonality, since transcendent commonality exists in first things in respect of secondary ones by virtue of a concept of things

235,1 that are caused which pertains to the cause. So how did we say that thinking consists in being acted on and in a commonality by mixture, so that there should somehow be a corresponding commonality in the case of things that act and things that are acted on? Transcendent and special causes bring all things into being,[400] but are not said to be productive by Aristotle, because they do not proximately start

5 coming to be. For what makes something is related to what comes to be, but those things are the causes of substance and being. So the question is, how does thinking consist in being acted on when the intellect is not acted on, as even Anaxagoras thinks? How will it not have something in common with things that produce or act, if it is acted on? For one thing acts and another is acted on by virtue of something they have in common, while the intellect is unmixed and

has nothing in common with anything else. The first problem is
something like this. He brings in another when he writes like this: 10

429b26 Also whether it is itself intelligible. Either all other
things will have intellect, if it is not by means of something else
that it is itself intelligible, and if what can be thought is specifically one and the same, or it will have something mixed with it,
which makes it intelligible just like other things

This problem pertains to the imperfect intellect, in so far as it is able
to think itself by virtue of being in potency, in its first meaning, but   15
more clearly to the already perfected one, about which it has been
said clearly 'and then it will be able to think itself',[401] clearly with
respect to the second meaning of in potency.[402] It is clear that what is
able to think itself will be not only thinking but being thought, and
at the same time intellect and intelligible object. It is also clear that
in this way it is assimilated both to the substantial intellect of the   20
soul and to the one superior to soul, as being brought to the immaterial through its indivisible union with itself. That is why the problem
is raised as common to the intellect's being simple and unmixed. For
if being an intelligible belongs to other things, both to physical forms
and simply to physical substances, but they do not all have intellect,
intellect and the intelligible would not be the same in form, that is
definition, even if they sometimes coincide in their substrate. In the   25
cases, then, where it does coincide, since it is not intelligible *qua*
intellect, it will have the characteristic of being intelligible by virtue
of something else which is common to other things too. So intellect
will be neither simple nor unmixed in respect of other things. For 'it
will have something mixed with it, which makes it intelligible just
like other things'. The 'being mixed' is there because of the addition
of 'intelligible' which differs from intellect by its own special nature,
and 'like other things' is added, extending the problem because of the   30
intellect's sharing something with them, though they are divided and
material. For other things are like that.

429b29 A distinction has been made before[403] in respect of being
acted on in virtue of something common, telling us that intellect
is in a way potentially the intelligibles, but in actuality nothing,
before it thinks. So like a writing tablet it must[404] have nothing
actually written on it: this is what happens in the case of   35
intellect.

With these words he takes up again the first question:[405] he keeps his
own hypothesis, that the intellect which proceeds from itself thinks
by being acted on, and agrees that this intellect has something in

236,1 common with objects of thought. And he shows that the intellect which is not yet perfect is nevertheless not entirely torn away from the intellect in act, both because it is of a nature to think and because it is able to receive intelligible forms, being clearly filled from the higher forms. 'For what acts is always of a higher status than what is acted on', as he will say himself.[406] Even if it is perfected, using its

5 own activity,[407] by the superior intellect, as thinking itself, being pure activity, shows, how is it not to a greater extent united with the pure intellect, and how is this not also the case with the intellect that proceeds but has been perfected and is already potentially able to operate on its own in respect of secondary things? This is the purpose of the replies to the first problem, but we must look at the words themselves. 'A distinction has been made before', he says, 'in respect

10 of being acted on in virtue of something common', because there is something in common between what is acted on in whatever way and what acts on it:[408] the former must be in potency what the thing acting on it is in act. That is why he says 'intellect is in a way potentially the intelligibles', this being clearly the one that thinks by being acted on, and the one that is still imperfect. And this is potential in a way but not simply, like matter, both because of the intellect's self-produced perfection under the agency of the intelligibles, and because it is not

15 just two, but in a way one, being the intellect that remains at rest and the one that proceeds, and so being in a way in act: but in that it proceeds, departs from itself and is still imperfect, it is potential and 'in actuality nothing before it thinks', before it becomes adequate to thinking on its own. This is the one that is likened to the tablet with nothing written on it: it too, being suitable for being written on, has not yet been written on. This is what our soul amounts to flowing

20 away from its own substance to the outside and, being borne towards not knowing and ignorance of itself and of every formal substance, it needs to be perfected under the agency of something other. That is by itself, but by itself *qua* other, since it has departed from itself and its own substance. So it is perfected by turning back to the substantial reason-principles in itself, seeking and finding the truth about things

25 that are in accordance with them, and these are stimulated to contemplation and perfect the part of it that proceeds to the outside. Therefore the intellect that proceeds is perfected by being written on, as it were, by acquiring something and from the outside. For it is perfected by substantial activity. 'This is what happens in the case of intellect', the one that is the subject of the discussion, clearly the one that flows out and is still imperfect or is perfected in disposition and

30 projection. For only the one that is substantial by its pure activity and remains in itself and operates from itself is perfect.

430a2 And it is itself intelligible like the intelligibles. [In the case of things without matter what thinks and what is being thought are the same. For theoretical knowledge and what is known in this way are the same].

He next deals separately with the second problem.[409] For it is precisely this, thinking itself or being able to think itself, that is characteristic of intellect. Therefore even the still imperfect intellect is intelligible as being potentially intelligible by virtue of the first level   35
of potentiality, and the perfected one is intelligible in a superior way by virtue of the second kind of potentiality, and is adequate to think itself on its own, both as being already perfect and as being in a state of equality with the substantial intellect and being close to it, it being intellect in act. For if even the perfected intellect is potential, it is so by the second level of potentiality. But if the intellect too is intelligible like the intelligibles, and the forms in matter are already intelligible,   237,1
it will have something in common with them and not be unmixed in respect of them. And it will not be simple, if the intelligible is specifically other than the intellect, as is shown by the being intelligible but not intellect being present to things in matter. For things which are the same in definition necessarily coincide. Look at the way Aristotle approaches this. 'In the case of things without matter', he   5
says, 'what thinks and what is being thought are the same', using the causal conjunction 'for' to indicate the reason why the intellect is intelligible. For it is entirely immaterial – it is difficult even to contrive the notion that it holds together some body – and turns to itself where even opinion, which is the last rational capacity of the soul,[410] is fully attended by belief: the assent to it as true is completed in accordance with opinion's returning to itself, judging as true its   10
understanding about things. Since therefore the intellect is immaterial, it is altogether intelligible in that it thinks itself. In the intellect in act what thinks and what is being thought are specifically the same, because every cognitive activity is determined by the object of cognition and is what the object is: this is already true of sense-perception, but applies to knowledge *a fortiori*. Indeed the better the form   15
of cognition, the greater is its unification with the object of cognition.[411] Since sense-perception is predominantly cognitive of things situated in matter, by virtue of the forms in those, but not of the forms in itself, for that reason it is not strictly the sense-objects. But knowledge is predominantly contemplative of the forms and reason-principles in itself, so that it can contemplate even things that are   20
caused from the viewpoint of the causes. So even if it moves over to the corresponding cognition of things that are caused, it is still the same as the objects of knowledge by virtue of the predominant apprehension of them in respect of the causes which are in it: the ones

in it, which are in the strict and primary sense objects of knowledge.
So 'theoretical knowledge and what is known in this way', in so far as
25 it is already being contemplated, and no longer in potency, 'are the
same', because the knowing reason turning to itself, having the object
of knowledge in itself and being determined in accordance with it in
the activity, sets the cognition in accordance with the determinant of
the object of cognition. That is so since there is one and the same
definition of the object of knowledge in act and of knowledge in act,
namely the definition of what is known. Saying that 'in the case of
30 things without matter what thinks and what is being thought are the
same', he adds 'for theoretical knowledge and the corresponding
object of knowledge are the same', intending that the knowledge
should be this intellect which he has already brought in, the one that
is imperfect while in potency but perfect when it is in act, and already
contemplating. For he is not using knowledge as a paradigm for
intellect, but because the words for knowledge and object of knowl-
35 edge are clearer: he is showing their mutual identity.

430a5 We must investigate the reason why it does not always
think.

What is immaterial is not altogether intelligible and always thinking,
and he does not maintain this, but only that in the case of immaterial
things the intelligible object is the same as the intellect, so that when
238,1 it is being thought in actuality it is also thinking in actuality, and
while it is potentially intelligible it is also potentially thinking. It is
none the less worth investigating the cause which brings it about that
some of the immaterial objects of thought do not always think, when
they are not actually objects of thought to themselves. The cause is
the procession through intermediates from the highest entities to the
5 lowest,[412] so that there should be no empty space. This is so since it
is necessary that the intermediates are superior to the lowest entities
as being more powerful and nearer to the things that exist primarily.
So the human soul is intermediate, or rather the reason of this kind
of soul, which he here calls intellect, intermediate between things
that are indivisible and divided, between those that are always in the
same condition and those which change entirely, and between those
10 that are entirely their own and those that exist in something else,
because it transcends the latter and does not attain the state of the
former:[413] in so far as it is on a higher level than things which are in
another it too is immaterial, but in so far as it does not attain the
state of the entities which are highest and remain in themselves it
neither always thinks simply nor is it thought in the pure sense.[414] It
is very clear that the activity of reason which departs from substantial
thinking in the direction of the imperfect and the potential is inferior.

And it seems to me that its substantial thinking itself is knocked out   15
of position in the projection of the life that proceeds, so that it
preserves its middle position in respect of the whole of itself, so that
it will do just this, project the intellect that proceeds to the outside,
and also be separate, which is what Aristotle says with the words 'and
being separated it is what it is', with 'being separated' not having a
place in the case of what has always been separated.415 How if it
always stays in the same condition, would it sometimes be sending   20
out from itself the imperfect intellect, sometimes be perfecting it and
sometimes bringing it back to itself? It is clear that our soul's substantial intellect does not simply remain in permanent turning to
itself, nor does it entirely depart from itself, like the passible intellect
which is the one that proceeds outside, so that it does not itself too
require another thing to perfect it. The substantial intellect has
relaxed its thinking to the extent that it does not simply think but is   25
sufficient to itself for its own perfection, sometimes so that it perfects
the intellect that proceeds, standing apart from that one at the
highest level, and with a complete retreat to itself when it is separated
and is what it is. The middle position is the reason why not even the
substantial intellect simply remains. Now the philosopher's discussion is sometimes about the intellect that has proceeded, which does   30
not always think, either because it stands apart from the substance
that perfects it as a result of the great extent of its outflowing, giving
itself as a whole to sense-perception and imagination and, to put it
simply, to the life of the body, and therefore remaining imperfect, or
because it is impeded from contemplation even if the intellect that
proceeds is already perfect. One of these happens because it occupies
itself intermittently with practical matters, because of the high
degree of division that appears in what proceeds, the other because   35
it produces much business because of the body and the fortunes that
befall it from outside, and also because of the imaginings that are
stimulated in an indeterminate way. About the immaterial intelligible he says that it is the same as the intellect, before he explains about
the intelligible in matter: in the middle he has made the point about
scientific reason because it does not always think, so that, having
completed the discussion of immaterial intelligibles he can go on to   40
the one about intelligibles in matter.

430a6 In the things that have matter each of the objects of   239,1
thought exists only416 potentially.

Not as being able to become an object of thought to itself (for this is
so only in the case of some immaterial objects of thought), nor because
it can sometimes become an object of thought to something else. For
even if it were always being thought by something else and never by

itself it is potential, just as the already living body is said to have life
5   potentially,⁴¹⁷ in so far as it does not live by itself or through its own
agency, but in an acquired way. The thing in matter which is intelligible to something else is imperfectly intelligible. For it is not adequate to being thought in its own right, if it is not what is thinking,
being other than it. Therefore it will be imperfectly intelligible,
needing something else to be thought, being potential belonging to
10 what is imperfect. So that what is said about immaterial objects of
thought and those in matter will in a way be homonymous, or like
things that are dependent on one thing.

430a7 So that they will not have intellect.

Clearly the intelligibles in matter, like the forms of those things and
composite substances. He adds the reason why they will not:

15   **430a7** For the intellect is the power of being such things without
their matter.

Showing that all intellect is immaterial and therefore not present in
things that are in matter, but that it happens to be the power of
material things, as what can potentially perfect them. Indeed in the
*Metaphysics*⁴¹⁸ it is not only in what is acted on but also in what acts
that he puts what is potential, and also in every cause which is
20 somehow potentially involved with what is caused, and which can
bring into being or perfect what is in potency. So it is reasonable that
the intellect is the potency of things in matter that are potentially
intelligible, in that it brings their potentiality to actuality in itself.
For just as he who measures is active with respect to what is being
measured, but does nothing to it, yet has the cognition of what size
it is from himself, so when one thinks things in matter one is active
20 in respect to them, but does nothing to them and is not acted on by
them, but is putting forward (*proballein*) the activity that cognizes
them in accordance with the causes of those things which are in one
as concepts.

430a8 But those things⁴¹⁹ will have intelligibility.

Intellects, since they are all immaterial, and all the immateriality is
their own and not something else's. Therefore intellect belongs to
30 itself, and that to which intellect belongs is intelligible. So all intellects will have the object of thought. And here, having completed the
discussion of the intellects that proceed he goes on to the one that
projects them and perfects them.

<CHAPTER 5>[420]

430a10 Since, as[421] in the whole of nature [there is something   240,1
in each kind which is matter (that is what is potentially all of
them), and something else which is cause and productive because it makes them all, related in the way that a craft is related
to its material, it is necessary that these differences should exist
in the case of the soul too. And there is a kind of intellect which
is such by becoming everything and another which is what it is
by producing everything, as a sort of disposition, like light. For
in some way light makes potential colours into actual colours.
And this intellect is separate and impassible and unmixed,
being in its substance activity. For what acts is always of a
higher status than what is acted on, as is the principle as
compared with the matter. Knowledge in act is the same as its
object. But knowledge in potency is prior in time in a single
person, but in general it is not prior even in time. But it
sometimes thinks and sometimes does not.[422] And when it is
separated it is only that which it is].

I think that not even this is said of the intellect that is participated
by soul or the one that is even superior to that, but rather about our
rational soul.[423] I make the first point because the whole treatise is
about the rational soul, the second because he himself clearly adds   5
'these differences exist in the soul too'. We shall adduce all the things
said after this which do not go beyond the consideration of the soul.
So, keeping to what has previously been said, after the secondary
intellect which he has already talked about, the one which departs
from the predominant substance of soul and therefore from the
activity that goes with it, and proceeds to secondary lives and contemplations, be they imperfect or perfect, but perfect in projection and   10
being perfected as by something else by the forms that remain in the
first kind of being, he now investigates the intellect that exists by the
same substantial activity and thinks the forms, not the ones that
proceed but those which remain in the substance of the soul itself.
For the inclination to the outside is brought down to a sort of division
(for the being outside is precisely this, some kind of division) and   15
proceeds to a secondary life in the soul, which is not what the first is,
and divides up the activity of the substance, not only of the first but
also of the activity that has been projected, so that the activity is no
longer substance, but merely in contact with substance, just as the
soul's ascent to its own highest substance and its remaining in it
unifies the activity with the substance because of the complete
turning inside. The 'inside' shows the indivisible bringing together.   20

But the summit of the soul is immediately joined with the intellective substance above it and the forms in it.[424] For all intellective substance above the soul is indivisible.[425] Hence the activity is what the substance is and the substance is activity not, clearly, in its specific nature but because the two are brought together indivisibly to be one.

25 So the summit of the soul, being joined to the intellect that is above it, has indivisibility to a high degree. And for this reason its activity is unified with its substance secondarily. So as in the case of the intellect that has proceeded and is not yet perfect its activity was likened to sense-perception,[426] not as being altogether the same (the difference was pointed out) but because of their being acted on from elsewhere, so now he likens the activity of the soul's highest and

30 substantial intellect to the intellect above it, not because it is exactly the same. Indeed he immediately brings in the difference, since he says that this intellect is sometimes active and sometimes not,[427] and that when it is separate this one is what it is,[428] whereas that one is always active and is always separate. If, to resume, the soul's highest substance remains altogether the same, the activity which does not

35 remain the same would not be what the substance is, if it sometimes thinks and sometimes does not think. And (i) if this its highest substance does not remain unmixed in its inclination to the secondary things, so that it will be intermediate in this respect too, as Iamblichus thinks in his own work *On the Soul*, not only between things divided and undivided but between things which are generated and ungenerated, perishable and imperishable, and (ii) so that this too

241,1 should happen, namely that it sometimes thinks and sometimes does not (acting of itself and remaining exactly the same it would always be being active in exactly the same way, and would not sometimes be projecting secondary functions and be involved with these and remain involved and inseparable from them, but would sometimes be being separated. Perhaps this is just what the separation is, the indestruc-

5 tible pure state of the substance, which Aristotle indicates when he writes 'and when it is separated it is what it is',[429] in as much as the faculty that is still not separated from the secondary things is not what it is) <given (i) and (ii)> it is reasonable, or rather necessary, that not only the activity but also the substance of the soul, and that the highest substance, I mean of our soul, should be somehow differentiated and loosened and, as it were, occupy a lower place in its

10 inclination to the secondary things. It will not depart from itself entirely (for it would not be remaining soul) but will no longer preserve its purity so that it keeps itself as the same and not the same at the same time, without the otherness changing it altogether or the sameness remaining pure and unchanged.[430] And so being divided in some way by the change and not remaining what it was, it undergoes

10 division of the activity from the substance so that it sometimes does

not exercise its activity. But when it has run up without admixture
to its own substance, and abandoned all its projection outside, when
it has been strengthened by its turning and picked up again the
measure appropriate to it, it is what it is and, being collected together
without parts by the high-level turning to itself, it unites its activity
too with its substance. And this highest perfection of the soul consists   20
in its complete separation from secondary lives. But in the inseparable involvement with these it is perfected and is perfect in a secondary
way, and the life that is already adequate to perfect the projected life,
either practically or theoretically, not being, clearly, imperfect would
itself be perfected, but it is not yet perfect in accordance with the
high-level measures in such a way as to be its own alone. But it leads
itself forward and goes up to its own high perfection according to the   25
measures of perfection for other things in virtue of which they exist.
Let us now go on to discuss the text itself.

430a10 Since as in the whole of nature there is something in
each kind which is matter (that is what is potentially all of
them), and something else which is cause and productive because it makes them all, related in the way that a craft is related
to its material, it is necessary that these differences should exist   30
in the case of the soul too.

Nature has not been taken as a more common term standing for any
kind of existence (for acting and being acted on do not occur in every
kind of existence,431 so that in everything there would be something
analogous to matter and what makes), but what has been defined
specifically as the principle of motion and rest. Matter and what   35
makes are in the things that exist according to nature and those that
incline to these things, acting and being acted on, strictly in the case
of the things in the realm of becoming, but also by analogy in the case
of the heavenly bodies and of our soul, whenever it proceeds to nature
(this kind of soul is also a subject for the physical philosopher432), since
when it remains purely in itself, it remains itself exalted, neither   242,1
acting nor being acted on nor having anything analogous to matter
and not being the subject of investigation by the physical philosopher,
but rather by the one occupying himself with metaphysics, as he
himself said in the *Parts of Animals*.433 We have set out the text which
shows this in the preface.434 So when our soul, having inclined
towards nature, projects the secondary lives in itself and from itself,   5
it no longer remains intact what it was, but has a part that is passible,
which is the lives that proceed outside, and an active or causative
part which is the life that produces things. And that is matter not
simply (for it is not like corporeal matter) but, as he himself said, in
its kind, that is by analogy. The cause of the producing is the life that

10   produces things, as if it were stretching out its activity to something
other which exists in potentiality and is subject to becoming. And the
one exists by becoming everything, the other by producing as many
forms as there are in – clearly – the intellectual soul that proceeds
outside. It is these forms by which the soul that proceeds is affected,
while the one that projects them brings them into being. He does well
to compare the craft with the maker and matter with the thing which
is being acted on, since craft, in the strict sense, is the disposition of
15   the soul which produces in accordance with reason[435] in the area of
material things.

> **430a14** And there is a kind of intellect which is such by becom-
> ing everything [and another which is what it is by producing
> everything, as a sort of disposition, like light. For in some way
> light makes potential colours into actual colours].

The 'such' is the one like matter. This refers to the lowest level. How
it is like matter he has shown: it is 'by becoming everything'. The other
is such as it is 'by producing everything as a sort of disposition, like
light. For in some way light makes potential colours into actual
20   colours'. And because the substance of the soul which produces the
secondary kinds of life does not put these forth somewhere outside,
but receives them in itself and does not remain entirely separate from
them, but is itself involved with them, and in some way comes to
belong to them, it is well compared with a disposition and with light,
as it was with a craft before because of its transcendent position. For
25   in its inclination to the secondary beings it both remains in itself in
a way, and proceeds to the outside, as has already been said.[436] The
craft applies rather to the characteristic of remaining and being
separate, the light and the disposition to the being inseparable and
being tied up with secondary things.[437] For light is inseparable from
the things that are being illuminated and the disposition from those
that have it. But as in its inclination to the outside it produces a
30   faculty and is in a way transcendent, and at the same time is joined
with the ones that proceed, it is rightly portrayed as producing, at the
same time as craft, as disposition and also as light. And it is worth
mentioning that, when he has likened it to a disposition by virtue of
its involvement with secondary things, he has added 'like light', and
then conducts the rest of the discussion about light and not simply
about the disposition, since the disposition which is rather a quality
35   is not at all appropriate for a substance which can be separated
whereas light, even if it is present to what is being illuminated,[438] is
so as an entelechy, and as being separated from what is at the time
receiving it. Even if in its inclination the soul's substantial intellect
is involved with the one that proceeds, it is nevertheless sometimes

separated and stands on its own, as he himself immediately adds. So
far he is explaining how the active or productive part of the soul is
comparable to light. By saying that light by being present makes   243,1
things which are colours in act, but objects of vision in potency, into
objects of vision in act, he shows the likeness to the intellect that
makes the forms in the passible intellect which are potentially knowable actually knowable, showing at the same time that they were not
in the passible part potentially in such a way as to be entirely[439]
non-existent, but as existing and yet not being cognizable, like colours   5
which are from time to time not illuminated.

430a17 And this intellect is separate and impassible and unmixed, being in its substance activity. For what acts is always
of a higher status than what is acted on, as is the principle as
compared with the matter.

'Separate' in the case of the intellect which is the subject of the present   10
investigation is not to be understood as 'the one that is always in a
state of separation' (he will add, with reference to it as being separated sometimes, 'when it has been separated it is only what it is'[440])
but as sometimes being already separated from all the activity that
is directed to the outside, or as being prepared for separation. In both
ways it is separate and impassible and unmixed, and in its substance
activity, in somehow pressing on towards these kind of pure existents   15
or being disposed according to them. But it is said to be separate not
only in respect of body or the faculties to do with body, but also in
respect of the rational and practical ones, and those that are theoretical in connection with projection in their departure from these.
It is impassible because it is not brought to perfection by something
else or through otherness or by participation, but because it is being
perfected or is already perfect in act by its own agency. In fact, even   20
if it is perfected by the superior intellect, it is so perfected not having
been torn away from it, but being joined to it and unified with it by
virtue of its own high substance, so that it is united in the best
possible way with what perfects it and, becoming what the thing that
perfects it is, it is adequate to perfect itself. So it will be separate in
its substance from the things which it does not require for its exist-   25
ence or its activity, even if it is still somehow mixed up with them in
so far as it brings them into existence by a kind of inclination.
'Unmixed' is the intellect that is not in any way involved, or the
one that is naturally like this and strives towards it. 'Being in its
substance activity' because of its undivided turning to itself, not
parting the activity from its substance, so that the substance can be
activity and the activity substance. For if the intellect that proceeds,
whenever it thinks itself, is the same as the object of thought, that is   30

as itself, and the activity is the same as its substance (for its substance is an object of thought, and the thinking is activity), by how much the more will this be true of the intellect that remains as a whole in itself and never departs from itself or the things that are above it? Whence, by virtue of its unification with the best things, it is productive of the intellect that proceeds on account of otherness, and is perfected as by something else and for this reason is acted on, and it is the principle
35   as perfecting cause of what is in potency, which is the matter, clearly being of higher status as being superior and because of this having a superior kind of unification. And why would anyone say the soul's intellect differs from the true intellect if, in addition to the rest, it were 'in its substance activity'? Perhaps just as the passible intellect
244,1 which is still imperfect was compared in respect of its impassibility and potentiality with the sensitive faculty – how it differed was defined later – so he applies what has been said, which in the first place was appropriate to the more divine intellect and then secondarily to the soul's substantial intellect, because of its kinship with it, to the soul's highest intellect, which was being compared with the higher
5   intellect: he brings in the difference next.

Let us for the moment comment on those points. On the one, how will this much vaunted separate intellect of the soul,[441] differ from the one that proceeds, if it too proceeds? Why would not the one that remains and the one that proceeds be the same? And the other, why is not the intellect that has proceeded also an object of thought as much as intellect, if being an object of thought is in every way a
10   property of intellect, even if being intellect is not necessarily a property of an object of thought? How can he call it intellect but not make it an object of thought since he wants the forms, which are the things that are thought, to be in it, so that it is intellect in its own right, but an object of thought by acquisition?[442] To this one must say, and it has already been said,[443] that the intellect that proceeds, being still imperfect, is neither intellect nor object of thought in act, but is both in potency and is being perfected from elsewhere, namely from
15   the substantial intellect. But the perfected one is intellect and object of thought in respect of being potential in the second way, so that it is capable of sometimes being active and thinking itself on its own account, but is passible because it is perfected by something else. So the object of thought which corresponds to it comes out with the intellect and is perfected with it. But the philosopher,[444] because of its special characteristic, puts the intelligible before the intellect, as
20   the former shows substance and the latter rather activity, and as the intelligible is an object for the intellect to aim at, while it aims at the intelligible as its end, and if the name of intellect also extends to imperfect being, but the name of intelligible does not. That he attributes rather to the forms which remain and perfect, and to those that

have been perfected in the intellect that has proceeded. These are the ones that he says are inscribed,[445] not the ones that are imperfect and in potency, but those that are already perfect and in act.

The former of the points we have brought up for comment has already, I think, been adequately cleared up before this. The soul's substance remains intact in its pure unification with itself and the high entities, but sometimes it undoes its unification and departs from itself in its inclination to the secondary things. It then remains, so that it may exist, but not intact, in so far as it is already putting forth (*proballein*) secondary lives from itself, while in putting these forth (*probolê*) it remains what it was, and does so even more in its deviation towards them. For the second form of life is a substance since even the lowest is. But that one is rational and intellective potentially, but nevertheless second to the one that produces it in so far as what is caused is inferior to the cause,[446] and in so far as what proceeds as a whole is inferior to what remains in some way, and also in so far as what is potential and is being perfected from elsewhere is inferior to what is in act and perfected from itself. Therefore even this never falls into ultimate imperfection, but into a looser kind of perfection. But what proceeds sometimes even becomes altogether imperfect. So he does well to say that our soul's intellect is double,[447] the one that remains and the one that proceeds, and this one is either imperfect or perfect, and the one that remains remains altogether or somehow.

And since these things have been put in order, let us now hear what the philosopher tells us about the difference between the intellect that receives its substance in respect of the highest part of the soul and the higher intellect, both the participated and the unparticipated one, since he has investigated what it has in common with it in terms of being separate and impassible and unmixed and being activity in substance.

430a19 Knowledge in act is the same[448] as its object. But knowledge in potency is prior in time in a single person, but in general it is not prior even in time. But it sometimes thinks and sometimes does not.[449] And when it is separated it is only that which it is.

In which he shows the first difference, that the soul's summit is not only intellect, but also reason: for knowledge is a rational form of cognition. But now he calls knowledge what he called intellect which is activity in its substance, showing that knowledge in act is the same as the object of knowledge, which is the thing known, but not as in the case of sense-perception another form apart from the sense-object. And again Plato's best interpreter[450] makes it clear to us what he means by saying that what always exists is 'apprehensible by intellect with reason',[451] that is that the highest form of the soul's cognition is at the same time intellection and knowledge. Intellect is simply the

15   higher one. This then is the first difference because of the reason's subordination to intellect, and that of cognition to the object of cognition. And just as what has come into being, when it exists, falls short of what exists without having come into being, because of its involvement with the potentiality of not being, so what sometimes thinks and sometimes does not think, even when it thinks, has the potentiality of sometimes not thinking, and does not have either intellection like that which always thinks, or the unification with the

20   object of thought. For the unification of the more accurate form of intellection is greater. The soul's intellect when it has been separated will be activity in its substance, but not in the same way as the intellect which is always separate. For our intellect, when it has not yet been separated, because of its cognition in respect of secondary things, which is unseparated,[452] does not unite its activity with its substance completely and to the extent that it is in its nature to do,

25   but still does so in a less perfect way, which he called being in potency, since it has the natural capacity to be perfected. And he says that the potential knowledge is prior in time in the single person. This is very true in the case of things that come into being: for every kind of coming into being proceeds from the imperfect to the more perfect. Therefore the imperfect, which is the potentiality in the one thing that is coming into being, is prior in time, since in the proximate cause what is in actuality must exist before what is potential in the thing that comes

30   into being by its agency. So the addition of 'in the single person' is a good one. In the case of things which are everlasting but sometimes think and again sometimes do not think, what is potential is not prior even in the individual. Why this rather than what is in act when they take turns with each other? Therefore Aristotle does not, in the case of the soul, think that the potency is prior in time, but that this truly belongs to it, that it sometimes thinks and sometimes does not think.

35   Indeed if in the composite human being the potency is prior, nevertheless this intellect is the soul's substance which is separable, as he immediately adds, giving us at the same time a third difference relating to the soul's intellect as compared with the higher one, and to the identity of the cognition with the object of cognition. For he says 'when it is separated', not always separate. It is agreed that the intellect which is not participated by soul is always separate, and so

246,1   too in every way is the participated one. For that one is not the soul's, but the soul belongs to that one. That one remains in itself and makes contact with its own soul without inclining. This soul of ours which by its inclination and deviation produces secondary lives, and is involved with them and lives not by the kind of life that remains alone,

but also by the kind of life that departs and proceeds from it, and then 5
is again being separated, when it is disposed according to what is at
rest in it alone, being, as he said, only what it is, and not anything
else such as the thing that thinks which comes into being in the
projection, which was in the unseparated life. Therefore even when
it has been separated, in so far as it is by nature such as to sometimes
live in an unseparated way, it will not even then have the being
separate in the same way as what is always separate. In so far as 10
thinking itself goes with what is separate and immaterial, and
thinking itself is activity in substance, in so far as the separation of
the soul's intellect is inferior to the separation in the superior one, to
that extent the identity of the activity with the substance falls short.

430a23 And this alone is immortal and everlasting. We do not
remember because this is impassible, while the passible intel- 15
lect is perishable, and without this it thinks nothing.[453]

It is worth commenting on the whole argument by which he is
encouraged to declare that the soul's substantial intellect is immortal
and everlasting, so that thereby we may admire his harmony with
Plato,[454] and also his greater working out of details, which Plato
handed down in a more general and synoptic way appropriate to his 20
earlier time. It is not the case that because he only used the word
'movement' of a continuous and divisible entelechy he was not prepared to attach it to the soul as not being divisible, since if you change
the word 'self-moved' and into 'self-living' and 'self-perfecting', 'self-
producing' and 'acted on', it will become clear that the whole argument starts from this point. Indeed even in Plato 'self-movement' 25
shows a certain duality in the soul.[455] The 'self-', which he also
habitually uses of the highest forms, applies to its being at rest and
to its formal and productive nature,[456] while to the 'moved' belong its
being passible, proceeding, being perfected and being determined. So
Aristotle starts from here and shows that the productive element in
the soul, which Plato himself had said was separable and impassible 30
and unmixed, is a principle and a kind of being that is causal and of
a higher status than matter and everything that comes into being (for
he has taken matter to stand for what comes into being), and also
that it is activity in its substance because of its indivisible combination with the form. From there he takes its being immaterial (for
everything that is in matter is divisible) and active with respect to
itself, and shows that everything immaterial thinks itself.[457] And 35
when he has shown that it is simultaneously thinking and object of
thought and simple, in so far as it does not think with a part of itself
and is not being thought with another part, but that the whole of it
does both, he shows that it is immortal and everlasting. For what is

separate and simple and its own and gives itself life and perfects itself, in such a way that in its inclination to the outside secondary lives and beings gush forth, is shown to be not only incapable of receiving death and destruction, but also to be predominantly the

247,1 bearer of life and being, and thereby immortal too. So the whole argument, to put it together concisely, is something like this: it is clear that the question is only about our soul. In our soul there is not only what is acted on but also what acts, the principle and cause of

5 the things that happen. Further what acts in the soul is able to think itself and unites its activity indivisibly with its substance. The principle and cause of the things that happen, and what is activity in its substance, is separable and simple. What is separable and simple belongs to itself and is not in anything other. This sort of thing cannot admit its opposite, lack of life and lack of substance (it will never

10 admit the contrary in itself nor in anything else, since it belongs only to itself). So what acts in the soul, being unable to admit death and destruction, turns out to be necessarily immortal and indestructible, not primarily because of its inability to admit them,[458] but, as has been said, on account of the fact that in its inclination to the outside it sources secondary substances and faculties.

This, as we have said, is discussed by Aristotle entirely in harmony

15 with Plato's exposition starting from the soul's being self-moved. That it is about the soul, and not about the intellect participated by it nor, *a fortiori*, about the unparticipated intellect, but about our soul, has already been commented on by us and one could deal with it from even more points of view. For how will potentiality and sometimes not thinking or sometimes being separated fit the entities above the partial soul? Nor is being immaterial and thinking and being thought

20 simultaneously or being completely separate in any way appropriate to those of our corporeal lives or, *a fortiori*, to the souls of other living beings or of plants. This then is, I think, clearly and necessarily concluded, that what only acts in the soul is immortal and everlasting. He has done well to add 'everlasting', as Plato added 'indestructible' in the *Phaedo*, so that we should not, like Boethus,[459] think that the

25 soul, like being ensouled, is immortal in so far as it does not stand firm in the face of advancing death, but departs when death advances on what is alive and is destroyed.[460] But why 'and this alone is everlasting'? It is because, as he indicates clearly, the passible intellect is perishable.

Someone might raise the question how that too, being intellect, is destroyed, if it too is immaterial. For every kind of intellect is held to

30 be immaterial, and for this reason every kind of intellect is intelligible, but it is not also the case that an immaterial form is also an intellect. The passible intellect is material and potential and precisely this, passible and imperfect intellect as a whole, so long as it is

passible. And for this reason it is perishable *qua* passible. It becomes immaterial and intellect in act and intelligible in contact with what acts, perfectly immaterial and perfect intellect in its ascent to the one that is active. So that the destruction of the passible intellect does not 35 consist in its moving out into not-being, but in the coming together with what exists in a superior way of the separated substance of the soul as it raises itself up to even the life that has proceeded,[461] which no longer proceeds but exists in the state of remaining as in its cause. Therefore the passible intellect *qua* passible is perishable. And as it were objecting to the soul having been shown to be everlasting, he 40 asks how we do not remember things before birth if it had previously existed everlastingly? By this it is clear again that his discussion is about the soul, and not about the higher intellect. For what sort of 248,1 problem would he have had about why we do not remember, if it is the things superior to us that are everlasting? And the solution to the objection is appropriate to soul, namely that the intellect that acts is impassible and for this reason immortal, while the passible intellect is perishable *qua* passible, as I said, as also when it is being brought together with what is at rest, and without the passible intellect, *qua* 5 passible and proceeding as far as corporeal lives, the impassible intellect clearly thinks none of the things that can be remembered, which is what Aristotle is talking about.

Those things, as he himself teaches us elsewhere,[462] are things that can be imagined. Therefore in thinking about things that can be remembered we do certainly need the reason that proceeds as far as the imagination, and without this[463] not even the impassible intellect 10 will think any of the things that can be remembered. The 'nothing' must not be understood simply as meaning that the impassible intellect thinks nothing without the passible one. For how will it still be separate, how unmixed, how activity in its substance? For even while it is still giving life to this body, the soul sometimes lives and thinks separately. 'What god is always', he says in the *Metaphysics* book lambda,[464] 'that we are sometimes', clearly as far as our power 15 allows. But god is always separate: and therefore we too are, even if only sometimes. We are the ones who are still living this physical life, when the soul is, even if only briefly, disposed to the body and the secondary lives, but in such a way as not to be attached to them.

Notes

1. Since Iamblichus it had been customary to assign a single *skopos* or purpose to each of the works of Plato and Aristotle: once done this limited the scope of possible interpretations. In the case of the *de Anima* the purpose of the work was of particular importance since, if it could be shown to be the rational soul, namely reason and the intellect that was part of the soul within the individual human being, interpretations which allowed the highest part of the soul to transcend the body-soul compound were thereby excluded. The matter is raised at the start of the commentary (1,21ff.) and recurs repeatedly: the question is now asked with respect to the third book in particular since that deals with the highest sections of the individual soul, so that the answer controls that to the question about the purpose of the whole *de Anima*. As the treatment of chapter 5 shows, the discussion is not without an element of circularity.

2. As opposed to immortal beings which have souls and in particular the heavenly bodies.

3. This sentence should be read in the light of the standard Neoplatonic doctrine that all entities strive towards a cognitive union with those above them. Thus by thinking about the highest level of our souls we may put ourselves in a position to understand superior souls and intellects.

4. That is the soul up to and including the faculty of sense-perception. This topic is, of course, continued in chapters 1 and 2 of book 3. That is convenient for Ps.-Simplicius' immediate argument, cf. 172,11-16. For Ps.-Simplicius' explanation of the continuation, cf. 173,2-3.

5. The Greek word here translated as 'soul' is *zôê*. While its normal, and basic, meaning is 'life', this writer frequently uses it to mean soul, faculty or activity: see index. Similar uses of *zôê*, though much less frequent, may be found in Philoponus' commentary on the *de Anima*, cf. e.g. 17,24, 214,24, and Priscian's *Metaphrasis*, 6,12; 29,5.

6. Throughout the commentary the commentator moves freely between the professed position that the soul is a single continuum and the expository convenience of treating it as if it can be cut into horizontal slices.

7. I translate *nous* as intellect throughout: it is used in a variety of senses, including deliberative and practical reason, in the former case often without qualification, as well as both human and supra-human forms of intellect.

8. All Neoplatonists believed that only intellect in the strict sense can know itself, because in the act of cognition it is identical with its objects, cf. e.g. Plotinus 5.3.3: the doctrine is derived from *de Anima* 3.7, 431a1-2. Reason, on the other hand, has its objects separate from themselves and each other, whereas in intellect, micro- and macrocosmically, they are all together and, *qua* intellects, identical with each other.

9. Reason is Ps.-Simplicius' addition. Whatever Aristotle thought, the commentator would not attribute any form of self-knowledge to a level of soul that was not at least somehow connected with reason and intellect.

10. i.e. sense-perception.

11. Ps.-Simplicius will attribute this belief to Iamblichus, cf. 174,39.

12. It is possible that Ps.-Simplicius is here thinking of the thesis in Plotinus 6.7.6 that even in the intelligible the forms of living beings must have sense-perception: on this difficult text see now P. Hadot, *Plotin. Traité 38. VI,7* (Paris 1988) ad loc. It is, however, more likely that he is referring to the semi-divine beings, demons and others, with which later Neoplatonists filled the space between humans and gods, cf. e.g. Iamblichus, *DM* 1.3 = 8.15-9.1 P. What the unapparent mortal beings are is even less clear: species unknown but assumed to exist?

13. Ps.-Simplicius is probably not yet talking about one sense perceiving the objects of another, the question discussed at 425a22f.

14. cf. Aristotle's remarks at *Sens.* 444b20-8.

15. Aristotle later puts worms, ants and bees together as not having imagination, cf. 428a9-11.

16. Of existence, or perfection.

17. Ps.-Simplicius seems to be making the point that even a lower animal, which may not even have all the senses, can still be perfect – or complete – as a member of its own kind.

18. While *horistikon* here and in the previous sentence may mean 'defines' it seems more likely in this instance to refer to the provision of form rather than the formulation of a definition. Hence 'determines', which I use for most occurrences of *horos* and its cognates. The widespread use of *horos* etc., in that sense, apparently peculiar to this commentary, is one of the features of it which indicate that it is not by the real Simplicius.

19. This is probably what the text means if *holôn* in line 40 is correct. Perhaps, as Steel suggests, it should be replaced by *atelôn*: the translation would then be '... determines the kinds of things that are imperfect too'.

20. One might ask why Ps.-Simplicius does not consider the possibility that it is made of more than one but fewer than all four elements.

21. This looks like a concession to hylozoism of the kind that Ps.-Simplicius will normally make only when discussing the lowest levels of the soul.

22. i.e. those on the surface of the body.

23. Reading *dusmetalêptikon* for *dusmetalêpton*.

24. Though I have translated the text as it stands, understanding *stoikheiôn* with *tôn allôn*, I suspect *stoikheiôn* should be read in place of *entelekheiôn*.

25. I capitalise Fire here, since it seems to mean something other than the element *tout court*: perhaps the commentator is talking about the *Sphere of Fire* that surrounds the air above the earth, cf. Aristotle, *Meteor.* 341b12-21 and Simplicius, *in Cael.* 42,22-7. It is called *hupekkauma*, something below the level of burning, because, as Aristotle there explains, it is in a state just below the threshold of actual combustion.

26. The problem here is that while this Fire appears to qualify for being a medium, for vision by its transparency and hearing by its permeability by sound, fire has been excluded from the elements which can be a medium.

27. i.e. Aristotle.

28. It is not clear whether this comment is Iamblichus' or the commentators' own. Both arguments are discussed above, 173,17-174,7.

29. It is not immediately clear whether the subject of this verb is Aristotle or Iamblichus, but since Aristotle does not say this in the text under discussion and the idea of a superior sort of sense-perception is Neoplatonic anyway (see next note), it is probably Iamblichus. In that case the whole passage down to the resumptive particles, *men oun*, in line 14 may represent Iamblichus' own views rather than just being the commentator's account of them.

30. The sense-perception of the heavenly bodies had been a topic of interest to

Neoplatonists since Plotinus, cf. *Enn.* 4.4.24,12ff. In this commentary they are already envisaged in the superhuman beings of 173,9.

31. These characteristics may be no more than logical consequences of the *apatheia*, 'not being subject to affections'.

32. This is true, for Ps.-Simplicius, only by way of contrast with what comes below, since all entities except the highest are dependent for their existence and power on what is above them.

33. 'Senses' and 'sense-perception' both translate *aisthêsis*, which in each case has to be understood from the context but cannot always have the same meaning.

34. It is therefore different, and so not an additional sense at the same level as the five.

35. Later the commentator will treat common sense as if it were on a higher level than the five special senses, cf. e.g. 195,30-3.

36. Taste and smell, not mentioned here, must come under the heading compound or composite. These senses are discussed at 154,37-158,8.

37. It is characteristic of late Neoplatonic commentary to divide discussion of a text into its general philosophical content (*praxis*, *pragmata* or *theôria*) and the significance of the actual words used, *lexis*: for an example cf. Olympiodorus, *in Cat.*, with explicit transitions from *theôria* to *lexis*, e.g. 28,20-1, 37,14-15. In this commentary the system is not yet firmly established (cf. nn. 280, 321), but its beginnings can already be seen in Proclus, cf. A.-J. Festugière, 'Modes de composition des Commentaires de Proclus', *Museum Helveticum* 20 (1963) 77-100.

38. I repunctuate: *aisthêsin* (*panta gar ... aisthêta estin*), removing the colon after *aisthêsin*, adding the parentheses, as in editions of Aristotle, and substituting a comma for the full stop after *estin*. With a full stop after *estin*, as printed by Hayduck, following his practice with all the lemmata, the sentence structure is disrupted.

39. cf. *GC* 2.2, 329b22-330b29.

40. Qualities that can undergo affections, *pathêtikai poiotêtes* are not mentioned in *Physics* 8, or elsewhere in the *Physics* apart from book 7, 244b5a, in a sentence restored to the text by Prantl from Simplicius, who quotes it at *in Phys.* 1057,24-6. Therefore *hebdomôi* should probably be read for *ogdoôi* – unless, of course, the commentator misremembered the book. *Pathêtikai poiotêtes* do figure several times in the *Categories*, e.g. 9a28; 35-6; 9b2-7.

41. The third premise is a version of 424a26-7, the conclusion comes at 425a9-10.

42. This probably means that it would be composed of some other element.

43. i.e. the existing sense-organs.

44. Ps.-Simplicius hereby excludes the possibility that the fifth element, *aithêr*, could be the material of a sense-organ.

45. I translate *dunamis* as 'power' rather than 'faculty' here and in the following lines because it refers to each sense rather than the faculty which controls all five of them.

46. Reading *autois* for *autê* (on which Hayduck rather pointlessly changed the accent from circumflex to grave): the latter makes no sense after *tis* while *khrômenê* needs an object.

47. An odd expression, since the Greek word *pêro-/ô-* entails the idea of impairment of a natural condition.

48. Deleting *to anapalin* in line 12, where it makes no sense: perhaps it has climbed up the page from line 14, where it is appropriate.

49. These words explain *amesos*, 'direct': Ps.-Simplicius is saying that there is no way the division could be done by interposing other terms.

50. If this parenthesis is meant to be part of the argument, it is circular.

51. I here use these three words to translate the term *sunaisthêsis* to avoid making any assumptions about the commentator's views on consciousness. [See also Editor's note on p. 148.]

52. I understand *aisthêsin* here, though the writer may have in mind something like *tên de allên aisthêtikên zôen*, in contrast to *tên haptikên zôên* of line 35. I suspect *haptomenê* (sc. *aisthêsis*) should be read rather than *haptomena* (sc. *zôa*).

53. i.e., here and just below, mediums.

54. At 425a2-8.

55. There is a certain inconcinnity in Aristotle's text, generally unremarked, because of the shift from 'more than one' (*pleiô*) to 'both' (*amphoin*).

56. At 176,37-8, but the mole is not mentioned there.

57. By Aristotle.

58. 177,1-3.

59. At 425a1-2.

60. While *akoê* and *osphrêsis* usually mean the senses, they may also mean the machinery that operates them, as here, or even the organs themselves, as in a well-known poem of Sappho, fr. 31 (Page), 11-12, where *akoê* is used in the plural. Ps.-Simplicius seems to be unaware of the fact that in the *de Sensu* Aristotle has the organ of smell made of fire, cf. 438b20-5.

61. Or perhaps, 'a substance between the two', i.e. air and water.

62. i.e. the fire of the lemma.

63. It is the *dio*, 'therefore', and not the modal *an*, which is relevant here, suggesting that *an* in line 9 is a mistake, and that it should be replaced by *dio* (the suggestion is Steel's).

64. Plutarch (the Athenian Neoplatonist, not to be confused with his better known namesake from Chaeronea) appears to have written the only commentary on the *de Anima*, or at least book 3 of it, between Alexander's lost commentary and those of Philoponus and the present commentator: on this see further pp. 9-10 of the introduction to this volume. On Plutarch's interpretation of this passage, for which Ps.-Simplicius provides the only evidence, see further D.P. Taormina, *Plutarco di Atene. L'uno, l'anima, le forme.* Symbolon 8 (Catania 1989) 195-6.

65. I translate *zôa* here and in the lemma as 'living beings' rather than the animals used by translators of Aristotle because that is clearly how Ps.-Simplicius took it, otherwise he could not have made the comment about zoophytes: that is not Aristotle's reason, and does not follow from what he says. Nor is it a useful explanation since Aristotle allows for ordinary animals with limited powers of sense-perception.

66. *ara*.

67. i.e. of their own volition and not in a random manner or one outside their own control.

68. This is not the point in Aristotle, who gives the mole as an example of a defective animal, cf. *HA* 4.8, 533a2-3, in a passage where he discusses eyes under the skin, 532b34-533a12.

69. Inserting *tên* after *pronoian*: the second article could easily have dropped out after the first, and without it it is difficult to make sense of the sentence. *Pronoia* here seems to stand for the caring nature of the previous sentence.

70. The commentator is assuming the Stoic theory of providence which sees it as an originative cause: it operates *proêgoumenôs*, 'primarily' or 'antecedently', or, as we might say, 'up front', cf. e.g. *SVF* II.1157. Thus any suggestion that it applies only after something has come into existence is inappropriate: what happens as a result of something having been brought into being in a certain way is a cause that follows, or is consequential, *aitia hepomenê* or *epakolouthousa*. On the meaning of *proêgoumenôs* cf. R.W. Sharples, 'Responsibility, chance and not-being (Alexander of Aphrodisias *mantissa* 169-72)', *BICS* 22 (1975) 49, with notes on pp. 60-1.

71. 'Progression' here translates *proödou*. For Neoplatonists *proödos* – typically rendered as 'procession' – usually implies movement from the higher and better to the lower and inferior.

72. Reading *autês* for *tês*.

73. 1.3, 270b26-31 (not 1.2 as Hayduck).

74. With the text as it stands *peri tên ousian autôn*, one would have to translate 'concerned with their substance in respect of ...', but this cannot be what the commentator means since he goes on to say that the senses cannot cognize substance. Therefore one must either read with a strong stress on the qualifications, which I do by translating '... only in respect of ...', or assume something has dropped out, e.g. *peri ta* by haplography before *peri tên*, translating '... the senses are concerned with <what attaches to> their substance ...'.

75. This parenthesis shows that 'nine' refers to the categories other than substance which are knowable through the senses and that Ps.-Simplicius is not, as might appear at first sight, working with a total of nine rather than the standard ten, as in Simplicius, *in Cat.* 11,6-7.

76. *kinêsei*, excised here by Ross against the testimony of MSS and commentaries, cf. 183,4.

77. Ps.-Simplicius has passed over the common sensibles listed by Aristotle and gone straight to the next question in the *de Anima*, perceiving the objects of one sense by means of another. It is curious that he does not use Aristotle's example of sweetness which he discusses below, at 184,17ff.

78. Ps.-Simplicius appears to have omitted a step in his explanation. The sensation that has happened before is the perception of the bitter by taste: what is missing is that it must have been seen as yellow at the same time, so that the sight of something yellow now carries with it the associated perception of something bitter.

79. Thus coming under cause and effect and therefore not incidental.

80. Thus the commentator has two kinds of sense-objects perceived directly, *kath' hauta*, but only those that are perceived by a single sense of which they are the specific objects are perceived directly *and* primarily. So size, shape etc. seem to overlap the direct:incidental division.

81. 'As it were', *hoion*, looks odd, since the thesis that there is a special sense for the common sensibles would certainly be an objection to the view that there are only five senses. It is not, however, an immediate objection to the conclusion of the previous section, that no sense would be missing in perfect living beings.

82. Though Ps.-Simplicius uses *entelekheia* here and *energeia* in line 6 (twice) I think there is no difference in meaning.

83. The word translated 'attention' is *probolê*. While most translators in this series have used the same translation, 'project', for this word, wherever it occurs, and similarly 'to project' for the associated verb *proballein*, I think those translations are not appropriate in all contexts. The choices I have made, together with the appropriate references, may be found in the Greek-English index. When the translation 'project' is not used, the occurrences of the Greek term will be indicated.

84. These words are given as a lemma in A, but are printed by Hayduck as part of the commentary on the previous lemma, though they do not belong to what goes before.

85. The lemma as printed by Hayduck has *kai to* twice: the articles do not, of course, show in the translation. Editors of Aristotle follow family E in omitting the first *to* and the second *kai*, which Ross and others report as being in Ps.-Simplicius' lemma. In fact it is not in A, so unless Hayduck found it elsewhere it is simply his mistake. It does not appear in Ps.-Philoponus' citation, *in DA* 458,24. Omitting the first *to* is supported by the previous *hoion megethos*.

86. The difference being, according to Ps.-Simplicius, that when we 'see' darkness nothing happens: we do not see light, cf. *in DA* 68,25-6. Aristotle himself describes darkness as unseeable, but an object of discrimination by the sense of sight, *DA* 2.10, 422a20-1.

87. With *autê*, 'itself', referring to the antecedent *stasin*, 'rest'. If it refers forward to the faculty then 'not by the perceiving faculty itself being moved'.

88. Reading *suneisagei* for *suneisagein*: in A, which does not usually abbreviate *-ein*, this final syllable is represented by a standard abbreviation.

89. *to (sunekhes)* is the reading of A, not *tôi* as reported by Hayduck.

90. I think this means simply that in a plurality the units which form it are juxtaposed and continuous in that way.

91. At 182,30-2.

92. i.e. the common sense's.

93. The two qualities, e.g. yellowness and sweetness.

94. Ps.-Simplicius seems not to be making the same point as Aristotle. While Aristotle's is that the common sensibles are not a kind of special sensible, the commentator is telling us that the perception of colour and the perception of a common sensible by sight are simultaneous.

95. i.e. the common sense produced by the unity of all the special senses.

96. i.e. the special senses.

97. The reference to the possibility of error indicates that 'what is left' refers to the identification as bile rather than to the quality (bitterness) that is not directly perceived.

98. i.e. one sense perceiving the common sensibles.

99. See n. 64. This passage is not in Taormina's collection of fragments.

100. The Greek is equivalent to *to plêthos tôn aisthêtôn diaphorôn ontôn*, 'the multiplicity of sense-objects which are different'.

101. For a Neoplatonist probably an implication that if body were better and less divided, division being a function of descent in the ontological scale, there would be no need for a plurality of senses.

102. i.e. with the special sensibles.

103. That is the other properties, previously and now again exemplified in *DA* by size and number: shape is not mentioned here.

104. I translate *hautê*, the reading of A, as well as the best MSS of Aristotle: Hayduck reads *autê*.

105. i.e. the sense of sight.

106. At 425b5.

107. Colour does not stand in the same relation to white and black as the common sensibles do to the special ones. Perhaps a scribe substituted *khrôma*, 'colour', for *megethos*, 'size' (cf. lines 3 and 8), here because of the adjacent colour terms: it would make sense to say that size stands to white and black as the common sensibles to the special ones.

108. 171,4-8. At the beginning of the commentary the purpose of the whole treatise is defined as being about the soul in mortal living beings, as opposed to that of the heavenly bodies, cf. 3,29-30.

109. The order of the words is different from the text of *DA* 424b25, but the meaning is the same.

110. Though it makes little difference to the meaning perhaps *monou* should be read for *monon* (187,28).

In what follows self-consciousness ('perceiving of perceiving') is explained as being due to the rational soul turning back towards itself (*epistrephein eis heautên*). The same verb is used for its turning back towards the source from which it derives its being; cf. n. 112 and indexes. (Ed.)

111. 'Penetrates' translates *diêkon*, a common Stoic term for one kind of matter penetrating or pervading another.

112. cf. Proclus, *Elements of Theology* 16: 'all that is capable of reverting upon itself has an existence separable from all body' (trans. Dodds).

113. In introducing reason into the discussion the commentator is going beyond Aristotle's claim that we perceive that we are perceiving by perception. In doing so he is apparently using two Neoplatonist theories: the first that higher entities exercise their power at levels below their own, to an extent that varies in proportion to their rank in the hierarchy (cf. e.g. Proclus, *ETh* 56 and 60), so that having reason influences the nature of our sensitive faculty; the second that what is perceived through the senses is referred to reason for processing, identification and validation, cf. H.J. Blumenthal, 'Plotinus and Proclus on the criterion of truth', in P.M. Huby and G.C. Neal (eds), *The Criterion of Truth. Essays in Honour of George Kerferd* (Liverpool 1989) 257-76, repr. in H.J. Blumenthal, *Soul and Intellect. Studies in Plotinus and later Neoplatonism* (London and Brookfield VT 1993) Study IX.

114. Reflexivity and self-knowledge become increasingly possible as one ascends the ontological scale, but in the fullest sense they are characteristic of intellect and can only happen at that level, cf. already Plotinus 5.3.4.3ff.

115. In referring to organs the commentator here perhaps also has in mind the faculties which work through the organs.

116. That is to say that our power of sense-perception is exceptional as compared with that of other beings that have it, and differs from the normal power by being, to the extent that it is, rational; hence it has the same name without being identical.

117. Here the commentator is limiting the self-awareness of vision to particular acts of seeing at any given time, saying that it can tell us nothing about the sense itself. That would then be in the province of reason. The sequel shows that for him the same applies, *mutatis mutandis*, to the other senses.

118. This is why it is not on the whole self-stimulating, even though most Neoplatonists thought of sense-perception as being more active than did Aristotle, cf. e.g. Plotinus 4.4.22,30-2, and E.K. Emilsson, *Plotinus on Sense-perception: a philosophical study* (Cambridge 1988) 126-33. Proclus took a more Aristotelian view, cf. H.J. Blumenthal, 'Proclus on perception', *Bulletin of the Institute of Classical Studies*, 29 (1982) 6-7.

119. *sunaisthêsis*; see n. 51.

120. Ps.-Simplicius splits into two what is a single argument in Aristotle, based on the mutual exclusivity of a further sense which, like the five, will cognize its own activity or having yet another sense that will do this, with the infinite regress that that entails.

121. Ps.-Simplicius goes beyond Aristotle, who confines his remarks on senses knowing their own activity to sight and hearing.

122. It is not clear whether this refers to all five, or just sight and hearing: possibly the *prôtai*, 'first', in line 25 is a mistake for *pente*, 'five' (CS): in that case the translation should read, 'then the five senses are ...'.

123. Ps.-Simplicius does not refer to Aristotle in the plural, and it is not clear to whom he is referring. The best candidates would be Alexander and Plutarch, though Plutarch is, at least sometimes, elsewhere cited by name.

124. It is not immediately clear what the commentator means by this. The most likely explanation seems to be that *qua* perceptible colours are potential until actually perceived, so that they are actualised by the sensitive faculty operating: the faculty works by making judgements about what happens in the sense organs. If this is correct Ps.-Simplicius is here simply assuming the Neoplatonic view of how sense-perception works, cf. e.g. Plotinus, 3.6.1,1-2; Proclus, *in Tim.* 2.83,28-9; 3.286,16-20.

125. Reason provides patterns against which sense-perception is able to identify its objects, cf. Plotinus 6.7.6,1-18; Proclus, *in I Eucl.* 13,13-18, and for further discussion my 'Plotinus and Proclus on the criterion of truth' (see n. 113).

126. This may include the cognitive activity of the higher soul as well: if so it is active *a fortiori*.

127. Understanding *zôên*.

128. cf. n. 125.

129. See above 189,34-8.

130. Though it does not show in translation, Ps.-Simplicius, as he sometimes does, has changed the order of the words in the original text. Nevertheless they are clearly meant to be a quotation.

131. Compare Proclus' thesis that all objects of cognition are cognized by the corresponding form of cognition, intelligible object by intellect, rational ones by reason, the objects of opinion by opinion and so on, cf. e.g. *Platonic Theology* 1.3 = 1.15,18-21 (Saffrey-Westerink).

132. The words quoted look as if they should form a separate lemma, but neither A nor the MS used by Asulanus writes them as such.

133. It might be more normal to speak of imagination imitating sense-perception since it retains and reproduces the data provided by sense-perception. Ps.-Simplicius appears to be putting it the other way round because he wants to stress the active nature of sense-perception.

134. i.e. an external object, not the body in which the sense or its organ is located.

135. 190,34 Hayduck prefers the *tauton* (with crasis and rough breathing on -*u*-) to the *to auto* of A and the E family of Aristotle, which I would restore.

136. It is unusual for Ps.-Simplicius to quote a previous lemma as he does here.

137. This is not what Aristotle says.

138. From an Aristotelian point of view this is hardly worth mentioning since there is only one thing, the unmoved mover, to which it does not apply. For a Neoplatonist, however, it applies to all the contents of intelligible being, in the strict sense.

139. cf. 172,4-8 and n. 1.

140. The point of these words, *to holon touto* is not clear: if they are not to be dismissed as a gloss they must mean (a) the sound taken together with the perception of it, as a whole, as opposed to sound simply, or on its own, or (b) the whole phrase, that is all the words in the lemma.

141. Lemma: Ross and other editors of Aristotle print the impossible form **eipeien*, weak aorist optative ending on a strong aorist stem, from C, presumably preferred as *lectio difficilior* to the *eipoi* of Ps.-Simplicius' lemma. A. Jannone, in the Budé edition, prints *eipoi*, apparently as an emendation.

142. Aristotle seems to have invented the word used here for hearing, *akousis*, for the purpose of this discussion, perhaps on the analogy of *psophêsis*, sounding, itself a rare word but attested for the fifth-century comic poet Cratinas. Their rarity is presumably why the commentator finds it necessary to explain what the words mean.

143. Ps.-Simplicius seems to be labouring this point, even by his standards, because he is engaged in the Neoplatonic quest to show that the sensitive soul is active and impassible, while at the same time giving due importance to the role of external stimuli in sense-perception.

144. 'The movement is in what is moved', *Phys.* 3.3, 202a13-14, explained and argued for in the rest of that chapter, 202a14-b29.

145. See n. 125 above.

146. Ps.-Simplicius seems to be making two points here: he is stressing, as ever, the active nature of sense-perception and also saying that the sense-organ's being acted on involves the actualisation of its potentiality to be affected by a sense-object.

147. This is the movement in the sense-organ, referred to in line 11 as *aisthêtikôs zôn*, 'being alive in a way pertaining to sense-perception'.

148. Though these remarks might suggest a form of idealism whereby the external world only really exists in the mind, they apply only to the external world *qua* object of perception: that remains potential until it is perceived. The other view is attributed to Democritus and rejected at 193,27-30.

149. While the sense of these words is clear in Greek, it is obscured in English for want of two different terms to distinguish (1) hearing=the sense and (2) hearing=what happens when the sense is in operation. In the translation, in the words 'hearing in act', 'hearing' has sense (1); in 'an act of hearing' it has sense (2).

150. Democritus is hardly an appropriate representative of 'earlier physical philosophers', whom one would otherwise take to be those before Parmenides, but Ps.-Simplicius may have taken the words to refer to all those earlier than Aristotle himself. Ps.-Philoponus, commenting on the same passage, says Aristotle is referring in a riddling way to 'Protagoreans', *Tous Prôtagoreious ainittetai, In de An.* 475,23. In any case Democritus did not think that the objects of sense had no existence of their own, but that the way their secondary qualities were perceived depended on the percipient subject, cf. Theophrastus, *de Sens.* 63-70 = DK 68A135, pp. 117,27-119,26. A less than careful reading of this report could easily produce Ps.-Simplicius' understanding of Democritus' theory.

151. This lemma should be read in A as translated, *ei dê*, and not *ei d'hê*, 'if the ...', as in our texts of Aristotle. The commentary that follows shows that the latter was not what Ps.-Simplicius thought the text should be, but the text in front of him may have divided the words in this way and so provided his starting point. He may, of course, have found it in Plutarch's commentary, with the comments he reports.

152. Ps.-Simplicius' approves what looks like an emendation by Plutarch to *ei dê*. This gives better sense with the word order Ps.-Simplicius has, viz. *sumphônia phônê tis*, since Aristotle has so far been talking about sound and not combinations of sounds. His order is the same as that of the MSS of Aristotle, the order printed by Ross, *phônê sumphônia tis* is based on Ps.-Philoponus and Sophonias: it gives the same sense as Plutarch's – or Ps.-Simplicius' – explanation of his text.

153. Both 'proportion' and 'ratio' translate *logos*, but the second explains how the first is produced. Later in the same section of the commentary (lines 37,38 and 195,2 and 10) *logos* is used in another of its senses, namely reason-principle, the formal representation of another level of reality.

154. Though it is not clear that the adjective *kritikos*, 'that discriminates', applies to both nouns, the fact that they are stated to be what sense-perception is, and that sense-perception certainly discriminates, strongly suggests that it does. *Logos*, 'proportion', is described as *kritikos* below, 195,10-11.

155. Understanding *dunamis*, since a sense, or even sense-perception in general, cannot be described as *ousiôdês logos*, a real reason-principle, or reason as something substantial. At best it can be called reason when some excuse is offered, as in the next line, to take account of the fact that it works under the influence of reason in those beings that have it.

156. On the relation of soul to Form and intellect in this commentary see Steel, *The Changing Self. A Study on the Soul in Later Neoplatonism: Iamblichus, Damascius and Priscianus* (Verhandelingen van de Koninklijke Academie voor Wetenschappen, Letteren en Schone Kunsten van België. Kl. der Lett. 40, 1978. Nr. 85/ Brussels 1978) 126-9.

157. In *DA* 1.4, 407b27-408a34.

158. Though in many cases 'discriminate' would be a better rendering of *krinein* and its cognates than 'judge', I have often retained this traditional translation because of the difficulty about using 'discriminate' with a direct object in English.

159. Undivided because belonging to the soul alone and therefore exempt from the division which is – Neoplatonically – characteristic of body, a view which was justified by interpretation of *Timaeus* 35A.

160. Ross prints *luei*, 'loosens' or 'undoes', rather than the *lupei*, 'hurts' or 'causes pain', of Ps.-Simplicius and the Aristotelian MSS. *Luei* is derived from Priscian, *Metaphr.* 22,26-7. Unless he found it in Theophrastus, this difference is another small piece of evidence for distinguishing Priscian from our commentator.

161. These words show clearly that Ps.-Simplicius regards the common sense as superior to the special ones in the hierarchy of the soul's faculties. Cf. his earlier remarks on it not being a sixth sense like the others, 175,5-10.

162. The limit being the end point of the relaying of information obtained through the senses for appraisal. Here it is the 'common sense': in other contexts it may be the reason.

163. Understanding *khrômatos*, 'of colour', from the previous sentence.

164. So Ps.-Simplicius is excluding the lower soul which informs the body as a whole to concentrate on the sensitive soul's relation to those parts of the body which it requires for its operations. How this works is explained in the following lines.

165. For the notion of the sense being in the sense organ in so far as it uses it cf. line 10 above. The commentator is here transferring to the level of the sensitive soul a distinction he has already made at the lowest level of soul to bridge the gap between Aristotelian and Platonic psychology, cf. n. 63 to ch. 1, splitting the faculty so as to allow a lower phase of it to be involved with the body, while maintaining the soul's impassibility by having a higher phase which uses the body, as it were, from above. For the idea of the soul using the body in sense-perception cf. Plotinus 4.7.8,2-4.

166. This combines Aristotle's idea that sense-perception receives the immaterial form of the object with the Neoplatonic notion that what is received in the sense-organs is translated into something like immaterial thoughts for the soul to process, cf. Plotinus 4.7.6,22-4.

167. At 428b28-31.

168. The commentator is clearly talking about immaterial activities.

169. That is, equipped with soul.

170. In other words in the indivisible point of time mentioned in line 22 above.

171. The idea that the common sense is comparable to the centre of a circle is already to be found in Plotinus, 4.7.6,11-15, but he found it in Alexander's *de Anima*, so that Ps.-Simplicius may have found it in Alexander's (lost) commentary. On Plotinus' dependence on Alexander here – one of the few points where it can be demonstrated – cf. P. Henry, 'Une comparaison chez Aristote, Alexandre et Plotin', in *Les Sources de Plotin* (Fondation Hardt. Entretiens sur l'Antiquité Classique 5, Vandœuvres 1960) 433-5.

172. cf. line 4, above. The word *peras*, 'limit', also occurs in the passage from Alexander referred to in the previous note, which may account for its use here.

173. Aristotle does not. One wonders whether Ps.-Simplicius himself has repunctuated the lemma, which editors of Aristotle print with a comma after 'we judge', *krinomen, tini kai aisthanometha hoti diapherei*: most editors and translators also accent the *tini* to be interrogative, 'with what', rather than indefinite, 'with something', have no comma before *hoti diapherei*, 'that they are different', and a heavy stop after it. In fact the comma before *hoti diapherei* seems to be Hayduck's own.

174. Understanding *antilambanetai* or *antilêptikê estin*.

175. It is very difficult to make sense of lines 5-8 as they stand. With Hayduck's text the translation would be something like this: 'For it is sense-perception that cognizes individual sense-objects, since opinion apprehends them together with sense-perception whenever it announces them as individuals, or does so through sense-perception, if it goes up from them to the universal or, when it also identifies individuals, it is operating together with imagination'. But (1) there is no obvious difference between opinion working with or through sense-perception, *met'aisthêseôs ê di'aisthêseôs*, (2) I see no clear meaning for opinion identifying individuals by opinion with sense-perception, since identification is not what sense-perception does (3) that is a function where imagination is necessary because (a) it presents information to the higher soul and (b) it is the basis of memory. I therefore propose deleting *hotan hôs atoma legêi* in line 6, where it makes little sense, as a doublet for the virtually equivalent *hotan ta atoma legêi* in lines 7 and 8.

Possibly *meta phantasias* means by using an image rather than the faculty of imagination: 'that does not affect what has been said above, since the image is there because the faculty is'.

176. Ps.-Simplicius has *prôton*, 'first', where Aristotle has *eskhaton*, 'last' or 'ultimate', because the commentator is looking at the process from the soul's end, Aristotle from the beginning of the process at the body's outer surface.

177. It is not clear whether Ps.-Simplicius is here talking about Aristotle's *sumphuton pneuma*, connate *pneuma*, or the Neoplatonic pneumatic vehicle which carries either the whole soul or, for those who unlike like Ps.-Simplicius believed in two, its lower faculties up to and including imagination. In either case we learn from his exposition of the chapters on motion that the, as it were, semi-material *pneuma* is given the role of link between the fully material body and immaterial soul, cf. 301,17ff. and Ps.-Philoponus, *in DA* 588,1-4. For further discussion cf. H.J. Blumenthal, 'Some Platonist readings of Aristotle', *Proceedings of the Cambridge Philological Society* n.s. 27 (1981) 9-12 and 'Soul vehicles in Simplicius', in S. Gersh and C. Kannengiesser (eds), *Platonism in Late Antiquity* (Christianity and Judaism in Antiquity 8, Notre Dame Indiana 1992) 182-6, repr. in *Soul and Intellect* (see n. 113), Study XVII.

178. Lines 17-18 below show that Ps.-Simplicius is not taking Aristotle's *aisthêtêrion*, 'organ of touch', in its obvious sense, but is interpreting it as if it were the sensitive soul, *hê aisthêtikê psukhê*.

179. These words come after the next lemma.

180. I take *kekhôrismenois* as an ethic dative with *endekhetai*, 'it is possible'. It would also be possible to take it as an instrumental dative with *krinein*, 'to judge', and translate: 'to judge with separate things'. In the end the point would be much the same, since it is that there must be a single thing exercising the judgement with the same part of itself at the same time.

181. *noerôs*, a level of existence and cognition the late Platonists introduced between discursive reason and intellect in the strict sense.

182. The argument so far seems to be this: either the percipient subject knows that, for example, a taste and a colour are not the same in a period of time, which is divisible; or he does so at an instant. In the first case he must not perceive the taste in one part and the colour in another part of that period, but both in all of it. In the second case he does not perceive the difference in time, since an instant is not time.

183. For sense-perception as a complete activity of the soul cf. perhaps already Theophrastus fr. 27,3-6 FHSG (53,5-9 Wimmer).

184. The commentator is probably thinking of the transition, *metabasis* or *diexodos*, that Neoplatonists frequently use to characterise the activity of the soul which reasons as opposed to the intellect which has direct apprehension of its objects, all simultaneously. This type of distinction goes back to Plotinus, cf. e.g. 5.3.17,23-4 and 5.9.6,7-10 and for further discussion H.J. Blumenthal, '*nous* and Soul in Plotinus: some problems of demarcation', in *Il neoplatonismo in oriente e in occidente* (Atti del convegno internazionale dell'Accademia dei Lincei, Rome 5-9.10.1970, Problemi attuali di scienza e di cultura, Rome 1974) 207-9, repr. in *Soul and Intellect* (see n. 105) Study II.

185. If we admit that we do not know the identity of this commentator we cannot say whether he did or did not actually write a commentary on the *Physics*. Priscian is not known to have done so. The real Simplicius, of course, did, and it is possible that this reference was added by a glossator who assumed that our commentator was the real Simplicius. It might, of course, be used as evidence that he was. For time made up of instants, like units, cf. *in Phys.* 728,20-3, for physical time, as explained by Iamblichus, allegedly reporting Archytas, 786,11-787,4. But the real Simplicius' *Physics* commentary does not really address the issues discussed here. On the commentator's reference see further Steel (1997) 122-3.

186. cf. e.g. 1.3,186a34-b35; 2.1,191b22-32.

187. The commentator appears to be switching between discussing 'inseparable' and 'undivided' because he is interpreting 'inseparable' as meaning 'undivided'.

188. It is not clear how this example of fire having opposite effects on different substances bears on the discussion of opposite sensible qualities.

189. I suspect the words *hê autê*, 'the same', should be deleted from line 8, where they may have been inserted under the influence of *hautê*, 'this', at the start of the sentence. The translation would then be: 'perceptual discrimination is not a movement, or ...'

190. The tongue is still the subject: in *tautês paskhousês*, line 12, *tautês* refers back to *glôssa*, 'tongue', in line 10.

191. Ps.-Simplicius comments on this lemma suggest that his text included *khronôi*, 'in time', as well as place and number, as in some MSS and the lemma in Ps.-Philoponus, cf. also his quotation in the commentary, 484,10-11. Ps.-Philoponus does not, however, have *topôi*, 'in place'. Jannone, in the Budé edition, has all three. On the other hand when Ps.-Simplicius is citing the text at lines 24-5 he cites only place and number.

192. Editors of Aristotle print these words as a question. In fact a straightforward denial of the preceding proposal is appropriate.

193. A comma is needed after *ou* in line 37 since the negative goes with *tôi einai*, 'in its being', cf. the lemma.

194. cf. *Metaphysics* Z 13, 1039a7, *hê entelekheia khôrizei*, 'the actuality separates'.

195. Neoplatonic psychology tended to be particularly interested in sense-perception for the light it throws on intellection, thus giving a different emphasis to their discussions and Aristotle's. The parallel is enshrined in the Greek language as well as in the philosophical tradition: thus *noein*, the philosophical word for thinking began its career in Homeric Greek with the meaning 'to see'. On this cf. esp. K. von Fritz, 'NOOS and NOEIN in the Homeric poems', *Classical Philology* 38 (1943) 79-93, and '*noos* and *noein* and their derivatives in Pre-Socratic Philosophy (excluding Anaxagoras)', *Classical Philology* I, 40 (1945) 223-42 and II, 41 (1946) 12-34.

196. These are Neoplatonic rather than Aristotelian points: higher, intelligible, being is characterised by lack of division and motion, which belong to the sensible world where what is undivided above becomes diffused and divided below.

197. *enülou*, 'in matter', make no sense here, since locomotion, even circular, does not belong to immaterial being: circular motion is the motion of the fifth element. While the received text could theoretically be defended by arguing that the spheres are immaterial, the next sentence indicates that they are not what the commentator is talking about. I suggest *aülou*, without matter.

198. For this Neoplatonic principle cf. n. 131 above.

199. Here again divisibility relates to ontological level. For the principle cf. Proclus, *ET* 61, and for the intermediate position of soul ibid. 190.

200. Ross has accepted Trendelenburg's *dis* against the MS consensus *dusi*, which is in Ps.-Simplicius' lemma. Since the whole discussion is about using one thing as two, *dusi* is almost certainly correct and should be restored to the text of Aristotle. *Dis* would undermine the argument, since the whole part of the point is that two things should be perceived at the same time, cf. 426b26-9. At the end of the lemma I translate Ross' *kekhôrismenôs*, the reading of A and some MSS of Aristotle. *Kekhôrismenois* here is Hayduck's emendation to make it conform with line 19: the comment does not have to reproduce the text.

201. Keeping the lemma *hen, heni* as in Ps.-Simplicius: Ross' *heni, hen* is a conjecture, but *hen* naturally picks up the preceding *duo* in 'it judges two things', cf. the previous lemma. 201,21 *hen, heni* against Ross' *heni, hen* (*DA* 427a14).

202. I read *autê hê aisthêtikê psukhê* for the dative *autêi têi aisthêtikê psukhê* which would depend on *khrêtai*: since the sensitive soul is the subject of this verb it makes no sense to have it as its object too.

203. The majority of MSS of Aristotle as well as Ps.-Philoponus have *krinein* or *tôi krinein* here: Ross follows those which have *tôi phronein*, 'by understanding', but, probably rightly, omits the article.

204. Aristotle sets up a faculty of appetition, *orexis* or *orektikon*, which subsumes both physiological drives and mental decisions to seek a goal: this faculty overlaps all three parts of Plato's soul, cf. 432b3-7. Plotinus regarded *orexis* as a separate faculty of the lower soul, cf. H.J. Blumenthal, *Plotinus' Psychology* (The Hague 1971) 31-7, and most later Platonists followed him in this. Ps.-Simplicius himself has both a rational and an irrational appetition, cf. 289,40-290,1. Aristotle discusses the role of his faculty, together with imagination, in initiating movement in 3.9-11.

205. Aristotle, while talking about the relation between thinking and imagination never actually calls imagination intellect. Platonists after Proclus frequently did so, some identifying it with the *pathêtikos nous* (to use their terminology), 'passible intellect', of *de Anima* 3.5; cf. Philoponus *in DA* 6,1-11, Ps.-Philoponus *in DA* 523,29-31, 542,1-18. Proclus, who did not accept the identification, refers to those who did, without identifying them, at *in I Eucl.* 52,20-53,20 (cf. also *in Tim.* 1.244,19-22, 3.158,5-11): some have assumed this refers to Aristotle himself, cf. e.g. G. Morrow, *Proclus: A Commentary on the First Book of Euclid's Elements* (Princeton 1970) 41 n. 6. On the whole question of imagination and passible intellect cf. Blumenthal, *'Nous pathêtikos* in later Greek philosophy', in H.J. Blumenthal and H.M. Robinson (eds), *Aristotle in the Later Tradition* (Oxford Studies in Ancient Philosophy. Suppl. vol., Oxford 1991) 197-205.

206. At 427b6-7, eighteen lines after the 'since' which begins the sentence.

207. cf. 427a9 and n. 187 above.

208. Fr. 31B106.

209. Fr. 31B108.

210. *Od.* 18,136.

211. Aristotle is here using *phronein* in a general sort of way to mean any kind of thinking, rather than the practical wisdom which it means when used in a technical sense, especially in the *Nicomachean Ethics*.

212. At *Theaet.* 151E,2-3.

213. Both Aristotle and, in a different way, the commentator seem to be misled by their assumption that words in Homer meant the same as in the classical language. Whereas *phronein* and the noun from which it is formed do often mean something like 'to think', *nous*, 'intellect', and its cognate verb usually do not: the noun has a meaning closer to 'disposition' or 'mind-set', as in the words Aristotle quotes at line 26, the verb generally means to perceive, cf. n. 187 above. Ps.-Simplicius' attempts at the end of this section to reconcile the Homeric poems with a proper distinction between sense-perception and thought should be read in this light.

214. The lines of Empedocles which Aristotle quotes do not in fact equate the two, and it is not clear why he thought they did, unless it was by focusing on the 'present' in 'men's wisdom grows according to what is present to them'.

215. '... of men who live on earth', as compared with the gods, *Od.* 136: 'feeble' is the commentator's addition from a few lines before: 'the earth nourishes nothing weaker than a man', line 130. Neither is in the text of the *de Anima*, so it is interesting to note that he either looked up the passage, or knew it anyhow. This explanation suggests the Neoplatonic – and Platonic – view that even the higher faculties can be impaired by excessive concentration on the physical world. On Aristotle's treatment of Homer and Empedocles see further Hicks, ad locc.

216. 1.2, 404b8-15; 405b11-15.

217. cf. 27,26-38; 33,5-15.

218. It is not clear whom Ps.-Simplicius has in mind. Of philosophers before Aristotle Democritus is the most likely candidate, cf. e.g. 404a28-9.

219. Though several of the Presocratics thought perception was of like by like, the reference to touching the unlike suggests that the commentator has Democritus as well as Empedocles in mind, since he too thought of sense-perception as a form of touching, cf. *Sens.* 442a29-b1.

220. Who were these? Alexander and Plutarch are the only known authors of commentaries on the *de Anima*, but since both are several times mentioned by name in this commentary the absence of a name here may indicate that the commentator has another, or others, in mind.

221. i.e. with both of the contraries or opposites.

222. At 427b11-12.

223. I have adopted CS' suggestion that *oikeiotês*, 'assimilation', should be emended to *enantiotês*, 'opposition': the former, though appropriate to the discussion of like by like cognition, is inappropriate here, and the lemma, as well as some of the preceding commentary, is about opposites. The error could easily have arisen from the other occurrences of *oikeio-* words in this section of the commentary. For the idea that opposition belongs to the living being cf. line 28, whose wording, *pôs oun to enantion autôi legei oikeioteron;*, could have helped produce the error here.

224. i.e. the soul with the body.

225. The word Ps.-Simplicius uses here, *rhopê*, like its virtual synonym *neusis*, always indicates inclination downwards and has a pejorative sense.

226. We have already noted the Neoplatonic view that too much concern for the body is deleterious to the operation of the higher soul, cf. n. 215 above. The point about thinking being a turning to oneself arises from another Neoplatonic view, that the intelligible world is to be found in each one of us as well as 'outside', cf. already Plotinus, 5.1.10,5-19, where Plotinus also talks about alienating oneself from the body if one is to rise to what is above. For the identity of thinking, truth, and being, cf. e.g. 5.5.3,1ff.

227. Though *theôria* in Neoplatonic texts most often means contemplation, of a higher entity by a lower one, it not infrequently retains the meaning of investigation or thinking about something, and I have so translated it in the comments on this lemma, and elsewhere where appropriate.

228. *tois atimôtatois huparkhei zôois*: perhaps Ps.-Simplicius has in mind *PA* 1.5, where Aristotle talks about not neglecting the study of any animals be they more or less prestigious, ... *mête atimôteron mête timiôteron*, 645a6-7, and not turning up one's nose in a childish manner at the investigation of the less prestigious ones, *peri tôn atimôterôn zôôn*, 645a15-16.

229. This may refer either to the collection of premises, or using the method of collection and division.

230. cf. 427b11-12.

231. Ross, following Madvig, excises thinking, *noêsis*, against the agreement of the Aristotle MSS, Ps.-Simplicius and Ps.-Philoponus (A has *noêsis* after *hupolêpsis*: Hayduck has restored it to the position it has in the direct tradition), presumably on the grounds that Aristotle should be saying that *hupolêpsis*, 'belief', is not the same as imagination, perhaps reinforced by the singular *touto men gar to pathos* – which actually refers to imagination in any case, as the commentator sees. He has an explanation for *noêsis*, but in terms Aristotle would almost certainly not have understood, since it is based on the understanding of *nous pathêtikos*, 'passible intellect', as imagination. Perhaps the right answer is Jannone's *hautê*, which would give the translation: 'this (i.e. imagination) is not thinking or belief'.

232. See previous note.

233. i.e. dismissing the images is not *eph' hêmin*, 'within our control', in the same way as summoning them.

234. While the word *tupôtikon*, 'subject to impressions', clearly has the connotation of impressions of a material type here, that will refer to the effect of sense-object on sense-organ. In the rest of the passage the noun *tupos* has the dematerialised sense it had acquired in Neoplatonic psychology, after Plotinus had carefully distinguished it from the literal sense to be found in Stoic psychology (which prefers the derivative *tupôsis*, 'making an impression'), cf. e.g. *SVF* I.58, II.59: the second passage is from Alexander's *de Anima*, 68,11-21, where he argues that the impression is not to be equated with imagination, which for him is 'something like an impression ... from our activities pertaining to sense objects', ibid. 4-6. For Plotinus' use of the term cf. e.g. 1.1.7,9-12, and for further discussion *Plotinus' Psychology* (see n. 204) 71ff.

235. Here too division is used as an indication of lower status.

236. Aristotle MSS are divided between *esti poiêsasthai* and *esti ti poiêsasthai*, A has the former. The extra *ti* could easily have fallen out after the final *-ti* of *esti*, or been inserted by dittography because of it. In any case the *ti*, 'something', could easily be understood even if it were not actually in the text.

237. While Alexander in his *de Anima* distinguishes memory and recollection, cf. 69,17-19, this particular point was presumably made in his commentary. Cf. also *Quaest.* 3.1.81,2-3: 'Recollection is finding something through a search for an image which was formed at some time in the body in which the sensitive soul is located'.

238. It is worth noting that later commentators tend to cite Alexander to disagree with him more often than to agree, cf. H.J. Blumenthal, 'Alexander of Aphrodisias in the later Greek commentaries on Aristotle's *de Anima*', in J. Wiesner (ed.), *Aristoteles. Werk und Wirkung* II (Berlin and New York 1987) 90-106, repr. in *Soul and Intellect* (see n. 113) Study XIV.

239. i.e. understand 'opinion' in the lemma to mean 'true opinion'.

240. Has the commentator misremembered *EN* 6.3, 1139b15-18 where Aristotle distinguishes five mental activities in which the soul tells the truth from two, belief and opinion, in which it may not? The five are discussed further at 1139b18-36: this, or some version of it could, however, be the discussion that Aristotle himself was referring to. Another candidate is *MM* 1.34.7, 1196b35-7 where belief replaces *tekhnê*, practical skill, in the similar list of five ways of arriving at truth: again there is nothing about varieties of belief. This is followed by a longer discussion than that of *EN*, at 1196b37-1197b11.

241. As the following words show the point of 'in the soul itself' is to limit the kind of thinking that is at issue, since there can be no question of sense-perception not being in the soul. This is in accordance with the restriction of the contents of book 3 to being about the rational human soul and the *de Anima* as a whole to the soul in mortal living beings, cf. 171,4-8 and n. 1.

242. This point seems too obvious to be worth making: if imagination and belief are not the same as the soul's thinking, they could hardly be the same as some higher kind of thought, but the commentator may have thought that Aristotle's text allowed at least the logical possibility of such an interpretation. One would expect at least an '*a fortiori*'.

243. For a modern endorsement of Ps.-Simplicius' explanation cf. M. Schofield, 'Aristotle on the Imagination', in G.E.R. Lloyd and G.E.L. Owen (eds), *Aristotle on Mind and the Senses* (Proceedings of the Seventh Symposium Aristotelicum, Cambridge 1978) 136 n. 58. (reprinted with minor revisions in J. Barnes, M. Schofield and R. Sorabji (eds), *Articles on Aristotle* 4: *Psychology and Aesthetics* (London 1979) 103-32: see 119 n. 42, and M.C. Nussbaum and A.O. Rorty (eds), *Essays on Aristotle's* De anima (Oxford 1992) 249-77: see 264 n. 42.)

244. Ross has added an interrogative <*ara*> before *mia tis*, 'some one', at the start of this lemma. I have not translated it.

245. To account for the accusative case of both nouns I understand *legei*, 'he says', following a suggestion of CS.

246. The contrast here seems to be between the faculty in itself and its operation, which is directed outwards.

247. This distinction between scientific knowledge and intellect assumes the standard characterisation of discursive thought being about lower, more divided and more diffusely deployed representations of what exists in a higher, undivided or (compact: all together) form in Intellect.

'Determinants' translates *horoi* which is here, as elsewhere in this commentary, equivalent to Forms: on this usage cf. Steel, *The Changing Self* (see n. 156) 127-9.

248. As a presentation.

249. With the MS (A) reading *energeiai* (dative), 'in act': Hayduck's genitive, *energeias*, which would have to be understood as the activity of sense-perception, appears to be simply a mistake.

250. This sentence only makes sense if 'living being' is taken in the sense it sometimes has of the lower part of the body-soul compound, in this context as far up as body plus sense-perception and the faculties below it.

251. Ps.-Simplicius seems to be trying to rescue a rather questionable point in Aristotle's argument by suggesting that there is a sort of toggle-switch between both actual and potential sense-perception on the one hand and imagination on the other. This makes little sense on either Aristotle's assumptions or his own, since the whole point of a power in potency is that it is there all the time whether it is currently being actualised or not.

252. Reading A's *progegenêsthai*. Hayduck's *prosgegenêsthai*, to have taken place in addition, gives the wrong sense and is apparently another mistranscription on his part.

253. Ps.-Simplicius is clearly commenting on the traditional text of Aristotle, *hoion murmêki ê melittêi ê skôlêki*: Ross' *skôlêki d' ou* is Torstrik's emendation, based on Themistius, *in DA* 90,7.

254. Again the commentary, 209,27-9, supports the traditional text, *tote ê alêthês ê pseudês*, against both Hicks' excision and Ross' emendation to *poteron alêthês ê pseudês*, 'whether it is true or false'.

255. Reading *hôrismenôs*, the reading of A: the untranslatable *hôrismenous* is another Hayduck mistake.

256. The commentator is here clearly trying to make sense of the received text (see n. 237), which presents two difficulties: (1) imagination is elsewhere attributed to bees, cf. *Metaph.* A.1, 980a27-b25, where they are described as intelligent (cf. also *PA* 648a6-7) in a passage implying they have memory, which entails possession of imagination, apparently denied to them here; (2) worms are never put on a level with ants and bees or given as an example of animals having some share in faculties above sense-perception. Torstrik's emendation does not help since it needlessly complicates what looks like a clear denial, with exempla, of the hypothesis of the previous sentence. With Ps.-Simplicius' comments here cf. Aristotle's own remarks at *DA* 433b31-434a7. Worms are already distinguished from ants and bees at 173,23-30.

257. cf. n. 254 above.

258. At 427b20-1.

259. Here again the immediate intuitive knowledge of intellect is contrasted with the discursive method of reason: on their objects cf. n. 247 above.

260. For the conditions of self-knowledge cf. n. 8 above.

261. Conviction, having been persuaded, and persuasion, are all clearly cognate in Greek.

262. Ross follows Biehl in bracketing these words as a repetition of 428a19-22, but they were in Ps.-Simplicius' text, and do not as the commentator explains, say the same. Most modern editors retain them: some for a reason that Ps.-Simplicius does not stress, namely the additional point that animals cannot have the conviction that goes with opinion because they do not reason.

263. cf. 209,19-24 above.

264. The Aristotle tradition has *oude ... oude ... oude* almost unanimously, so does Ps.-Philoponus. Ps.-Simplicius and Themistius have *oute … oute … oute*: it makes little difference.

265. cf. *Soph*. 264A-B, where Plato's word *summixis* is closer to the commentator's *mixis* than is Aristotle's *sumplokê*. The *Philebus* passage he has in mind is probably 39B, which is not quite parallel, but talks of opinions resulting from sense-perception producing images (*eikones*, not *phantasiai*), more appropriate to 'imagination … produced by sense-perception; for 'opinion with sense-perception' cf. also *Tim*. 52A, where they do not describe imagination, but rather a way of knowing about the sensible world.

266. The interpretation of Aristotle in such a way as to show that apparent differences with Plato are not real, but result from misunderstanding or superficial reading of the text of Aristotle is one of the central concerns of this commentary – and many others; on this cf. this commentary's opening remarks, esp. 1,15-16, where the truth may be taken to mean Platonist philosophy; see further above, Introduction, pp. 7-8.

267. Hayduck prints *diakekrinomenôs*, an unlikely hybrid of perfect and present participial stems: it should be corrected to *diakekrimenôs*, which is what A has, but the meaning is not affected.

268. I read *hoion* for *hoson* in line 10: *hoson* makes little sense, while it is appropriate to indicate that the Stoic-type mutual interpenetration of one material object by another is only an inexact parallel to what happens when immaterial entities or, as here, activities, are 'mixed'.

269. Punctuate with comma instead of stop after *eiê*: the following words cannot stand on their own, but form a transition from this sentence to the next one.

270. Or perhaps just the character Timaeus.

271. Plato, *Tim*. 35A. This text, with some differences in interpretation, became the standard Neoplatonic account of the soul's nature, and was used to emphasise its intermediate position between fully intelligible and corporeal existence. Some, like Plotinus, found four kinds of existence in Plato, distinguishing being divided distributed among and in bodies (*peri ta sômata* and *en* [or *epi*] *sômasi meristê*) cf. the discussion in 4.2 and Proclus, *in Tim*. 2.152,9-24, others, like Ps.-Simplicius here, only three; cf. also 27,38-28,4, 254,25-9. See further H.-R. Schwyzer, 'Zu Plotins Interpretation von Platons Timaeus 35A', *Rheinisches Museum* n.F. 84 (1935) 360-8.

272. Here the commentator maintains Aristotle's clear separation of imagination and opinion, and so departs from the position of Proclus in particular. Proclus, and probably his master Plutarch, tended to blur the distinction between opinion and imagination, cf. H.J. Blumenthal, 'Plutarch's exposition of the *de Anima* and the psychology of Proclus', in *De Jamblique à Proclus* (Fondation Hardt. Entretiens sur l'Antiquité Classique 21, Vandœuvres 1974) 133-47, repr. in *Soul and Intellect* (see n. 113), Study XII.

273. Ross writes *dioti*, 'because', for the MSS and Ps.-Simplicius' *dêlon*, 'it is clear'.

274. Hayduck has *ekeinou, houper estin, homou kai hê aisthêsis*: the OCT prints *ekeinou, eiper estin, hou kai hê aisthêsis*. I retain Hayduck's text but would remove the comma after *estin* (for what it is worth: A has no punctuation at this point).

275. *Cat*. 4a26-b2.

276. The following lines of *DA*, 428b11-15 are quoted under the next lemma, at 214,30-7.

277. 'Pure', *kathara*, here and in the expression 'pure judgement' at lines 32-3 below means uncontaminated by any element of passibility.

278. On *pneuma* and the soul's vehicles cf. 197,11-12 and n. 166. 'This solid instrument', *to stereon touto organon*, is probably an allusion to the not uncommon practice of referring to the body as if it were a second or third vehicle for a soul which already has one or two semi-material ones. In such contexts the body is sometimes called the shell-like vehicle or body, cf. e.g. Proclus, *in Tim.* 3.298,27-299,4, Ps.-Philoponus *in DA* 482,11-12. It is, however, strange at first sight to find the commentator talking about the *pneuma* which is the basis for imagination being affected by our rational activities, since for those who have two soul vehicles, as he does, these would be based on the higher vehicle. His meaning must therefore be that the lower vehicle is affected by rational activity in so far as this may also affect the imagination. For further discussion see H.J. Blumenthal, 'Soul vehicles in Simplicius' (see n. 177).

279. If Iamblichus is correctly reported here he would seem to have given a more materialist account than one might expect of how imagination handles the results of the operations of higher faculties: Plotinus talked about reflections, as in a mirror, cf. 1.4.10,6-19.

280. This is one of the relatively few examples in this commentary of the division of the discussion of a text into general considerations, *theôria*, and the exposition of the actual words, *lexis*: on this division cf. n. 37.

281. The dots (...) here and in the following lines are, of course, mine and not the commentator's: they are used to show how he is reading his text.

282. What comes thereafter includes negatives, so I have inserted one here. Aristotle goes on '... be able to be present without sense-perception or in things which do not perceive' (see next lemma).

283. 'At the beginning', *tên arkhên*, is a comment on *aisthanomenois*, things which are perceiving, the point being that sense-perception is the start of a process which may lead to imagination or ratiocination. To conform with his own doctrine the commentator should have said 'and <sometimes> to our rational faculties'.

284. I accept Hayduck's *tôi* for *tên*, but that requires that the accusative *prosekhê* be changed to the – to a copyist – homophonous dative *prosekhei*. Another solution would be to keep the words of the MS but change the order, from *tên ge prosekhê kai dia sômatikên pathên* to *dia tên ge prosekhê kai sômatikên pathên*.

285. Reading *hoti*, 'because', as does Asulanus in the Aldine and his translation: A's *hote*, 'when', gives no good sense.

286. For the idea that the heavenly bodies, or the cosmos as a whole, have sense-perception and imagination, cf. already Plotinus, 4.4.6-17 *passim* and Proclus, e.g. *in Tim.* 2.83,3-15. For this commentator, who locates human imagination in the soul-vehicle, *okhêma*, it is natural that the heavenly bodies' imagination should be in their *okhêma*, namely the celestial spheres in which they are set. What they have will be a higher form of what exists here, which is described as a *prolêpsis*, a conception prior in the sense of hierarchically and axiologically, rather than, as usually, temporally superior.

287. cf. 314,12-21 and *DA* 434a5-10.

288. At 427b11-12.

289. Light is *phôs*, contracted from *phaos*: in addition to the normal genitive *phôtos*, which does not show a connection, there is another commonly used form, *phaous*, which has some resemblance to *phantasia*, 'imagination'. Such resemblances were the usual – unsafe – basis of ancient etymology, but in this case there is a real connection, even if matters are more complicated than Aristotle or Ps.-Simplicius thought.

290. I read *aisthêton*, 'sense-object', with the MSS of Aristotle, for *aisthêtikon*, 'sensitive faculty', cf. 216,3-4.

291. I have added numbers in this section to show the articulation of the commentary.

292. Aristotle, of course, says nothing about impressions on *pneuma*.

293. I have taken these words out of Hayduck's text and given them as a separate lemma: they appear to be marked as such in A at the beginning but not at the end.

294. cf. above n. 185. Apart from a further reference at 28,19-20 we have no more evidence for a *Metaphysics* commentary by the author of this one: that would remain true even if he were, after all, to be Priscian. The fact that there is no reference to one in the extent writings of Priscian is far from conclusive, since their extent is so small. The real Simplicius may have written one: a case, not completely conclusive, for its existence is made by I. Hadot in 'Recherches sur les fragments du commentaire de Simplicius sur la Métaphysique d'Aristote', in I. Hadot (ed.), *Simplicius. Sa vie, son oeuvre, sa survie* (Actes du Colloque international sur les oeuvres et la pensée de Simplicius. Paris 28.9-1.10.1985. Peripatoi 15, De Gruyter, Berlin and New York 1987) 225-45. (See also n. 185 on the references to a *Physics* commentary.)

295. For Ps.-Simplicius' method cf. the remarks in the preface to this commentary, 1.18-20, '... keeping everywhere, to the best of my ability, to the truth of things according to the guidance given by Iamblichus in his own writings on the soul'.

296. Now that the commentator has moved to the part of the *de Anima* that deals with the higher faculties of the human soul it becomes necessary for him to discuss their relation with the purely intelligible world as conceived by late Neoplatonists. These relations, or some of them, are governed by reciprocal or unilateral participation, with the entities concerned arranged in triads of terms relating as A, A and B, B (or sometimes A, not A and not B, B): the highest member of the triad is unparticipated, the middle one participates in that above and is participated by that below, the lowest merely participates. Sometimes it is not immediately clear whether the highest level of the human soul is or is not below the intellect which only participates, cf. e.g. 218,29-31. For an early and clear presentation of the system cf. e.g. Proclus, *ElTh* 23 and 24.

297. On the soul's status with respect to divisibility cf. 200,27 and nn. 159, 271, 354, 425.

298. cf. e.g. *SVF* II 114 and Long and Sedley 28D. For the Stoics it was, of course, material, cf. *SVF* II 394 = Alexander, *DA* 17,15-18,10.

299. Being adjacent to intellect, on which souls depend, entails being adjacent to forms of which Intellect consists and with which it is identical.

300. Aristotle's method of moving from lower to higher levels, exemplified throughout the *de Anima*, is the reverse of that found in independent, i.e. not directly exegetical, Neoplatonic writings.

301. I propose to read *hoti*, 'which', hence 'this', referring back to the previous sentence, rather than the MS *hopote*, 'when' or 'since'.

302. At 429a23.

303. cf. 1,21ff and 172,4-8 with n. 1.

304. The text of A, printed by Hayduck, looks like a simple grammatical error: the feminine article and adjective *tên prôtên* cannot agree with the masculine *logon*. So they should be corrected to the masculines *ton prôton*, a correction implicit in Asulanus' translation. The *prôton* which now stands in the text should then be deleted, being presumably an attempt to equip *logon* with the article required by the position of *tês psukhês*.

305. The words are those of *DA* 430a18.

306. That is because it thereby becomes assimilated to intellect where that is the case, a Neoplatonic explanation of an Aristotelian dictum.

307. Punctuating with a comma after *holôs*, and none after *autos* and *logôi*.

308. *genesiourgos*, that exists in the realm of becoming, and in particular the sublunary world, and can produce life or motion of the same kind, cf. book 1 of this commentary, 95,1, and 287,30; Simplic. *In Phys.* 1122,6.

309. Does this mean that the soul is substantially and permanently changed by incarnation, or only that the shock of incarnation causes temporary disruption? In the former case the commentator falls into the same group as Iamblichus, Hierocles, Damascius and Priscian, who all held this view of the results of the soul's embodiment. It was not shared by other late Platonists such as Plotinus, Proclus and the real Simplicius. For further discussion cf. C. Steel, *The Changing Self* (see n. 156) 63-9, 93-8, favouring the first alternative; and I. Hadot, 'La doctrine de Simplicius sur l'âme raisonnable humaine dans le commentaire sur le manuel d' Epictète', in H.J. Blumenthal and A.C. Lloyd (eds), *Soul and the Structure of Being in Late Neoplatonism: Syrianus, Proclus and Simplicius* (Liverpool 1982) 51-63, who, however, finds admittedly ambiguous evidence for substantial change in the real Simplicius too (on this see Steel's addendum, op. cit. 171, and Blumenthal in the discussion to Hadot's paper, pp. 71-2, and 'The psychology of (?) Simplicius' commentary on the *de Anima*', ibid. 91-2, arguing for the second).

310. *Platôni* should be emended to *Plôtinôi*. Neoplatonic commentators do not simply contradict Plato, and while the beginning of the discussion to which Hayduck refers at *Phaedo* 79Cff. could be taken to mean that the soul remains permanently unchanged, the rest of it merely says that it is like what remains permanently unchanged, namely the forms. The view to which Ps.-Simplicius objects is, on the other hand, an appropriate characterisation of Plotinus' notorious and admittedly unorthodox position that the individual human soul has a part permanently in the intelligible, cf. 4.8.1,1-3, a position to which Ps.-Simplicius has already objected at the beginning of the commentary, cf. 6,12-15 where he uses the same words to describe it: *menein ti autês ... aei hôsautôs ...*: here he writes *menein aei hôsautôs*. This emendation was first proposed by Steel, *The Changing Self* (see n. 156) 39 n. 26, where he gives other arguments to support it.

311. This comment, unlike some, does indicate clearly that Ps.-Simplicius did not think that we had an intellect below the series of unparticipated, participating and participated, and participating intellects: its purpose here is to show that Aristotle is not talking about even the last of these, but only a soul which participates it. Even Plotinus would admit that soul *qua* soul, i.e. *psukhê* and not *nous*, is subject to change.

312. It is not clear who is the subject of this verb. Plotinus and Porphyry are the likeliest candidates.

313. Delete *hê*.

314. *Hupolêpsis* defined by Aristotle *On the Soul* 3.3, 427b25, as the genus comprising scientific understanding (*epistêmê*), opinion (*doxa*) and practical understanding (*phronêsis*). (Ed.)

315. On the description of imagination as (passive) intellect cf. n. 205.

316. 427b27-8.

317. 429a6-8.

318. I am accepting a suggestion of CS that *gnôristika* be emended to *hôristika*, 'determinative' or 'able to determine': it makes no sense to say that forms are capable of cognizing sensible objects. On the meaning of *hôristikos* see n. 18.

319. Here again *horos* means a form, or an object of knowledge, cf. n. 247, and for the expression *(meta)bainein kath' horous*, Steel (1997) 113.

320. *eidos ti*. This passage, printed as fr. 8 Ross, is the only evidence for this expression of Aristotle's later abandoned view that the soul was a separate substance. Ps.-Simplicius' comments show that he thought it was no different from Aristotle's mature concept of the soul, not surprisingly given his efforts to assimilate Aristotle's view to Plato's. For a recent discussion of soul in the *Eudemus* cf. J.M. Rist, *The Mind of Aristotle. A study in philosophical growth*. (*Phoenix* suppl. vol. 25. Toronto, Buffalo and London 1989) 165-70.

321. Another example of the *lexis/theôria* organisation of commentary.

322. That cannot be the correct explanation for a commentator who assumes that Aristotle basically accepted the Platonist view of the relation between body and soul.

323. It seems odd that the sensitive faculty is not included here: has the word for it, *to aisthêtikon*, simply dropped out by *homoioteleuton*?

324. cf. 219,27-32.

325. I propose to delete *all'*, 'but', here because there is no finite verb after it.

326. At 427b14-17.

327. At 429a13ff: perhaps Ps.-Simplicius has chapter 5 in mind too.

328. Being able to act without being enabled to do so by a higher level of soul or being is a mark of superiority to what cannot do this.

329. A case can be made for translating *poiein* as 'making', cf. L.A. Kosman, 'What does the maker mind make?', in M.C. Nussbaum and A.E. Rorty (eds), *Essays on Aristotle's De Anima* (Oxford 1992) 343-58.

330. cf. 430a12-13.

331. 430a18.

332. cf. 430a10-14, but the being acted on by an intelligible object, rather than a kind of intellect, is Neoplatonic, an easy transition given that for these Platonists intellects were intelligible objects and, in the intelligible itself, vice-versa.

333. The identity of these interpreters is not clear. Plotinus and Porphyry may be intended, since they held that the highest part of our soul is an intellect which transcends the sensible individual and which later Platonists, but not they themselves, would have described as unparticipated. Plotinus, of course, wrote no commentaries on Aristotle as such (and there is no good evidence that Porphyry wrote one on the *de Anima*), but by Ps.-Simplicius' time anything he wrote on the same subject as a work of Aristotle's could be treated as such, cf. esp. Ps.-Philoponus, *in DA* 535,1-539,1.

Another possible candidate is Iamblichus, who would then be talking about an intellect above ours, cf. 313,1-4 and Steel, *The Changing Self* (see n. 156) 142-3.

334. cf. again 1,22ff. and 172,4-8, also 218,31-2.

335. 430a13-14.

336. 430a15.

337. These last words are again a Neoplatonic translation of Aristotle.

338. Asulanus has *cognitio*, so presumably read *gnôsis*, not a major change from *genesis* and, at first sight, an attractive emendation. Nevertheless *genesis*, 'coming to be', fits better with the preceding *ginetai*, 'comes to be'.

339. In fact Aristotle does not say 'being acted on', *paskhein*, but 'becoming', *ginesthai*. 430a14-15.

340. An imprecise quotation (cf. the lemma), which does not, however, distort the sense of Aristotle's words.

341. cf. 90,14-18.

342. i.e. the one that takes place in sense-perception.

343. Understanding *ousias* with *tês*, but possibly the latter should be deleted, in which case the translation would be '(to the investigation) of what thinks …'.

344. That is, reason deals with the formal aspect of objects and so treats them as universals and not as discrete objects, as sense-perception does: on this point the commentator's views do not deviate from Aristotle's.

345. For intellect (*nous*) being that with which we apprehend definitions cf. Aristotle, *EN* 6.8, 1142a25-6 and 6.11, 1143a35-7. Proclus, *In Tim.* 1.428,29-30, uses the same words, *nous ... hôi tous horous ginôskomen* as Ps.-Simplicius uses here.

346. Ps.-Simplicius takes the *touto*, 'that', with which Aristotle says the intellect is not identical, as being the higher intellect, while Aristotle himself clearly means the intellect's object. For the commentator that could be what is above intellect, and it is this interpretation that he has read into the text.

347. Some translate *aisthêtikon* here as 'the sensitive faculty', which it certainly can mean, but what follows indicates that a more general translation is appropriate.

348. 429a13-14.

349. In the preceding words, at 428a13.

350. At 429b5-7.

351. cf. n. 347 above.

352. 429a17.

353. This may be deliberately ambiguous: it could be either the organ or the faculty.

354. By virtue of having a soul whose composition includes the indivisible, cf. n. 297.

355. DK 59 B 12,18-19. Aristotle with his *amigê<s>*, 'unmixed', has summarised, or paraphrased Anaxagoras' words which are *nous de estin apeiron kai autokrates kai memeiktai oudeni khrêmati*, 'mind is infinite (or unbounded) and self-controlling and is not mixed with anything'. In his comments on this lemma Ps.-Simplicius uses Aristotle's word with no indication that it is just paraphrase. The real Simplicius, to whom we owe the fragment (cf. *in Phys.* 164,24-5), might well have introduced the actual text of Anaxagoras.

356. Here, and throughout his discussion, the commentator takes 'unmixed' as meaning not mixed with any of its – intelligible – objects. Anaxagoras almost certainly meant that it was not mixed with any other of all the components of his world, intellect being made of a finer, and hence superior material, cf. the rest of fr. 12. Nor did he have any notion of intelligible objects as opposed to objects of the senses, a difficulty in using him in the explanation of Aristotle's mind which does not seem to have occurred to this commentator who, like other Neoplatonists, will not have been aware that the Presocratics had not yet arrived at a concept of the immaterial.

357. Because it is below the intelligibles, and not on the same level.

358. Those in which, as in everything but intellect, cf. fr. 11, there is something of everything, cf. fr. 6.

359. i.e. so that it can handle the sensible world as well as the intelligible, which it would not be able to do if it were operating at the higher, purely intelligible, level.

360. The reference is not clear, but similar things are said at 218,42ff., 222,6ff., 224,22ff.

361. The commentator's point is that the negation should not apply to intellect. Cf. Hicks' note, ad loc: the *mêde* ('<and> not') goes, not with *autou* ('of it'), but with *einai phusin* ('there is a nature [or characteristic]'), 'mind has not even any characteristic save this, that it has potentiality'. (I have added the translations in parentheses.)

362. Something appears to have dropped out of the text here, since 'this kind of', *ton toiouton*, requires a noun to indicate what it is that is called intellect. The easiest supplement would be *noun*, which could easily have dropped out of *kaleisthai legei ton toiouton tês psukhês <noun> noun*, 'he says that the *nous* of the soul (i.e. reason) is called *nous*, (i.e. intellect)'. On this double use of *nous* see the next note; cf. too the wording of 429a22, *ho ... kaloumenos tês psukhês nous*, 'the so-called intellect of the soul', and Aristotle's own explanation (see next lemma). Another possibility (CS) is *ton toiouton tês psukhês <logon>*.

363. A distinction taken up from the beginnings of Neoplatonism to make it possible to use *nous*, 'intellect', of both the discursive reason and the intuitive intellect, cf. e.g. Plotinus, 1.1.8,1-3.

364. I have added 'it': the grammatical subject is the intellect that stands in the words that come before the parentheses in which editors of Aristotle put 'I mean ... concepts': see previous lemma.

365. For this attempt to explain Aristotle's entelechy in terms of a compromise between hylomorphism and dualism cf. 90,29-91,4.

366. cf. 413a9, where many modern commentators take it as an undigested residue of Aristotle's earlier dualist psychology. For the dualist Platonist commentators it was, however, a suitable illustration of the soul's relation to the body as they saw it, cf. this commentary 96,3-15. Philoponus, who was more inclined to try to interpret Aristotle on his own terms makes heavy weather of the remark, cf. *in DA* 224,12-225,31, but cannot accept Alexander's view, for which he is the only source, that Aristotle was in two minds.

367. The beneficiaries of this approval have never been satisfactorily identified. While Ps.-Philoponus, *in DA* 524,6-16, firmly attributes the idea to Plato himself, our commentator says nothing on this question. Some modern commentators refer to Plato's *Parmenides*. However, as Ross points out, ad loc., though that dialogue talks about Ideas being thoughts, 132B – a suggestion which is, incidentally, rejected – it also contains statements incompatible with this view of the Forms' location, cf. e.g. 133C and 134B, which deny that they can be in us. The best candidates would seem to be Platonist contemporaries of Aristotle's, but not Plato himself.

368. At 429a26-7.

369. This is hardly what Aristotle is trying to say, as it might have been had he been a late Platonist. Rather it is his explanation of why sense and intellect react to strong stimuli in different ways.

370. *hôs eskhatois ikhnesi tôn eidôn*. For this view of the sensible world being characterised by traces – literally footmarks – of the forms cf. Proclus, *in Tim.* 1.383,17-22, *Platonic Theol.* 5.63,5-8.

371. This clearly refers to Aristotle, as do all unspecified references to 'the philosopher' in this commentary: contrast 'the philosopher Plutarch', at e.g. 186,26.

372. I understand *apo*, 'from', here: perhaps it has dropped out of the text either before (as compounding preposition) or after *merizomenên* because of its proximity to *apomerizetai* in the previous line.

373. cf. *DA* 86,20-3, though Ps.-Simplicius may have been working with Alexander's lost commentary, with which his independent *de Anima* must not be confused.

374. Not, in so many words, in the *de Anima*: if Ps.-Simplicius was using Alexander's commentary here it is the more likely that his other criticisms of Alexander in this set of comments were based on it.

375. *autoenergêtos*, which indicates that what is being perfected must play its own part in the 'process', cf. 236,5. On the meaning of this term cf. Steel, *The Changing Self* (see n. 156) 148-50.

376. This characterisation of the activity of intellect, answering the question of what it was that Aristotle's supreme intellect thought, was already standard in the Middle Platonic period, cf. Alcinous, *Did.* 10 = 164,26-7 H. (pp. 22-3 Whittaker), and may go back much further. On its possible origins see now J.M. Dillon, *Alcinous. The handbook of Platonism* (Oxford 1993) 94-5, ad *Did.* 9,12-13.

377. Ps.-Simplicius may still be thinking of Alexander: for his views on 'change' without real change cf. *Quaest.* 3.3, 84,20-33, à propos *DA* 2.5, 416b32-3.

378. At first sight it would appear that these words should be put in parentheses, as they are by the editors of Aristotle but not by Hayduck: they are not part of the structure of the sentence, while the words that follow them are clearly the main clause to the causal clause introduced by *epei*, 'since'. The colon after *to hudati einai*, 'the essence of water', should be replaced by a comma after the parenthesis, that after *kai sarka*, 'and flesh', should be removed. This gives punctuation etc. as ... *hudati einai (houtô de kai eph' heterôn pollôn, all' ouk epi pantôn: ep' eniôn gar tauton esti), to sarki einai kai sarka ê allôi* .... With Hayduck's punctuation the text would be saying that in some cases flesh and the essence of flesh are the same, which makes no sense, and is inconsistent with what has just been said about water. The cases where they are the same are ones where matter is not involved, cf. *Metaph.* 7, 1033a33-b7. Nevertheless his comments at 231,38-40 show that the commentator did have his text punctuated as Hayduck prints it, since he complains precisely about the inappropriateness of the example and has difficulty in making some sense of his lemma.

It is not immediately clear what the subject of *krinei*, 'judges', is, but it can hardly be intellect, and if it were people in general one might expect *krinomen*, 'we judge': in practice the meaning of that would not be much different from having soul as the subject, as I would prefer. On this matter cf. Rodier, ad loc.

379. i.e. 'this form in this matter': I have kept the literal translation because Ps.-Simplicius' discussion, 231,41-232,10 starts from the unspecified demonstrative.

380. i.e. to the intellect in question.

381. I think one must assume that one of three successive *êtas* has dropped out, and restore it, reading *êi ê hê* for *êi hê*, otherwise the remark makes no sense, since the soul that stays in itself is closer to the ideas and not further from them, as that which proceeds.

382. The idea that certain kinds or levels of being are cognized by different cognitive powers appropriate to the objects is a common theme in Proclus, who perhaps codified it. In his work *oikeiôs*, 'appropriately', became almost a slogan in such contexts: for one of the fuller lists cf. *Plat. Theol.* 1,3 (=1.15,17-21 S-W). Closely related to this is the notion that each cognitive faculty has a different way of cognizing its objects, cf. e.g. *in Tim.* 1.352,15-19. The origin of this scheme is, of course, Platonic, and may be found particularly in the Divided Line, cf. *Rep.* 511D-E.

383. Once again one has to say that Aristotle doesn't: the interest in different degrees of division, *merismos*, at different levels of being is a Neoplatonic and not an Aristotelian concern, and the same may be said about procession.

384. This is a special case of the general Neoplatonic doctrine that the cause is other than the effect, already neatly formulated in Plotinus', *to aition ou tauton tôi aitiatôi*, 'the cause is not the same as what is caused', 6.9.6,54-5.

385. Ps.-Simplicius' complaint arises directly from the unsatisfactory way the text before him was punctuated – or the way he read it if it was not, cf. n. 347 above.

A more scholarly commentator might have found a better way out of the difficulty which Ps.-Simplicius rightly finds in the text as he had it.

386. Since the commentator has produced three examples I propose emending *autou*, 'of it, its', to *autôn*, 'of them', their, which could easily have been changed to the singular under the influence of the other four neuter singulars in the same clause.

387. This is not quite what Plato says but cf. *Gorg.* 465A, *Theaet.* 202B-C.

388. cf. n. 382 above.

389. This source of possible confusion was seen as such from the beginning of Neoplatonism, cf. e.g. Plotinus, 5.9.2,21-2, and Blumenthal, *Plotinus' Psychology* (see n. 204) 104-5.

390. 232,26-8.

391. It is by no means clear that real Pythagoreans talked in such terms. The importance of the imagination in mathematics was emphasised by Proclus in his commentary on the first book of Euclid's *Elements*, cf. esp. *in I Eucl.* 54,14-56,23, though the theme is not exclusive to that work, cf. *in Tim.* 2.237,11-15.

392. Aristotle is our earliest source for this doctrine, and may well have been the commentator's too, cf. esp. *Metaph.* 1, 987b27-9 and 14, 1090a20-3.

393. For mathematics dealing with abstractions cf. *DA* 403b14-15 and *Metaph.* 11, 1061a28-9.

394. This view of the effects of mathematics is genuinely Platonic, cf. esp. *Rep.* 525B-526B, 527A-B.

395. i.e. the being straight and the straight.

396. In Book 7, 1031a15-b11, where a variety of arguments are deployed to make the point that they are the same.

397. Perhaps it is worth recalling that any kind of transcendent intellect has been excluded from the start as not being part of what the *de Anima* is about.

398. The higher intellect in us, which thinks intuitively, rather than the so-called intellect which thinks discursively and can handle objects other than purely immaterial ones.

399. cf. 429a18-19, where Anaxagoras is cited for the view that intellect is *amigês*, 'unmixed' and n. 355 above.

400. This late Neoplatonic doctrine would hardly have been immediately comprehensible to Aristotle. For one formulation cf. Proclus, *ElTh* 61. The word translated 'bring ... into being' is *hupostatika*, used by the commentator of causes of being, as opposed to *poiêtika*, 'productive', derived from the ordinary word for 'make' or 'produce', *poiein*; cf. 70,29-31, 112,5-14 and Steel, Introduction (1997) 113-14.

401. 429b9.

402. The two meanings of *dunamei*, 'potentially' or 'in potency', are distinguished in *DA* 2.5, 417b29-418a4, where they are exemplified by the difference between a boy and an adult being potentially a general.

403. In book 2, ch. 5, at 417b2-16.

404. Hicks, followed by Ross, adopted a conjecture of Cornford's, reading *d<unam>ei*, 'potentially', for *dei*, 'it must', universally read by MSS of Aristotle as well, but to say that the tablet has nothing *potentially* written on it would weaken the point. Moreover the commentator says nothing about that, though one might expect that he would have done so had his text presented him with this extra problem.

405. Of the two identified at 234,28-30.

406. At 430a18-19.

407. *autoenergêtos*, which I translate 'using its own activity' rather than 'by its own activity' to avoid confusion here. On its meaning see n. 375 above.

408. Explained by Aristotle at *GC* 1.7, 323b29-324a9.

409. cf. 234,28-30 above.

410. Late Neoplatonists had no generally accepted view on the position of *doxa*, 'opinion', or even its identity, since it was sometimes identified with imagination: when it was it tended to be seen as the highest level of the irrational soul rather than the lowest level of the rational one. On this question in the preceding period cf. Blumenthal, 'Plutarch's exposition of the *de Anima*' (see n. 272) 134-47. Ps.-Simplicius himself kept *doxa* and imagination apart, cf. 211,33ff.

411. While the starting point for this notion is Aristotle's identification of knower and known in intellection, this is a Neoplatonic development. For one expression of the view cf. Proclus, *ElTh* 173.

412. This again is nothing to do with Aristotle, but reflects the late Neoplatonic tendency to see all reality as based on a triadic structure.

413. Neoplatonists from Plotinus on thought of the soul as an intermediate entity, cf. *Enn.* 4.8.7,5-9, Proclus, *in Tim.* 3.254,10-17, and saw the discursive reason in particular, *qua* the soul's distinctive power, as occupying this position, cf. e.g. Philoponus, *in DA* 2,21-4. For further discussion see H.J. Blumenthal, 'Simplicius and others on Aristotle's discussions of reason', in J. Duffy and J. Peradotto (eds), *Gonimos. Neoplatonic and Byzantine Studies presented to Leendert G. Westerink at 75* (Buffalo 1988) 108-19.

414. This and the following discussion must be read in the light of the Neoplatonic controversy about the position of our intellect: Plotinus had maintained that it remains transcendent, and was followed by Porphyry. Later Neoplatonists argued that both the intermittent nature of intellection and human imperfection required that the highest part of the soul should descend with the rest, cf. e.g. Proclus, *in Tim.* 3.333,29ff. and the doxography at Ps.-Philoponus, *in DA* 535,1ff. See also nn. 309-10 above.

415. It looks as if the commentator, who is occasionally given to writing rhetorically, is here playing on the apparent similarity of the noun for 'place', *khôra*, and *khôrizô*, the verb meaning 'to separate', which is derived from the cognate adverb *khôris*, 'separately' or 'apart'.

416. *monon*, which appears in only *y* of the MSS of the *de Anima*, is perhaps therefore a gloss, but a perfectly sensible one which clarifies the point.

417. The commentator is here introducing his own special reading of Aristotle's definition of the soul, the first entelechy of a body potentially having life: for Neoplatonists the body already has soul, and so life, since body is a combination of matter and the lowest level of soul, cf. Plotinus' translation of the Aristotelian doctrine, at 4.7.8[5],1-5, and Ps.-Simplicius commentary on the definition at 90,29-91,4, where he splits Aristotle's entelechy into two, what informs the body, and gives it life, and what uses that body, as a way of bridging the gap between Aristotelian and Platonic psychology.

418. cf. 5.12, 1019a15-23, 9.1, 1046a9-19.

419. *ekeinois*: texts of Aristotle have the singular *ekeinôi*, but the reading *ekeinois* is secured for Ps.-Simplicius by the following comments which are about plural intellects.

420. Given how much discussion this chapter has generated from Theophrastus to the present day, Ps.-Simplicius' commentary on it is surprisingly short, a mere 8½ *CAG* pages, or some 5% of his commentary on book 3: that is roughly the same proportion as Ps.-Philoponus, his lengthy discussion of previous views notwithstanding – another surprise. By contrast Themistius, who even departs from his periphrastic method for this chapter alone, gives it about 11 out of 46½, some 24% of his exposition of book 3, and Averroes about 13%.

421. Retaining *hôsper* against Ross, but with all other authorities except possibly Themistius.

422. On the text of this sentence see n. 449 below.

423. The commentator is here simply reiterating what he regards as an axiom for the interpretation of the *de Anima*, cf. n. 1.

424. This is because there are no gaps in being, and because every soul must depend on what is above it – as must every intellect. In the case of soul what is immediately above will be *noeron*, 'intellective', cf. e.g. Proclus, *ElTh* 183 with 193.

425. In view of the following discussion it might be worth recalling that indivisibility is for the Neoplatonists a characteristic of intellect as opposed to soul, cf. already Plotinus' fourth treatise, 4.2.1,17-34.

426. At 429a13. The commentary on that text pays special attention to the kind of intellection that sense-perception can be compared with at 223,17ff.

427. 430a22: on the text here see note on the lemma beginning at 430a19 (below n. 449).

428. cf. 430a22-3: the words used here are not quite a quotation, Aristotle has *khôristheis d'esti monon touth' hoper esti*, 'and when it is separated it is only that which it is': Ps.-Simplicius has *estin houtos*, 'this one (sc. intellect) is what it is'.

429. cf. n. 383 above.

430. Ps.-Simplicius is here talking in terms of the well-known passage in Plato's *Timaeus*, 35A-B, on the composition of the soul. On its interpretation cf. n. 271. Plato is more than usually prominent in the commentary on this chapter.

431. cf. Aristotle, *GC* 1.7, 324b4-24.

432. cf. *DA* 403a24-8.

433. *PA* 1, 641a17-b10.

434. 2,6-28.

435. For this characterisation of *tekhnê*, 'craft' or 'skill', cf. Aristotle, *EN* 6.4, 1140a3-10.

436. e.g. at 240,7ff.

437. I suspect that all the genitives after *pros* in this sentence should be accusatives, but the genitive might just be possible in the sense required.

438. i.e. the transparent.

439. Reading *pantê<i>*, as in A: Hayduck's *panta* is wrong, and in any case the following words show that the adverb is needed.

440. At 430a22-3.

441. The target of this remark is the Plotinian undescended intellect: on this cf. n. 310.

442. Aristotle, not having believed in forms, cannot possibly have wanted this – a good example of the results of the conviction that his philosophy was Platonist.

443. e.g. at 223,20-40.

444. Aristotle, see n. 371.

445. Presumably the commentator has in mind 429b30-430a2, which does not say quite the same.

446. cf. n. 384 above.

447. This again is not quite what Aristotle says, but the formulation was part of the vocabulary of Neoplatonic interpretations of this chapter, cf. e.g. Ps.-Philoponus *in DA* 3, 535,14.

448. Ps.-Simplicius' lemma reads *he autê d'estin*, while all MSS of Aristotle have *to auto d'estin*, giving knowledge in act is the same thing as its object. There is little or no difference in the meaning, but the text our commentator has is a more direct way of putting the point. Ross wants to excise the whole of this lemma down to the words *hote d'ou noei*, 'sometimes it does not think', on the grounds that they occur again in ch. 7, 431a1-3: the words *all' oukh* (see next note) *hote men noei hote d'ou noei* do not, however, occur there. In any case Ps.-Simplicius' commentary makes it quite clear that his text had all the words in the lemma.

449. The ensuing exposition is clearly based on the text as printed by Hayduck. Most MSS of Aristotle begin the sentence with a negative, *all' oukh*, 'it is not the case that ...', assumed also, according to Ross, in the discussions reported by Ps.-Philoponus 535,1ff., and by that commentator himself: in fact some of the views reported there seem to be based on the text without the negative. In any case it is probably (probably because there is a doubt as to the subject of the verbs) the positive version that post-Porphyrian Platonists would have wished to read, since the negative would entail either Plotinus' view that the human intellect has not descended, or have to be read as a reference to the intellect above ours, which Ps.-Simplicius in this part of the commentary and elsewhere repeatedly says is not what Aristotle was talking about: hence presumably Torstrik's view that the negative had been removed by Platonists for doctrinal reasons, a view that perhaps underestimates these commentators' ability to find the meaning they wanted in more or less any text! Further there is a contrast between the state of intellect envisaged in this sentence, and the next which considers it when it has been separated: intellect in that state would be the first to be a candidate for being described as having permanent intellection.

450. Aristotle!

451. *Tim.* 28A.

452. Reading *deutera*, neuter plural and meaning 'secondary things' for A's *deuteran*, the feminine singular adjective for which it is difficult to supply an appropriate noun. One could only supply *gnôsin*, 'cognition': the translation would then be 'cognition unseparated in respect of the second kind of cognition'.

453. *outhen noei*, or 'nothing thinks'. Ps.-Simplicius commentary indicates that he takes the words to mean 'it thinks nothing', cf. 248,9-11, so I have translated it that way even though I think Aristotle means 'nothing thinks'.

454. Demonstrating the agreement between Plato and Aristotle which they assumed to hold in most matters was one of the main aims of most Neoplatonist commentators, cf. Introduction, pp. 13-14.

455. A comment perhaps based on Aristotle's discussion of self-movement in *Physics* 8, cf. esp. 254b7ff. The reference to Plato is clearly to the argument for the soul's immortality in the *Phaedrus*, 245C-246A, but it should be noted that Plato does not anywhere use the late Neoplatonists' standard term *autokinêtos*, 'self-moved', but the non-technical *to auto heauto kinoun*, 'what moves itself'.

456. 'Self', *auto(s)* is of course part of the normal Forms vocabulary in Plato, but the remarks that follow may indicate a less than completely precise recall of *Sophist* 248E-249A: if so it is odd that a text which was such a favourite with the Neoplatonists should be misremembered, if it was misremembered rather than misrepresented to fit this commentator's own views about self-motion in so far as it applies to the soul. For a brief discussion of this matter cf. Steel (1997) 117-18.

457. 'Everything immaterial ...' goes beyond what Aristotle says, but is implicit in the Neoplatonic account of the hypostasis Intellect which is structured on principles based on Aristotle's analysis of intellection here.

458. Ps.-Simplicius' argument here is not, of course, drawn from the text at issue, but from the last argument for immortality in Plato's *Phaedo*, 105C-107A. This use of Plato's arguments and vocabulary facilitates the conclusion that Aristotle's account agrees with Plato's – as in the *Phaedrus*. Typically Ps.-

Simplicius shows no awareness that the *Phaedrus* argument may be meant to supersede those in the *Phaedo*, and is quite at ease in using the one dialogue to illustrate points arising from the other.

459. Presumably the syncretising first century BC Peripatetic, rather than the Academic who lived in the previous century when the Academy were sceptics. I know of no other evidence for Ps.-Simplicius' report. Identification with the Peripatetic is argued for by H.B. Gottschalk, 'Boethus' psychology and the Neoplatonists', *Phronesis* 31 (1986) 254-6.

460. All this has little to do with the *de Anima*, but as we have seen, the commentator has slid into talking about the *Phaedo*, cf. n. 458. Gottschalk, op. cit. 245-6, suggests that Ps.-Simplicius' source for this argument, which may derive from Strato, is Porphyry's work *On the soul, against Boethus* in 5 books, from which most of the other evidence about him comes, including the only other named testimonium. The texts in question, preserved by Eusebius, may now be found in A. Smith's edition of Porphyry's fragments (*Porphyrii Philosophi Fragmenta*, Teubner 1993) nos. 242-50.

461. I insert a comma after *anäiresin*, and remove the one Hayduck prints after *ousias* in the next line.

462. cf. *Mem*. 450a23-5.

463. The reference of *toutou*, 'this', is notoriously unclear. Ps.-Simplicius' interpretation is a function of the identification of passible intellect as imagination. For some discussion of this interpretation and its history cf. Blumenthal, '*Nous pathêtikos* in later Greek philosophy' (see n. 205).

464. At 12.7, 1072b25.

Editor's addition to n. 51 (p. 122)

[*Sunaisthêsis, sunaisthanesthai*, are standardly used by the commentators of self-awareness. Themistius sometimes uses the term differently, but apparent exceptions often turn out not to be exceptions. Thus (i) the terms are used of perceiving   darkness and light, including light through the eyelids, of perceiving dimness and colourlessness and an absence of objects of touch. But, elaborating Aristotle in *DA* 425b20-2, the commentators take it that these things are perceived through our awareness of our success or failure in trying to see or feel: Priscian in Theophrastum 5,6; Ps.-Simplicius *in DA* 106,17; 135,3 and 7; 181,24 and 27. (ii) Awareness of common sensibles is called *sunaisthêsis* only when it is thought of as being due to awareness of an internal change (*kinêsis*) within us: Priscian in Theophrastum 21,34. (iii) Alexander, commenting that different observers do not have *sunaisthêsis* of each other's sensibles, uses the word *sunaisthêsis* precisely because he is talking not of external sensibles, which they can perfectly well see in common, but of their perceptual experiences. (iv) Alexander also makes *sunaisthêsis* responsible for judging distance in hearing because distance is judged from the intensity of the (inner) blow. (Ed.)]

Appendix
The Commentators*

The 15,000 pages of the Ancient Greek Commentaries on Aristotle are the largest corpus of Ancient Greek philosophy that has not been translated into English or other European languages. The standard edition (*Commentaria in Aristotelem Graeca*, or *CAG*) was produced by Hermann Diels as general editor under the auspices of the Prussian Academy in Berlin. Arrangements have been made to translate at least a large proportion of this corpus, along with some other Greek and Latin commentaries not included in the Berlin edition, and some closely related non-commentary works by the commentators.

The works are not just commentaries on Aristotle, although they are invaluable in that capacity too. One of the ways of doing philosophy between A.D. 200 and 600, when the most important items were produced, was by writing commentaries. The works therefore represent the thought of the Peripatetic and Neoplatonist schools, as well as expounding Aristotle. Furthermore, they embed fragments from all periods of Ancient Greek philosophical thought: this is how many of the Presocratic fragments were assembled, for example. Thus they provide a panorama of every period of Ancient Greek philosophy.

The philosophy of the period from A.D. 200 to 600 has not yet been intensively explored by philosophers in English-speaking countries, yet it is full of interest for physics, metaphysics, logic, psychology, ethics and religion. The contrast with the study of the Presocratics is striking. Initially the incomplete Presocratic fragments might well have seemed less promising, but their interest is now widely known, thanks to the philological and philosophical effort that has been concentrated upon them. The incomparably vaster corpus which preserved so many of those fragments offers at least as much interest, but is still relatively little known.

The commentaries represent a missing link in the history of philosophy: the Latin-speaking Middle Ages obtained their knowledge of Aristotle at least partly through the medium of the commentaries. Without an appreciation of this, mediaeval interpretations of Aristotle will not be understood. Again, the ancient commentaries are the unsuspected source of ideas which have been thought, wrongly, to originate in the later mediaeval period. It has been supposed, for example, that Bonaventure in the thirteenth century invented the ingenious arguments based on the concept of infinity which attempt to prove the Christian view that the universe had a beginning. In fact, Bonaventure is merely repeating arguments devised

---

* Reprinted from the Editor's General Introduction to the series in Christian Wildberg, *Philoponus Against Aristotle on the Eternity of the World*, London and Ithaca, N.Y., 1987.

by the commentator Philoponus 700 years earlier and preserved in the meantime by the Arabs. Bonaventure even uses Philoponus' original examples. Again, the introduction of impetus theory into dynamics, which has been called a scientific revolution, has been held to be an independent invention of the Latin West, even if it was earlier discovered by the Arabs or their predecessors. But recent work has traced a plausible route by which it could have passed from Philoponus, via the Arabs, to the West.

The new availability of the commentaries in the sixteenth century, thanks to printing and to fresh Latin translations, helped to fuel the Renaissance break from Aristotelian science. For the commentators record not only Aristotle's theories, but also rival ones, while Philoponus as a Christian devises rival theories of his own and accordingly is mentioned in Galileo's early works more frequently than Plato.[1]

It is not only for their philosophy that the works are of interest. Historians will find information about the history of schools, their methods of teaching and writing and the practices of an oral tradition.[2] Linguists will find the indexes and translations an aid for studying the development of word meanings, almost wholly uncharted in Liddell and Scott's *Lexicon*, and for checking shifts in grammatical usage.

Given the wide range of interests to which the volumes will appeal, the aim is to produce readable translations, and to avoid so far as possible presupposing any knowledge of Greek. Notes will explain points of meaning, give cross-references to other works, and suggest alternative interpretations of the text where the translator does not have a clear preference. The introduction to each volume will include an explanation why the work was chosen for translation: none will be chosen simply because it is there. Two of the Greek texts are currently being re-edited – those of Simplicius *in Physica* and *in de Caelo* – and new readings will be exploited by

1. See Fritz Zimmermann, 'Philoponus' impetus theory in the Arabic tradition'; Charles Schmitt, 'Philoponus' commentary on Aristotle's *Physics* in the sixteenth century', and Richard Sorabji, 'John Philoponus', in Richard Sorabji (ed.), *Philoponus and the Rejection of Aristotelian Science* (London and Ithaca, N.Y. 1987).
2. See e.g. Karl Praechter, 'Die griechischen Aristoteleskommentare', *Byzantinische Zeitschrift* 18 (1909), 516-38 (translated into English in R. Sorabji (ed.), *Aristotle Transformed: the ancient commentators and their influence* (London and Ithaca, N.Y. 1990); M. Plezia, *de Commentariis Isagogicis* (Cracow 1947); M. Richard, 'Apo Phônês', *Byzantion* 20 (1950), 191-222; É. Evrard, *L'Ecole d'Olympiodore et la composition du commentaire à la physique de Jean Philopon*, Diss. (Liège 1957); L.G. Westerink, *Anonymous Prolegomena to Platonic Philosophy* (Amsterdam 1962) (new revised edition, translated into French, Collection Budé; part of the revised introduction, in English, is included in *Aristotle Transformed*); A.-J. Festugière, 'Modes de composition des commentaires de Proclus', *Museum Helveticum* 20 (1963), 77-100, repr. in his *Études* (1971), 551-74; P. Hadot, 'Les divisions des parties de la philosophie dans l'antiquité', *Museum Helveticum* 36 (1979), 201-23; I. Hadot, 'La division néoplatonicienne des écrits d'Aristote', in J. Wiesner (ed.), *Aristoteles Werk und Wirkung* (Paul Moraux gewidmet), vol. 2 (Berlin 1986); I. Hadot, 'Les introductions aux commentaires exégétiques chez les auteurs néoplatoniciens et les auteurs chrétiens', in M. Tardieu (ed.), *Les règles de l'interprétation* (Paris 1987), 99-119. These topics are treated, and a bibliography supplied, in *Aristotle Transformed*.

translators as they become available. Each volume will also contain a list of proposed emendations to the standard text. Indexes will be of more uniform extent as between volumes than is the case with the Berlin edition, and there will be at least three of them: an English-Greek glossary, a Greek-English index, and a subject index.

The commentaries fall into three main groups. The first group is by authors in the Aristotelian tradition up to the fourth century A.D. This includes the earliest extant commentary, that by Aspasius in the first half of the second century A.D. on the *Nicomachean Ethics*. The anonymous commentary on Books 2, 3, 4 and 5 of the *Nicomachean Ethics*, in *CAG* vol. 20, is derived from Adrastus, a generation later.[3] The commentaries by Alexander of Aphrodisias (appointed to his chair between A.D. 198 and 209) represent the fullest flowering of the Aristotelian tradition. To his successors Alexander was The Commentator *par excellence*. To give but one example (not from a commentary) of his skill at defending and elaborating Aristotle's views, one might refer to his defence of Aristotle's claim that space is finite against the objection that an edge of space is conceptually problematic.[4] Themistius (*fl.* late 340s to 384 or 385) saw himself as the inventor of paraphrase, wrongly thinking that the job of commentary was completed.[5] In fact, the Neoplatonists were to introduce new dimensions into commentary. Themistius' own relation to the Neoplatonist as opposed to the Aristotelian tradition is a matter of controversy,[6] but it would be agreed that his commentaries show far less bias than the full-blown Neoplatonist ones. They are also far more informative than the designation 'paraphrase' might suggest, and it has been estimated that Philoponus' *Physics* commentary draws silently on Themistius six hundred times.[7] The pseudo-Alexandrian commentary on *Metaphysics* 6-14, of unknown

3. Anthony Kenny, *The Aristotelian Ethics* (Oxford 1978), 37, n.3: Paul Moraux, *Der Aristotelismus bei den Griechen*, vol. 2 (Berlin 1984), 323-30.
4. Alexander, *Quaestiones* 3.12, discussed in my *Matter, Space and Motion* (London and Ithaca, N.Y. 1988). For Alexander see R.W. Sharples, 'Alexander of Aphrodisias: scholasticism and innovation', in W. Haase (ed.), *Aufstieg und Niedergang der römischen Welt*, part 2 *Principat*, vol. 36.2, *Philosophie und Wissenschaften* (1987).
5. Themistius *in An. Post.* 1,2-12. See H.J. Blumenthal, 'Photius on Themistius (Cod. 74): did Themistius write commentaries on Aristotle?', *Hermes* 107 (1979), 168-82.
6. For different views, see H.J. Blumenthal, 'Themistius, the last Peripatetic commentator on Aristotle?', in Glen W. Bowersock, Walter Burkert, Michael C.J. Putnam, *Arktouros*, *Hellenic Studies Presented to Bernard M.W. Knox* (Berlin and N.Y., 1979), 391-400; E.P. Mahoney, 'Themistius and the agent intellect in James of Viterbo and other thirteenth-century philosophers: (Saint Thomas Aquinas, Siger of Brabant and Henry Bate)', *Augustiniana* 23 (1973), 422-67, at 428-31; id., 'Neoplatonism, the Greek commentators and Renaissance Aristotelianism', in D.J. O'Meara (ed.), *Neoplatonism and Christian Thought* (Albany N.Y. 1982), 169-77 and 264-82, esp. n. 1, 264-6; Robert Todd, introduction to translation of Themistius *in DA* 3.4-8, in *Two Greek Aristotelian Commentators on the Intellect*, trans. Frederick M. Schroeder and Robert B. Todd (Toronto 1990).
7. H. Vitelli, *CAG* 17, p. 992, s.v. Themistius.

authorship, has been placed by some in the same group of commentaries as being earlier than the fifth century.[8]

By far the largest group of extant commentaries is that of the Neoplatonists up to the sixth century A.D. Nearly all the major Neoplatonists, apart from Plotinus (the founder of Neoplatonism), wrote commentaries on Aristotle, although those of Iamblichus (c. 250–c. 325) survive only in fragments, and those of three Athenians, Plutarchus (died 432), his pupil Proclus (410–485) and the Athenian Damascius (c. 462–after 538), are lost.[9] As a result of these losses, most of the extant Neoplatonist commentaries come from the late fifth and the sixth centuries and a good proportion from Alexandria. There are commentaries by Plotinus' disciple and editor Porphyry (232–309), by Iamblichus' pupil Dexippus (c. 330), by Proclus' teacher Syrianus (died c. 437), by Proclus' pupil Ammonius (435/445–517/526), by Ammonius' three pupils Philoponus (c. 490 to 570s), Simplicius (wrote after 532, probably after 538) and Asclepius (sixth century), by Ammonius' next but one successor Olympiodorus (495/505–after 565), by Elias (fl. 541?), by David (second half of the sixth century, or beginning of the seventh) and by Stephanus (took the chair in Constantinople c. 610). Further, a commentary on the *Nicomachean Ethics* has been ascribed to Heliodorus of Prusa, an unknown pre-fourteenth-century figure, and there is a commentary by Simplicius' colleague Priscian of Lydia on Aristotle's successor Theophrastus. Of these commentators some of the last were Christians (Philoponus, Elias, David and Stephanus), but they were Christians writing in the Neoplatonist tradition, as was also Boethius who produced a number of commentaries in Latin before his death in 525 or 526.

The third group comes from a much later period in Byzantium. The Berlin edition includes only three out of more than a dozen commentators described in Hunger's *Byzantinisches Handbuch*.[10] The two most important are Eustratius (1050/1060–c.1120), and Michael of Ephesus. It has been suggested that these two belong to a circle organised by the princess

8. The similarities to Syrianus (died c. 437) have suggested to some that it predates Syrianus (most recently Leonardo Tarán, review of Paul Moraux, *Der Aristotelismus*, vol.1 in *Gnomon* 46 (1981), 721-50 at 750), to others that it draws on him (most recently P. Thillet, in the Budé edition of Alexander *de Fato*, p. lvii). Praechter ascribed it to Michael of Ephesus (eleventh or twelfth century), in his review of *CAG* 22.2, in *Göttingische Gelehrte Anzeiger* 168 (1906), 861-907.

9. The Iamblichus fragments are collected in Greek by Bent Dalsgaard Larsen, *Jamblique de Chalcis, Exégète et Philosophe* (Aarhus 1972), vol. 2. Most are taken from Simplicius, and will accordingly be translated in due course. The evidence on Damascius' commentaries is given in L.G. Westerink, *The Greek Commentaries on Plato's Phaedo*, vol. 2, Damascius (Amsterdam 1977), 11-12; on Proclus' in L.G. Westerink, *Anonymous Prolegomena to Platonic Philosophy* (Amsterdam 1962), xii, n. 22; on Plutarchus' in H.M. Blumenthal, 'Neoplatonic elements in the de Anima commentaries', *Phronesis* 21 (1976), 75.

10. Herbert Hunger, *Die hochsprachliche profane Literatur der Byzantiner*, vol. 1 (= *Byzantinisches Handbuch*, part 5, vol. 1) (Munich 1978), 25-41. See also B.N. Tatakis, *La Philosophie Byzantine* (Paris 1949).

Anna Comnena in the twelfth century, and accordingly the completion of Michael's commentaries has been redated from 1040 to 1138.[11] His commentaries include areas where gaps had been left. Not all of these gap-fillers are extant, but we have commentaries on the neglected biological works, on the *Sophistici Elenchi*, and a small fragment of one on the *Politics*. The lost *Rhetoric* commentary had a few antecedents, but the *Rhetoric* too had been comparatively neglected. Another product of this period may have been the composite commentary on the *Nicomachean Ethics* (*CAG* 20) by various hands, including Eustratius and Michael, along with some earlier commentators, and an improvisation for Book 7. Whereas Michael follows Alexander and the conventional Aristotelian tradition, Eustratius' commentary introduces Platonist, Christian and anti-Islamic elements.[12]

The composite commentary was to be translated into Latin in the next century by Robert Grosseteste in England. But Latin translations of various logical commentaries were made from the Greek still earlier by James of Venice (*fl. c.* 1130), a contemporary of Michael of Ephesus, who may have known him in Constantinople. And later in that century other commentaries and works by commentators were being translated from Arabic versions by Gerard of Cremona (died 1187).[13] So the twelfth century resumed the transmission which had been interrupted at Boethius' death in the sixth century.

The Neoplatonist commentaries of the main group were initiated by Porphyry. His master Plotinus had discussed Aristotle, but in a very independent way, devoting three whole treatises (*Enneads* 6.1-3) to attacking Aristotle's classification of the things in the universe into categories. These categories took no account of Plato's world of Ideas, were inferior to Plato's classifications in the *Sophist* and could anyhow be collapsed, some

---

11. R. Browning, 'An unpublished funeral oration on Anna Comnena', *Proceedings of the Cambridge Philological Society* n.s. 8 (1962), 1-12, esp. 6-7.

12. R. Browning, op. cit. H.D.P. Mercken, *The Greek Commentaries of the Nicomachean Ethics of Aristotle in the Latin Translation of Grosseteste, Corpus Latinum Commentariorum in Aristotelem Graecorum* VI 1 (Leiden 1973), ch. 1, 'The compilation of Greek commentaries on Aristotle's Nicomachean Ethics'. Sten Ebbesen, 'Anonymi Aurelianensis I Commentarium in *Sophisticos Elenchos*', *Cahiers de l'Institut Moyen Age Grecque et Latin* 34 (1979), 'Boethius, Jacobus Veneticus, Michael Ephesius and "Alexander" ', pp. v-xiii; id., *Commentators and Commentaries on Aristotle's Sophistici Elenchi*, 3 parts, *Corpus Latinum Commentariorum in Aristotelem Graecorum*, vol. 7 (Leiden 1981); A. Preus, *Aristotle and Michael of Ephesus on the Movement and Progression of Animals* (Hildesheim 1981), introduction.

13. For Grosseteste, see Mercken as in n. 12. For James of Venice, see Ebbesen as in n. 12, and L. Minio-Paluello, 'Jacobus Veneticus Grecus', *Traditio* 8 (1952), 265-304; id., 'Giacomo Veneto e l'Aristotelismo Latino', in Pertusi (ed.), *Venezia e l'Oriente fra tardo Medioevo e Rinascimento* (Florence 1966), 53-74, both reprinted in his *Opuscula* (1972). For Gerard of Cremona, see M. Steinschneider, *Die europäischen Übersetzungen aus dem arabischen bis Mitte des 17. Jahrhunderts* (repr. Graz 1956); E. Gilson, *History of Christian Philosophy in the Middle Ages* (London 1955), 235-6 and more generally 181-246. For the translators in general, see Bernard G. Dod, 'Aristoteles Latinus', in N. Kretzmann, A. Kenny, J. Pinborg (eds), *The Cambridge History of Latin Medieval Philosophy* (Cambridge 1982).

of them into others. Porphyry replied that Aristotle's categories could apply perfectly well to the world of intelligibles and he took them as in general defensible.[14] He wrote two commentaries on the *Categories*, one lost, and an introduction to it, the *Isagôgê*, as well as commentaries, now lost, on a number of other Aristotelian works. This proved decisive in making Aristotle a necessary subject for Neoplatonist lectures and commentary. Proclus, who was an exceptionally quick student, is said to have taken two years over his Aristotle studies, which were called the Lesser Mysteries, and which preceded the Greater Mysteries of Plato.[15] By the time of Ammonius, the commentaries reflect a teaching curriculum which begins with Porphyry's *Isagôgê* and Aristotle's *Categories*, and is explicitly said to have as its final goal a (mystical) ascent to the supreme Neoplatonist deity, the One.[16] The curriculum would have progressed from Aristotle to Plato, and would have culminated in Plato's *Timaeus* and *Parmenides*. The latter was read as being about the One, and both works were established in this place in the curriculum at least by the time of Iamblichus, if not earlier.[17]

Before Porphyry, it had been undecided how far a Platonist should accept Aristotle's scheme of categories. But now the proposition began to gain force that there was a harmony between Plato and Aristotle on most things.[18] Not for the only time in the history of philosophy, a perfectly crazy proposition proved philosophically fruitful. The views of Plato and of Aristotle had both to be transmuted into a new Neoplatonist philosophy in order to exhibit the supposed harmony. Iamblichus denied that Aristotle contradicted Plato on the theory of Ideas.[19] This was too much for Syrianus and his pupil Proclus. While accepting harmony in many areas,[20] they could see that there was disagreement on this issue and also on the issue of whether God was causally responsible for the existence of the ordered

14. See P. Hadot, 'L'harmonie des philosophies de Plotin et d'Aristote selon Porphyre dans le commentaire de Dexippe sur les Catégories', in *Plotino e il neoplatonismo in Oriente e in Occidente* (Rome 1974), 31-47; A.C. Lloyd, 'Neoplatonic logic and Aristotelian logic', *Phronesis* 1 (1955-6), 58-79 and 146-60.

15. Marinus, *Life of Proclus* ch. 13, 157,41 (Boissonade).

16. The introductions to the *Isagôgê* by Ammonius, Elias and David, and to the *Categories* by Ammonius, Simplicius, Philoponus, Olympiodorus and Elias are discussed by L.G. Westerink, *Anonymous Prolegomena* and I. Hadot, 'Les Introductions', see n. 2 above.

17. Proclus in *Alcibiadem 1* p. 11 (Creuzer); Westerink, *Anonymous Prolegomena*, ch. 26, 12f. For the Neoplatonist curriculum see Westerink, Festugière, P. Hadot and I. Hadot in n. 2.

18. See e.g. P. Hadot (1974), as in n. 14 above; H.J. Blumenthal, 'Neoplatonic elements in the de Anima commentaries', *Phronesis* 21 (1976), 64-87; H.A. Davidson, 'The principle that a finite body can contain only finite power', in S. Stein and R. Loewe (eds), *Studies in Jewish Religious and Intellectual History presented to A. Altmann* (Alabama 1979), 75-92; Carlos Steel, 'Proclus et Aristotle', Proceedings of the Congrès Proclus held in Paris 1985, J. Pépin and H.D. Saffrey (eds), *Proclus, lecteur et interprète des anciens* (Paris 1987), 213-25; Koenraad Verrycken, *God en Wereld in de Wijsbegeerte van Ioannes Philoponus*, Ph.D. Diss. (Louvain 1985).

19. Iamblichus ap. Elian *in Cat.* 123,1-3.

20. Syrianus *in Metaph.* 80,4-7; Proclus *in Tim.* 1.6,21-7,16.

physical cosmos, which Aristotle denied. But even on these issues, Proclus' pupil Ammonius was to claim harmony, and, though the debate was not clear cut,[21] his claim was on the whole to prevail. Aristotle, he maintained, accepted Plato's Ideas,[22] at least in the form of principles (*logoi*) in the divine intellect, and these principles were in turn causally responsible for the beginningless existence of the physical universe. Ammonius wrote a whole book to show that Aristotle's God was thus an efficent cause, and though the book is lost, some of its principal arguments are preserved by Simplicius.[23] This tradition helped to make it possible for Aquinas to claim Aristotle's God as a Creator, albeit not in the sense of giving the universe a beginning, but in the sense of being causally responsible for its beginningless existence.[24] Thus what started as a desire to harmonise Aristotle with Plato finished by making Aristotle safe for Christianity. In Simplicius, who goes further than anyone,[25] it is a formally stated duty of the commentator to display the harmony of Plato and Aristotle in most things.[26] Philoponus, who with his independent mind had thought better of his earlier belief in harmony, is castigated by Simplicius for neglecting this duty.[27]

The idea of harmony was extended beyond Plato and Aristotle to Plato and the Presocratics. Plato's pupils Speusippus and Xenocrates saw Plato as being in the Pythagorean tradition.[28] From the third to first centuries B.C., pseudo-Pythagorean writings present Platonic and Aristotelian doctrines as if they were the ideas of Pythagoras and his pupils,[29] and these forgeries were later taken by the Neoplatonists as genuine. Plotinus saw the Presocratics as precursors of his own views,[30] but Iamblichus went far beyond him by writing ten volumes on Pythagorean philosophy.[31] Thereafter Proclus sought to unify the whole of Greek

21. Asclepius sometimes accepts Syranius' interpretation (*in Metaph.* 433,9-436,6); which is, however, qualified, since Syrianus thinks Aristotle is realy committed willy-nilly to much of Plato's view (*in Metaph.* 117,25-118,11; ap. Asclepium *in Metaph.* 433,16; 450,22); Philoponus repents of his early claim that Plato is not the target of Aristotle's attack, and accepts that Plato is rightly attacked for treating ideas as independent entities outside the divine Intellect (*in DA* 37,18-31; *in Phys.* 225,4-226,11; *contra Procl.* 26,24-32,13; *in An. Post.* 242,14-243,25).

22. Asclepius *in Metaph.* from the voice of (i.e. from the lectures of) Ammonius 69,17-21; 71,28; cf. Zacharias *Ammonius, Patrologia Graeca* vol. 85 col. 952 (Colonna).

23. Simplicius *in Phys.* 1361,11-1363,12. See H.A. Davidson; Carlos Steel; Koenraad Verrycken in n. 18 above.

24. See Richard Sorabji, *Matter, Space and Motion* (London and Ithaca, N.Y. 1988), ch. 15.

25. See e.g. H.J. Blumenthal in n. 18 above.

26. Simplicius *in Cat.* 7,23-32.

27. Simplicius *in Cael.* 84,11-14; 159,2-9. On Philoponus' *volte face* see n. 21 above.

28. See e.g. Walter Burkert, *Weisheit und Wissenschaft* (Nürnberg 1962), translated as *Lore and Science in Ancient Pythagoreanism* (Cambridge Mass. 1972), 83-96.

29. See Holger Thesleff, *An Introduction to the Pythagorean Writings of the Hellenistic Period* (Åbo 1961); Thomas Alexander Szlezák, *Pseudo-Archytas über die Kategorien*, Peripatoi vol. 4 (Berlin and New York 1972).

30. Plotinus e.g. 4.8.1; 5.1.8 (10-27); 5.1.9.

31. See Dominic O'Meara, *Pythagoras Revived: Mathematics and Philosophy in Late Antiquity* (Oxford 1989).

philosophy by presenting it as a continuous clarification of divine revelation[32] and Simplicius argued for the same general unity in order to rebut Christian charges of contradictions in pagan philosophy.[33]

Later Neoplatonist commentaries tend to reflect their origin in a teaching curriculum:[34] from the time of Philoponus, the discussion is often divided up into lectures, which are subdivided into studies of doctrine and of text. A general account of Aristotle's philosophy is prefixed to the *Categories* commentaries and divided, according to a formula of Proclus,[35] into ten questions. It is here that commentators explain the eventual purpose of studying Aristotle (ascent to the One) and state (if they do) the requirement of displaying the harmony of Plato and Aristotle. After the ten-point introduction to Aristotle, the *Categories* is given a six-point introduction, whose antecedents go back earlier than Neoplatonism, and which requires the commentator to find a unitary theme or scope (*skopos*) for the treatise. The arrangements for late commentaries on Plato are similar. Since the Plato commentaries form part of a single curriculum they should be studied alongside those on Aristotle. Here the situation is easier, not only because the extant corpus is very much smaller, but also because it has been comparatively well served by French and English translators.[36]

Given the theological motive of the curriculum and the pressure to harmonise Plato with Aristotle, it can be seen how these commentaries are a major source for Neoplatonist ideas. This in turn means that it is not safe to extract from them the fragments of the Presocratics, or of other authors, without making allowance for the Neoplatonist background against which the fragments were originally selected for discussion. For different reasons, analogous warnings apply to fragments preserved by the pre-Neoplatonist commentator Alexander.[37] It will be another advantage of the present translations that they will make it easier to check the distorting effect of a commentator's background.

Although the Neoplatonist commentators conflate the views of Aristotle

32. See Christian Guérard, 'Parménide d'Elée selon les Néoplatoniciens', in P. Aubenque (ed.), *Etudes sur Parménide*, vol. 2 (Paris 1987).

33. Simplicius *in Phys.* 28,32-29,5; 640,12-18. Such thinkers as Epicurus and the Sceptics, however, were not subject to harmonisation.

34. See the literature in n. 2 above.

35. ap. Elian *in Cat.* 107,24-6.

36. English: Calcidius *in Tim.* (parts by van Winden; den Boeft); Iamblichus fragments (Dillon); Proclus *in Tim.* (Thomas Taylor); Proclus *in Parm.* (Dillon); Proclus *in Parm.*, end of 7th book, from the Latin (Klibansky, Labowsky, Anscombe); Proclus *in Alcib. 1* (O'Neill); Olympiodorus and Damascius *in Phaedonem* (Westerink); Damascius *in Philebum* (Westerink); *Anonymous Prolegomena to Platonic Philosophy* (Westerink). See also extracts in Thomas Taylor, *The Works of Plato*, 5 vols. (1804). French: Proclus *in Tim.* and *in Rempublicam* (Festugière); *in Parm.* (Chaignet); Anon. *in Parm* (P. Hadot); Damascius *in Parm.* (Chaignet).

37. For Alexander's treatment of the Stoics, see Robert B. Todd, *Alexander of Aphrodisias on Stoic Physics* (Leiden 1976), 24-9.

with those of Neoplatonism, Philoponus alludes to a certain convention when he quotes Plutarchus expressing disapproval of Alexander for expounding his own philosophical doctrines in a commentary on Aristotle.[38] But this does not stop Philoponus from later inserting into his own commentaries on the *Physics* and *Meteorology* his arguments in favour of the Christian view of Creation. Of course, the commentators also wrote independent works of their own, in which their views are expressed independently of the exegesis of Aristotle. Some of these independent works will be included in the present series of translations.

The distorting Neoplatonist context does not prevent the commentaries from being incomparable guides to Aristotle. The introductions to Aristotle's philosophy insist that commentators must have a minutely detailed knowledge of the entire Aristotelian corpus, and this they certainly have. Commentators are also enjoined neither to accept nor reject what Aristotle says too readily, but to consider it in depth and without partiality. The commentaries draw one's attention to hundreds of phrases, sentences and ideas in Aristotle, which one could easily have passed over, however often one read him. The scholar who makes the right allowance for the distorting context will learn far more about Aristotle than he would be likely to on his own.

The relations of Neoplatonist commentators to the Christians were subtle. Porphyry wrote a treatise explicitly against the Christians in 15 books, but an order to burn it was issued in 448, and later Neoplatonists were more circumspect. Among the last commentators in the main group, we have noted several Christians. Of these the most important were Boethius and Philoponus. It was Boethius' programme to transmit Greek learning to Latin-speakers. By the time of his premature death by execution, he had provided Latin translations of Aristotle's logical works, together with commentaries in Latin but in the Neoplatonist style on Porphyry's *Isagôgê* and on Aristotle's *Categories* and *de Interpretatione*, and interpretations of the *Prior* and *Posterior Analytics*, *Topics* and *Sophistici Elenchi*. The interruption of his work meant that knowledge of Aristotle among Latin-speakers was confined for many centuries to the logical works. Philoponus is important both for his proofs of the Creation and for his progressive replacement of Aristotelian science with rival theories, which were taken up at first by the Arabs and came fully into their own in the West only in the sixteenth century.

Recent work has rejected the idea that in Alexandria the Neoplatonists compromised with Christian monotheism by collapsing the distinction between their two highest deities, the One and the Intellect. Simplicius (who left Alexandria for Athens) and the Alexandrians Ammonius and

---

38. Philoponus *in DA* 21,20-3.

Asclepius appear to have acknowledged their beliefs quite openly, as later did the Alexandrian Olympiodorus, despite the presence of Christian students in their classes.[39]

The teaching of Simplicius in Athens and that of the whole pagan Neoplatonist school there was stopped by the Christian Emperor Justinian in 529. This was the very year in which the Christian Philoponus in Alexandria issued his proofs of Creation against the earlier Athenian Neoplatonist Proclus. Archaeological evidence has been offered that, after their temporary stay in Ctesiphon (in present-day Iraq), the Athenian Neoplatonists did not return to their house in Athens, and further evidence has been offered that Simplicius went to Harrān (Carrhae), in present-day Turkey near the Iraq border.[40] Wherever he went, his commentaries are a treasurehouse of information about the preceding thousand years of Greek philosophy, information which he painstakingly recorded after the closure in Athens, and which would otherwise have been lost. He had every reason to feel bitter about Christianity, and in fact he sees it and Philoponus, its representative, as irreverent. They deny the divinity of the heavens and prefer the physical relics of dead martyrs.[41] His own commentaries by contrast culminate in devout prayers.

Two collections of articles by various hands have been published, to make the work of the commentators better known. The first is devoted to Philoponus;[42] the second is about the commentators in general, and goes into greater detail on some of the issues briefly mentioned here.[43]

39. For Simplicius, see I. Hadot, *Le Problème du Néoplatonisme Alexandrin: Hiéroclès et Simplicius* (Paris 1978); for Ammonius and Asclepius, Koenraad Verrycken, *God en wereld in de Wijsbegeerte van Ioannes Philoponus*, Ph.D. Diss. (Louvain 1985); for Olympiodorus, L.G. Westerink, *Anonymous Prolegomena to Platonic Philosophy* (Amsterdam 1962).

40. Alison Frantz, 'Pagan philosophers in Christian Athens', *Proceedings of the American Philosophical Society* 119 (1975), 29-38; M. Tardieu, 'Témoins orientaux du *Premier Alcibiade* à Harrān et à Nag 'Hammādi', *Journal Asiatique* 274 (1986); id., 'Les calendriers en usage à Harrān d'après les sources arabes et le commentaire de Simplicius à la *Physique* d'Aristote', in I. Hadot (ed.), *Simplicius, sa vie, son oeuvre, sa survie* (Berlin 1987), 40-57; id., *Coutumes nautiques mésopotamiennes chez Simplicius*, in preparation. The opposing view that Simplicius returned to Athens is most fully argued by Alan Cameron, 'The last day of the Academy at Athens', *Proceedings of the Cambridge Philological Society* 195, n.s. 15 (1969), 7-29. P. Foulkes, 'Where was Simplicius', *JHS* 112 (1992), 143. R. Thiel, 'Simplikios und das Ende der neuplatonischen Schule in Athen', Akademie der Wissenschaften und der Literatur Mainz: *Abhandlungen der geistes- und sozialwissenschaftlichen Klasse*, no. 8, 1999.

41. Simplicius *in Cael.* 26,4-7; 70,16-18; 90,1-18; 370,29-371,4. See on his whole attitude Philippe Hoffmann, 'Simplicius' polemics', in Richard Sorabji (ed.), *Philoponus and the Rejection of Aristotelian Science* (London and Ithaca, N.Y. 1987).

42. Richard Sorabji (ed.), *Philoponus and the Rejection of Aristotelian Science* (London and Ithaca, N.Y. 1987).

43. Richard Sorabji (ed.), *Aristotle Transformed: the ancient commentators and their influence* (London and Ithaca, N.Y. 1990). The lists of texts and previous translations of the commentaries included in Wildberg, *Philoponus Against Aristotle on the Eternity of the World* (pp. 12ff.) are not included here. The list of translations should be augmented by: F.L.S. Bridgman, Heliodorus (?) in *Ethica Nicomachea*, London 1807.

I am grateful for comments to Henry Blumenthal, Victor Caston, I. Hadot, Paul Mercken, Alain Segonds, Robert Sharples, Robert Todd, L.G. Westerink and Christian Wildberg.

English-Greek Glossary

a fortiori: *meizonôs*
able, be: *dunasthai, endekhesthai*
able to perceive: *aisthêtikos,*
    antilêptikos
abolish: *anäirein*
above, be: *epanabebêkenai,*
    huperekhein
absence: *endeia, sterêsis*
abstraction: *aphairesis*
absurd: *adunaton, atopon*
accept: *anekhomai, prosïesthai*
acceptance: *apodokhê*
accident: *to sumbebêkos*
accompany: *akolouthein,*
    episumbainein
account: *logos*
accrue: *proïenai*
accurate: *akribês*
accustomed, be: *eiôthenai*
act, be in: *energein*
act: *energein, poein*
acting on (noun): *poiêsis*
action: *praxis, to prakton*
active: *drastêrios, energêtikos*
activity: by one's own (adv.),
    autenergêtikôs
activity: *energeia, entelekheia, zôê*
actuality: *energeia, entelekheia*
add: *eisagein, epagein, epipherein,*
    prostithenai
addition: *prosthesis*
adduce: *epagein, kinein*
adjacent: *ekhomenos, sunhêmmenos*
advance: *epienai*
affected, to be: *paskhein, pathainesthai*
affection: *pathê, pathos, peisis*
affections, able to cause: *pathêtikos*
affections, free from, not subject to:
    apathês
affinity: *oikeiotês*
afraid, be: *phobeisthai*
agree: *homologein*
agreement: *sumphônia*

aim at: *hiesthai*
air: *aêr*
alive, be: *zên*
alive: *zôtikos*
allow: *sunkhôrein*
alteration: *tropê*
analogy: *analogia*
anger: *orgê*
animal: *zôion*
answer: *apodosis*
ant: *murmêx*
antecedent (noun): *to proêgoumenon*
antecedent propositions: *hêgoumena*
    proêgoumena
apart, be: *exïstasthai*
appear together: *sunanaphainesthai*
appetition: *orexis*
apply: *pherein*
apply to (intrans.): *prosêkein*
apply to (trans.): *katêgorein*
apprehend: *antilambanein, gnôrizein*
apprehend, able to: *antilêptikos*
apprehended, able to be: *katalêptikos:*
    kataléptos
apprehensible: *kataléptos*
apprehension: *antilêpsis, sunesis*
approach (noun): *apantêsis*
appropriate: *oikeios, prepon, prosêkôn*
approve: *epainein*
archetypal: *prôtotupos*
argument: *epikheirêma, logos,*
    sullogismos
arise: *sunïstamai*
arousal: *egersis*
arrive at: *apoteleutan*
article: *arthron*
artificial creation: *plasmatia*
artificial production, to do with:
    tekhnikos
assent (noun): *sunkatathesis*
assent (vb.): *homologein, suntithesthai*
asserting premise: *axiousa protasis*
assertions, to make: *diïskhurizesthai*

Index of Passages

References are to the notes to the translation.